SchoolGirls

Doubleday

■

New York
London
Toronto
Sydney
Auckland

■

SchoolGirls

Young Women,
Self-Esteem,
and the
Confidence Gap

■

Peggy Orenstein

in association with the
American Association of
University Women

PUBLISHED BY DOUBLEDAY
a division of Bantam Doubleday Dell Publishing Group, Inc.
1540 Broadway, New York, New York 10036

DOUBLEDAY and the portrayal of an anchor with a dolphin are
trademarks of Doubleday, a division of Bantam Doubleday Dell
Publishing Group, Inc.

Book Design by Nancy Field

Library of Congress Cataloging-in-Publication Data

Orenstein, Peggy.
    Schoolgirls : young women, self-esteem, and the confidence gap /
  by Peggy Orenstein in association with the American Association of
  University Women. — 1st ed. in the United States of America.
       p.   cm.
    Includes bibliographical references.
    1. Teenage girls—United States—Psychology.   2. Self-esteem in
  adolescence—United States.   3. Self-perception in adolescence—United
  States.   I. American Association of University Women.   II. Title.
  HQ798.O74   1994
  305.23′5—dc20   94-9883   CIP

To Steven

Acknowledgments

■

■

■

For me, the writing process has always involved many people: people who gave me opportunity, who broadened my thinking, people who critiqued my manuscript, who offered sustenance and love and, sometimes, told me to stop whining and get back to work. Without them—without my colleagues, friends, and family—this book could never be.

I owe great debts to my agent, Sandra Dijkstra, and to Sheila Buckmaster, formerly of the AAUW, who saw the potential of this project and forged our alliance; to Doubleday's Wendy Goldman; and to Ashley Craddock, Heidi Frieze, and Tina Plaza, who offered invaluable research and translation assistance.

My friends have chewed over my ideas with me endlessly, commented on drafts, and provided more moral support than I could ever repay. In particular, I'd like to thank Eva Eilenberg, Ruth Halpern, Peg-bo Edersheim, David Fallek, Neal Karlen, Connie Matthiessen, Sarah Weir, Dvora Honigstein, Catherine Taylor, and Barbara Swaiman (who has been my friend since we were "schoolgirls"). And, of course, thank you to Beatsy, Mel,

Leslie, David, Debbie, and John Orenstein for their love and faith.

In a book such as this, I believe it is especially important to acknowledge a group of people who may or may not remember me: the teachers who made a lasting impact on my life. Thank you to Susan Hanson, the late Betty Ann Long, Richard Rosch, Miriam Kagol, and Oberlin's Katherine Linnehan. And to Carrie Jensen, my eighth-grade English teacher at Westwood Junior High, who once told me to send her an autographed copy of my first book—it's waiting for you.

Finally, there are three people for whom I reserve special gratitude. My editor, Deb Futter, has given freely of her time, her editorial wisdom, and her friendship. Doug Foster read every word of every draft; his insight and guidance permeate this and all my work. Steven Okazaki has not only been a fine editor, but has endured my tears, shared my triumphs, fed, loved, and even married me during the time I worked on this project. One could not ask for a truer soul mate. This book is dedicated to him, and the standard of equity to which he holds me.

Contents

Contents

Introduction:
The Bad News about
Good Girls

.
.
.

The bell rings, as it always does, at 8:30 sharp. Twenty-eight sixth graders file into their classroom at Everett Middle School in San Francisco, straggling a bit since this is the first warm day in months—warm enough for shorts and cutoffs, warm enough for Stüssy T-shirts.

The students take their seats. Heidi, who wears bright green Converse sneakers and a matching cap, pulls off her backpack and shouts, "Did everyone bring their permission slips? You have to bring them so we can have the pizza party."

"Pizza," moans Carrie, who has brown bangs and a permanently bored expression. "That has milk. I'm allergic to milk."

Heidi looks stunned. "You can't eat pizza?"

The drama is interrupted as Judy Logan, a comfortably built woman with gray-flecked hair and oversized glasses, steps to the front of the classroom. She tapes two four-foot lengths of butcher paper to the chalkboard. Across the top of one she writes: "MALES," across the other: "FEMALES."

Ms. Logan is about to begin the lesson from which her entire middle school curriculum flows, the exercise that explains why she makes her students bother to learn about women, why the bookshelves in her room are brimful with women's biographies, why her walls are covered with posters that tout women's achievements and draped with quilts that depict women through history and women in the students' own lives.

It's time for the gender journey.

"Ladies and gentlemen," Ms. Logan says, turning toward the children and clasping her hands. "I'd like you to put your heads down and close your eyes. We're going to take a journey back in time."

Ms. Logan's already soothing voice turns soft and dreamy. "Go back," she tells her students. "Forget about everything around you and go back to fifth grade. Imagine yourself in your classroom, at your desk, sitting in your chair. Notice who your teacher is, what you have on, who's sitting around you, who your friends are.

"Continue your journey backward in time to third grade. Picture your third-grade teacher, your place in class. Imagine yourself in your room at home. What do you like to do when you have free time? What kind of toys do you play with? What books are you reading?"

The children go further back, to the first magical day of kindergarten, then further still, remembering preschool, remembering their discovery of language, remembering their first toddling steps. Then Ms. Logan asks her students to recall the moment of their birth, to imagine the excitement of their parents. And then, when the great moment arrives . . .

They are each born the opposite sex.

The class gasps.

"Gross," offers Jonathan with great enthusiasm.

"Yuck," adds Carrie. "That's worse than being allergic to milk."

"You are born the opposite sex," Ms. Logan repeats firmly, and then asks her students to imagine moving forward through their lives again, exactly as they were and are, except for that one crucial detail.

Again they imagine themselves walking on tiny, uncertain feet. Again they imagine speaking, entering kindergarten. Again they envision their clothes as third graders, their toys, their books, their friends.

"I can't do this," says Jonathan, who has braces and short blond hair. "I just picture myself like I am now except in a pink dress."

"This is stupid," agrees Carrie. "It's too hard."

"Just try," says Ms. Logan. "Try to imagine yourself in fourth grade, in fifth grade." By the time thirty minutes have elapsed, the students are back in their classroom, safe and sound and relieved to find their own personal anatomies intact.

"Without talking," Ms. Logan says, "I'd like you to make a list, your own personal list, not to turn in, of everything that would be different if you were the opposite sex."

The students write eagerly, with only occasional giggles. When there is more horseplay than wordplay, Ms. Logan asks them to share items from their lists with the class. The offerings go up on the butcher paper.

"I wouldn't play baseball because I'd worry about breaking a nail," says Mark, who wears a San Jose Sharks jersey.

"My father would feel more responsibility for me, he'd be more in my life," says Dayna, a soft-spoken African American girl.

Luke virtually spits his idea. "My room would be *pink* and I'd think everything would be *cute*."

"I'd have my own room," says a girl.

"I wouldn't care how I look or if my clothes matched," offers another.

"I'd have to spend lots of time in the bathroom on my hair and stuff," says a boy whose own hair is conspicuously mussed. The other boys groan in agreement.

"I could stay out later," ventures a girl.

"I'd have to help my mom cook," says a boy.

"I'd get to play a lot more sports," says Annie, a freckled, red-haired girl who looks uncomfortable with the entire proposition. Many of the students are, in fact, unsettled by this exercise. Nearly a third opt to pass when their turns come, keeping their lists to themselves.

"I'd have to stand around at recess instead of getting to play basketball," says George, sneering. "And I'd worry about getting pregnant."

Raoul offers the final, if most obvious comment, which cracks up the crowd. "I'd have to sit down to go to the bathroom."

At this point the bell rings, although it is not the end of the lesson. The students will return after a short break to assess the accuracy of their images of one another. But while they're gone, I scrutinize the two butcher paper lists. Almost all of the boys' observations about gender swapping involve disparaging "have to"s, whereas the girls seem wistful with longing. By sixth grade, it is clear that both girls and boys have learned to equate maleness with opportunity and femininity with constraint.

It was a pattern I'd see again and again as I undertook my own gender journey, spending a year observing eighth-grade girls in two other Northern California middle schools. The girls I spoke with were from vastly different family structures and economic classes, and they had achieved varying degrees of academic success. Yet all of them, even those enjoying every conceivable advantage, saw their gender as a liability.

Sitting with groups of five or six girls, I'd ask a variation on Ms. Logan's theme: what did they think was lucky about being a girl? The question was invariably followed by a pause, a silence. Then answers such as "Nothing, really. All kinds of bad things happen to girls, like getting your period. Or getting pregnant."

Marta, a fourteen-year-old Latina girl, was blunt. "There's nothing lucky about being a girl," she told me one afternoon in her school's cafeteria. "I wish I was a boy."

■

Shortchanging Girls:
What the AAUW Survey Reveals

■

Like many people, I first saw the results of the American Association of University Women's report *Shortchanging Girls, Shortchanging America* in my daily newspaper. The headline unfurled across the front page of the San Francisco *Examiner:* "Girls' Low Self-Esteem Slows Their Progress," and the New York *Times* proclaimed: "Girls' Self-Esteem Is Lost on the Way to Adolescence."[1] And, like many people, as I read further, I felt my stomach sink.

This was the most extensive national survey on gender and self-esteem ever conducted, the articles said: three thousand boys and girls between the ages of nine and fifteen were polled on their attitudes toward self, school, family, and friends. As part of the project the students were asked to respond to multiple-choice questions, provide comments, and in some cases, were interviewed in focus groups. The results confirmed something that many women already knew too well. For a girl, the passage into adolescence is not just marked by menarche or a few new curves. It is marked by a loss of confidence in herself and her abilities, especially in math and science. It is marked by a scathingly critical attitude toward her body and a blossoming sense of personal inadequacy.

In spite of the changes in women's roles in society, in spite of the changes in their own mothers' lives, many of today's girls fall into traditional patterns of low self-image, self-doubt, and self-censorship of their creative and intellectual potential. Although all children experience confusion and a faltering sense of self at adolescence, girls' self-regard drops further than boys' and never catches up.[2] They emerge from their teenage years with reduced expectations and have less confidence in themselves and their abilities than do boys. Teenage girls are more vulnerable to feelings of depression and hopelessness and are four times more likely to attempt suicide.[3]

The AAUW discovered that the most dramatic gender gap in self-esteem is centered in the area of competence. Boys are more likely than girls to say they are "pretty good at a lot of things" and are twice as likely to name their talents as the thing they like most about themselves. Girls, meanwhile, cite an aspect of their physical appearance.[4] Unsurprisingly, then, teenage girls are much more likely than boys to say they are "not smart enough" or "not good enough" to achieve their dreams.[5]

The education system is supposed to provide our young people with opportunity, to encourage their intellectual growth and prepare them as citizens. Yet students in the AAUW survey reported gender bias in the classroom—and illustrated its effects —with the canniness of investigative reporters. Both boys and girls believed that teachers encouraged more assertive behavior in boys, and that, overall, boys receive the majority of their teachers' attention. The result is that boys will speak out more readily, and are more willing to "argue with my teachers when I think I'm right."[6]

Meanwhile, girls show a more precipitous drop in their interest in math and science as they advance through school. Even girls who like the subjects are, by age fifteen, only half as likely as boys to feel competent in them. These findings are key: researchers have long understood that a loss of confidence in math usually *precedes* a drop in achievement, rather than vice versa.[7] A confidence gap, rather than an ability gap, may help explain why the numbers of female physical and computer scientists actually went down during the 1980s.[8] The AAUW also discovered a circular relationship between math confidence and overall self-confidence, as well as a link between liking math and aspiring to professional careers—a correlation that is stronger for girls than boys. Apparently girls who can resist gender-role stereotypes in the classroom resist them elsewhere more effectively as well.

Among its most intriguing findings, the AAUW survey revealed that, although all girls report consistently lower self-esteem than boys, the severity and the nature of that reduced self-worth vary among ethnic groups. Far more African American girls retain their overall self-esteem during adolescence than white or Latina girls, maintaining a stronger sense of both personal and familial importance. They are about twice as likely to be "happy with the way I am" than girls of other groups and report feeling "pretty good at a lot of things" at nearly the rate of white boys.[9] The one exception for African American girls is their feelings about school: black girls are more pessimistic about both their teachers and their schoolwork than other girls. Meanwhile, Latina girls' self-esteem crisis is in many ways the most profound. Between the ages of nine and fifteen, the number of Latina girls who are "happy with the way I am" plunges by 38 percentage points, compared with a 33 percent drop for white girls and a 7 percent drop for black girls. Family disappears as a source of positive self-worth for Latina teens, and academic confidence, belief in one's talents, and a sense of personal importance all plummet.[10] During the year in which *Shortchanging Girls, Shortchanging America* was conducted, urban Latinas left school at a greater rate than any other group, male or female.[11]

■
Self-Esteem: Cutting Through the Hype
■

Although ideas about the importance of self-esteem have been knocking around academic literature since the late nineteenth century, the phrase has become the buzzword of the 1990s, helped by the ascendance to best-seller status of Gloria Steinem's *Revolution from Within: A Book of Self-Esteem*. Like Steinem, I started out a critic of the self-esteem evangelists. I was suspicious of any movement that stressed personal transformation over structural change, especially for women. Self-esteem sounded to me like another way to blame the victim, warm fuzzy style. We do girls a disservice, I reasoned, if we encourage them to feel good about themselves rather than targeting the overarching institutions, policies, and cultural attitudes that make them (understandably) feel worthless. And self-esteem by what means? By whose measure? Wily advertising executives dangle improved self-esteem as enticement to join one of the diet industry's two billion dollars' worth of weight loss programs or to risk the dangers of plastic surgery. How terribly clever, I thought: the people who robbed women of their self-esteem now want to sell it back to us! I believed that the sole feminist work that needed to be done was on the politics of the external. But spending time in the world of girls (and reflecting on the world of women) convinced me that the internal need not, and indeed should not, be ignored.

Self-esteem has been defined in many ways by psychological theorists, as well as by Madison Avenue. For the purposes of this book, I employ the definition put forth in the work of Susan Harter and Morris Rosenberg. To them, self-esteem is derived from two sources: how a person views her performance in areas in which success is important to her (so if appearance is more important to a girl than academic success, gaining a few extra pounds may damage her self-esteem more than an F in math) and how a person believes she is perceived by significant others, such as parents, teachers, or peers.[12] In their book *Lifeprints*, writer Caryl Rivers and psychologists Grace Baruch and Rosalind Barnett, put women's self-esteem on continuums of confidence and inferiority, competence and incompetence, pride and shame.[13]

Girls with healthy self-esteem have an appropriate sense of their potential, their competence, and their innate value as individuals. They feel a sense of entitlement: license to take up space in the world, a right to be heard and to express the full spectrum of human emotions. The fact that, in study after study, women and girls are less likely to feel those things than men and boys should be no surprise. We live in a culture that is ambivalent toward female achievement, proficiency, independence, and right to a full and equal life. Our culture devalues both women and the qualities which it projects onto us, such as nurturance, cooperation, and intuition. It has taught us to undervalue ourselves. Too often we deride our own abilities. We denigrate our work and discount success. We don't feel we have the right to our dreams, or, if we achieve them, we feel undeserving. Small failures may confirm our own sense of inevitable failure, making us unable to take necessary risks. We learn to look outward for markers of acceptability and are particularly vulnerable to putting our self-esteem in the hands of lovers or husbands, to believing that only someone else's approval can confer worth.

■

Seeking the Source:
Entering Girls' Worlds

■

When I first read about the AAUW survey, I felt deeply troubled. This was a report in which children were talking directly to us about their experience, and I didn't like what I heard. Like the girls in Judy Logan's class, these girls had internalized the limitations of gender. As a feminist, I took this as a warning. As a journalist, I wanted to find out more. According to the survey, middle school is the beginning of the transition from girlhood to womanhood and, not coincidentally, the time of greatest self-esteem loss.[14] So, with the support of the AAUW, I went back to eighth grade.

I chose to work on this project in California, which has the largest school system in the country. California, along with Minnesota and several other states, has been on the cutting edge of both gender-fair and multicultural education and perhaps there is less bias here than there might be elsewhere. But I wanted to see what was working in classrooms as well as what was not.

School administrators are leery of journalists, and teachers even more so. It was not easy to find educators (or parents) who were willing to put up with a year's scrutiny, even though, since I was writing about children, I promised to change the names of everyone involved.* I interviewed over one hundred and fifty girls and spoke with nearly a dozen administrators before settling on two schools, fifty miles apart, in which I would spend the 1992–93 school year. My criteria were simple: I chose the schools based on their racial and economic makeup and the willingness of the administrators, teachers, and students to participate. Both of the schools' student handbooks included written sexual harassment policies, and some teachers in each school were aware of a bias in favor of boys and were struggling with solutions. Among the girls, I strove for a cross section of ethnicity, class, and family structure, although I also knew that, inevitably, someone would be excluded. The AAUW survey focused on the country's largest ethnic groups—Caucasians, African Americans, and Latinos. I have also stayed within those parameters. The Latinas in the AAUW study were predominantly Mexican American. Likewise, the Latina girls in the schools I visited were largely Mexican American and Central American. Also, none of the girls I interviewed expressed (or were willing to express) sexual feelings toward other girls during our conversations. An emerging lesbianism or bisexuality in a relentlessly heterosexual world would add another strand to a girl's developing sense of self. Like the AAUW survey, I focused on coeducational public institutions, in part because of the belief that to effect true change, we must alter the way we raise our boys as well as our girls.

Initially, I had hoped to find schools whose student population was racially and economically diverse. But California's education system, like that of other states, has become increasingly segregated in the last twenty-five years. By one measure, California's is among the top five most segregated school systems in the

---

* The exception to this is Judy Logan at Everett Middle School, although her students are pseudonymous.

country for African American and Latino students.[15] Most schools I visited were divided not only by race but by economic class as well. Inevitably, the schools I chose reflect that system-wide inequity. Weston is a suburban middle school with a reputation for excellence. Although its student body is overwhelmingly white, I was attracted by its broad class range. Audubon Middle School serves a beleaguered urban community that is nearly 90 percent ethnic minority, mostly poor or working poor. The circumstances of the girls at Audubon cannot reflect the entirety of the experience of girls of color, any more than the Weston girls reflect every aspect of white girls' experience. However, I found it especially important to include young women who are devalued by class and race as well as gender. The popular research on girls has too often addressed only the needs of white and privileged girls, or assumed that while there are vast differences between boys and girls, the ethnic and economic differences among girls are irrelevant. But since nearly one third of the students in our public education system are children of color, and they are disproportionately concentrated in urban schools,[16] it is essential to include their experiences.

During the spring of 1992, principals, counselors, and teachers at each school submitted the names of girls who might be willing to participate in a long-term, in-depth project. I met with them in small groups, usually of three to five girls. I asked specific questions about their favorite classes, as well as more open-ended questions, such as to complete the phrase "The best thing about being a girl is . . ." I asked if they would be willing to be interviewed alone, throughout the next school year, and requested parental permission from those who agreed. From that smaller group, I tried to select girls who represented a range of family configurations, educational engagement, personality styles, and perspectives on femininity; girls who, although their stories are very specific, could offer windows into a collective experience.

Shortchanging Girls, Shortchanging America concentrated on the ways in which the education system—often unwittingly —inhibits, restricts, diminishes, and denies girls' experience. As I delved into my research, though, I found my own vision broadening. The strands that make up the self are intricately interwoven. They include school, but they also include family life. They encompass the ways boys treat girls as well as girls' reaction to emerging sexual desire and new consciousness of sexual exploitation and abuse. It seemed to me that the girls in the AAUW survey were telling us that, at adolescence, at the moment of transformation from girlhood to womanhood, they learn in a new and profound way that boys are still central in every aspect of the culture. I began to wonder, if girls feel a reduced sense of self, how is that expressed in their attitudes toward all the vital threads of their lives?

In school, I wondered how educators were trying to combat girls' flagging self-confidence, and what they were doing— consciously or unconsciously—to undercut it. What forces, in particular, inhibited girls' achievement in science, where the gender gap looms widest, as well as in math, where girls' confidence dwindles regardless of ability. What role did boys, and girls' attitudes toward them, play in diminishing girls' self-regard? What benefits did black girls derive from a stronger sense of self, and what were the sources of their academic loss of faith? How did the self-esteem crisis deepen for Latinas?

I wondered, too, how girls were absorbing the lessons of their mothers' lives. What were girls learning at home about a woman's place? How were they affected by "the second shift" that sociologist Arlie Hochschild has so eloquently described: the month of twenty-four-hour days a year more than her mate that a working wife will spend on housework and child care?[17] What were parents' aspirations for their daughters?

As they entered adolescence, I also wondered how girls were negotiating their relationships with their bodies. How did girls feel about the way they looked (an aspect which is still central—*too* central—to girls' self-esteem). Did girls feel entitled to an appetite for food? Did they feel entitled to their emerging sexual appetites or, as Simone de Beauvoir has said, do teenage girls' bodies still become Other to themselves?[18] Were adolescent power relationships between boys and girls, especially those revolving around sex and desire, changing?

During the 1992–93 school year, I spent four days a week with the girls I had chosen to follow. I sat in their classrooms, visited their homes, went to school dances and plays, to athletic events and community centers. I interviewed parents, teachers, and friends. I ate school lunches. From the outset I emphasized that I was a journalist, a temporary observer of their lives, and, as such, could not give them advice. I also promised to keep our conversations confidential during the course of the reporting, although, as the reader will see, I could not always keep that promise.

I developed great affection and concern for all of the girls, although our relationships, as well as my access to them, varied tremendously. The hectic nature of both school and personal life at Audubon, as well as the students' distrust of adult authority —especially white adult authority—made establishing trust especially difficult at that school. The girls there were reluctant to allow me to observe them with peers, although they were happy to speak to me in private. Their parents, too, were less willing to talk to me. Several had no phones, making contact difficult. When we could arrange interviews, they were hesitant to meet at home, concerned about my safety in the housing projects where they lived.

The girls at Weston often inquired about their counterparts at Audubon, although the reverse was not true. They asked whether I was frightened in the hallways of what they called an "inner-city school" and wondered if all of the students there were on drugs or in gangs. Although that vision was sadly distorted, the issues in the urban girls' lives were, in fact, quite different from those of the suburban girls. The pressures of poverty, discrimination, and the inadequacy of education facing all students at Audubon often overshadowed the gender differences reported in the AAUW survey. Nonetheless, the strategies children pursued to maintain self-esteem in such an atmosphere were frequently dictated by gender. As the school year progressed, I found that the schism in the lives of the girls at the two schools pervaded my reporting and it became part of my story as well.

I was astonished by how consistently articulate and insightful the girls were, including those who were doing poorly in school. Much of the time, as I followed them through their eighth-grade year, the girls seemed happy, successful, faced squarely toward productive futures. And I found that heartening and hopeful. But there was something else there, too even for the most successful girls. One girl repeatedly dismissed her academic triumphs but willingly embraced her failures. Another's paralyzing vision of perfection made her afraid even to cough in class. A third had suffered a bout of bulimia. Yet another carried the burden of her mother's unhappy marriage. And another's waning interest in school corresponded to her increasing desire to join a gang. Both images were true, the excitement of progress in young women's lives as well as the defeat of stasis. Too often, I realized, our eagerness to see the first can prevent us from truly seeing the second.

■

Double Vision: Confronting Myself

■

I was unprepared for how much the journey into gender would become a journey into myself, how much the voices of the AAUW survey echoed my own. While writing this book, I began to look at myself in the way I looked at many of these girls: with a kind of double vision. There is the lens of success, through which I see the perfect daughter, who always obeyed her parents, was always a leader at school, pulled good grades, went to a good college, landed prestigious jobs, achieved and thrived.

If I were writing about that self, I could celebrate the distance traveled in the generation between my mother's and my own. My mother is sixty-four. She was an elementary school teacher as a young woman, but quit to become a homemaker and raise her own children. I am thirty-two—half her age. Since I left home for college at seventeen, she has made running observations about the differences between us. She is in awe of the opportunities I've had, the options that she could not even have imagined at my age. Sometimes, my mother wonders who else she might have become had she grown up when I did, although, she adds, she is satisfied with the course of her life. She marvels at my dedication to my career (at the very existence of my career), at my ease in traveling the globe alone, at the accomplishments of my girlfriends. She is intrigued and somewhat discomfited by other doors that have opened, particularly those involving sexual freedom.

I could write that story, and it would be true. It would be true about me, about my friends, about the friends of my friends. But there is another book I could write. It would be about how, in spite of all of our success, in spite of the fact that we have attained the superficial ideal of womanhood held out to our generation, we feel unsure, insecure, inadequate. I resist applying this lens to my life, and I have tried hard to avoid it, to remain unseeing even when the feelings it reveals threaten to overwhelm me. I wouldn't look through it at thirteen, when I lowered my hand in math class, never to raise it again, out of a sudden fear that I might answer incorrectly and be humiliated. I wouldn't look through it at sixteen when I winnowed forty pounds from my body, refusing food and binging on laxatives, eventually losing the ability to eat at all. I wouldn't see it when I declined to try out for my college newspaper, even though I dreamed of becoming a journalist. Nor would I see it at twenty-one, when I became paralyzed during the writing of my senior thesis, convinced that my fraudulence was about to be unmasked. Back then, I went to my adviser and told her of the fears that were choking me.

"You feel like an impostor?" she asked. "Don't worry about it. All smart women feel that way."

It was part of the answer, and it stayed with me for years. It allowed me to continue not to look. I felt this way because I was a smart woman, I'd tell myself, and our culture undermines smart women, so just shut up and ignore it—it's normal. As long as I pushed forward with the politics of the external, I thought I could ignore the politics of the internal, but they continued to dog me at every turn.

It was not until I began this project that I truly confronted my own conflicts and recognized their depths. It was not until I saw how these vibrant young women were beginning to suppress themselves that I realized how thoroughly I, too, had learned the lessons of silence, how I had come to censor my own ideas and doubt the efficacy of my actions. At times, the pain of discovery was so acute that I wanted to turn away, to simply discontinue the work. But in the end, writing this book, and working with these young women, has helped me to begin mending those contradictions, as I hope it will for other adult readers.

Twenty years have elapsed between my adolescence and that of the girls in this book. They have many more role models than I ever did, and seemingly fewer barriers to equality. Yet during the course of our many conversations it was clear that, regardless of race and class, they still had learned to see boys as freer, with fewer concerns, ultimately more powerful. Girls' diminished sense of self means that, often unconsciously, they take on a second-class, accommodating status. Few of the girls I spoke with had ever been told that girls "can't" do what boys can—most were overtly encouraged to fulfill their potential. Yet all, on some level, had learned this lesson anyway.

"I once had a dream that sums it up," Evie, a student at Weston, said to me one day. "I dreamed that I worked for a guy who did science in a white coat. He did the experiments, and I wrote the paper. That's the way it is, right? The guy does the work and we finish the job. That's how we'll end up, the girls."

Without a strong sense of self, girls will enter adulthood at a deficit: they will be less able to fulfill their potential, less willing to take on challenges, less willing to defy tradition in their career choices, which means sacrificing economic equity. Their successes will not satisfy and their failures will be more catastrophic, confirming their own self-doubt. They will be less prepared to weather the storms of adult life, more likely to become depressed, hopeless, and self-destructive. In order to raise healthier girls, we must look carefully at what we tell them, often unconsciously, often subtly, about their worth relative to boys'. We must look at what girls value about themselves—the "areas of importance" by which they measure their self-esteem —as well as the potential sources of strength and competence that, too often, they learn to devalue.

It's time for the gender journey.

SchoolGirls

Part I
Weston Middle School

■

1
Learning Silence:
Scenes from the
Class Struggle

■

■

■

Weston, California, sits at the far reaches of the San Francisco Bay Area. The drive from the city takes one through a series of bedroom communities, carefully planned idylls in which, as the miles roll by, the tax brackets leap upward, the politics swing right, and the people fade to white. But Weston is different: once an oddly matched blend of country folk and chemical plant workers, this is an old town, the kind of place where people still gather curbside under the bunting-swathed lampposts of Maple Street to watch the Fourth of July parade. Many of the businesses in Weston's center—doughnut shops, ladies' clothing stores, a few hard drinkers' bars, and picked-over antiquaries—haven't changed hands in over thirty years. There are a few fern bars and one café serving espresso here, but if people want high tone, they go to the city.

Not that Weston has remained suspended in time. The ram-shackle houses downtown may still be populated by the families of mechanics, plant workers, and, in shoddy apartment complexes, a small community of working poor, but the hills that ring the town's edge have been gobbled up by tract homes where young professionals have hunkered down—a safe distance from urban ills—to raise their children. There's even a clean, modern supermarket by the freeway, built expressly for the new suburbanites, with a multiplex cinema across the street for their occasional evenings out.

The only place where Weston's two populations converge regularly is at Weston Middle School, a crumbling Spanish-style edifice just up the street from the post office, city hall, and, more important to the student body, a McDonald's. This is the town's sole middle school, and as such, it serves nearly nine hundred students a year from this disparate population. The bumper stickers on the cars dropping off the children reflect the mix: Toyota vans advertising the local NPR affiliate pull up behind rusty pickups that proclaim: "My wife said if I buy another gun she'll divorce me; God, I'll miss her!" There is also a staunch Christian population here—Mormons, Seventh-Day Adventists, and other, less austere sects whose cars remind other residents that "Jesus Loves You!"

In recent years, Weston Middle School has fulfilled its mandate well: the school entrance is draped with a "California Distinguished School" banner, earned last year by the students' estimable standardized test scores as well as the staff's exemplary performance. The teachers are an impressive, enthusiastic group who routinely seek methods of instruction that will inspire a little more engagement, a little more effort on the part of their pupils: an eighth-grade history teacher uses a karaoke microphone to juice up his lessons; an English teacher videotapes students performing original poems to bring literature to life; a science teacher offers extra credit to students who join him in cleaning up the banks of a local river. There is also some concern about gender issues in education: Weston's history teachers have embraced the new, more inclusive textbooks adopted by the state of California; in English, students write essays on their views about abortion and read, among other books, *Streams to the River, River to the Sea,* a historical novel which recasts Sacagawea as an intrepid female hero.

Yet the overt curriculum, as fine as it may be, is never the only force operating in a classroom. There is something else as well. The "hidden curriculum" comprises the unstated lessons that students learn in school: it is the running subtext through which teachers communicate behavioral norms and individual status in the school culture, the process of socialization that cues children into their place in the hierarchy of larger society. Once used to describe the ways in which the education system works to reproduce class systems in our culture, the "hidden curriculum" has recently been applied to the ways in which schools help reinforce gender roles, whether they intend to or not.

▪

The Daily Grind:
Lessons in the Hidden Curriculum
▪

Amy Wilkinson has looked forward to being an eighth grader forever—at least for the last two years, which, when you're thirteen, seems like the same thing. By the second week of September she's settled comfortably into her role as one of the school's reigning elite. Each morning before class, she lounges with a group of about twenty other eighth-grade girls and boys in the most visible spot on campus: at the base of the schoolyard, between one of the portable classrooms that was constructed in the late 1970s and the old oak tree in the overflow parking lot. The group trades gossip, flirts, or simply stands around, basking in its own importance and killing time before the morning bell.

At 8:15 on Tuesday the crowd has already convened, and Amy is standing among a knot of girls, laughing. She is fuller-figured than she'd like to be, wide-hipped and heavy-limbed with curly, blond hair, cornflower-blue eyes, and a sharply up-turned nose. With the help of her mother, who is a drama coach, she has become the school's star actress: last year she played Eliza in Weston's production of *My Fair Lady*. Although she earns solid grades in all of her subjects—she'll make the honor roll this fall—drama is her passion, she says, because "I love entertaining people, and I love putting on characters."

Also, no doubt, because she loves the spotlight: this morning, when she mentions a boy I haven't met, Amy turns, puts her hands on her hips, anchors her feet shoulder width apart, and bellows across the schoolyard, "Greg! Get over here! You have to meet Peggy."

She smiles wryly as Greg, looking startled, begins to make his way across the schoolyard for an introduction. "I'm not exactly shy," she says, her hands still on her hips. "I'm *bold.*"

Amy is bold. And brassy, and strong-willed. Like any teenager, she tries on and discards different selves as if they were so many pairs of Girbaud jeans, searching ruthlessly for a perfect fit. During a morning chat just before the school year began, she told me that her parents tried to coach her on how to respond to my questions. "They told me to tell you that they want me to be my own person," she complained. "My mother *told* me to tell you that. I do want to be my own person, but it's like, you're interviewing me about who *I* am and she's telling me what to say—that's not my own person, is it?"

When the morning bell rings, Amy and her friends cut off their conversations, scoop up their books, and jostle toward the school's entrance. Inside, Weston's hallways smell chalky, papery, and a little sweaty from gym class. The wood-railed staircases at either end of the two-story main building are worn thin in the middle from the scuffle of hundreds of pairs of sneakers pounding them at forty-eight-minute intervals for nearly seventy-five years. Amy's mother, Sharon, and her grandmother both attended this school. So will her two younger sisters. Her father, a mechanic who works on big rigs, is a more recent Weston recruit: he grew up in Georgia and came here after he and Sharon were married.

Amy grabs my hand, pulling me along like a small child or a slightly addled new student: within three minutes we have threaded our way through the dull-yellow hallways to her locker and then upstairs to room 238, Mrs. Richter's math class.

The twenty-two students that stream through the door with us run the gamut of physical maturity. Some of the boys are as small and compact as fourth graders, their legs sticking out of their shorts like pipe cleaners. A few are trapped in the agony of a growth spurt, and still others cultivate downy beards. The girls' physiques are less extreme: most are nearly their full height, and all but a few have already weathered the brunt of puberty. They wear topknots or ponytails, and their shirts are tucked neatly into their jeans.

Mrs. Richter, a ruddy, athletic woman with a powerful voice, has arranged the chairs in a three-sided square, two rows deep. Amy walks to the far side of the room and, as she takes her seat, falls into a typically feminine pose: she crosses her legs, folds her arms across her chest, and hunches forward toward her desk, seeming to shrink into herself. The sauciness of the playground disappears, and, in fact, she says hardly a word during class. Meanwhile, the boys, especially those who are more physically mature, sprawl in their chairs, stretching their legs long, expanding into the available space.

Nate, a gawky, sanguine boy who has shaved his head except for a small thatch that's hidden under an Oakland A's cap, leans his chair back on two legs and, although the bell has already rung, begins a noisy conversation with his friend Kyle.

Mrs. Richter turns to him, "What's all the discussion about, Nate?" she asks.

"He's talking to *me,"* Nate answers, pointing to Kyle. Mrs. Richter writes Nate's name on the chalkboard as a warning toward detention and he yells out in protest. They begin to quibble over the justice of her decision, their first—but certainly not their last—power struggle of the day. As they argue, Allison, a tall, angular girl who once told me, "My goal is to be the best wife and mother I can be," raises her hand to ask a question. Mrs. Richter, finishing up with Nate, doesn't notice.

"Get your homework out, everyone!" the teacher booms, and walks among the students, checking to make sure no one has shirked on her or his assignment. Allison, who sits in the front row nearest both the blackboard and the teacher, waits patiently for another moment, then, realizing she's not getting results, puts her hand down. When Mrs. Richter walks toward her, Allison tries another tack, calling out her question. Still, she gets no response, so she gives up.

As a homework assignment, the students have divided their papers into one hundred squares, color-coding each square prime or composite—prime being those numbers which are divisible only by one and themselves, and composite being everything else. Mrs. Richter asks them to call out the prime numbers they've found, starting with the tens.

Nate is the first to shout, "Eleven!" The rest of the class chimes in a second later. As they move through the twenties and thirties, Nate, Kyle, and Kevin, who sit near one another at the back of the class, call out louder and louder, casually competing for both quickest response and the highest decibel level. Mrs.

Richter lets the boys' behavior slide, although they are intimidating other students.

"Okay," Mrs. Richter says when they've reached one hundred. "Now, what do you think of one hundred and three? Prime or composite?"

Kyle, who is skinny and a little pop-eyed, yells out, "Prime!" but Mrs. Richter turns away from him to give someone else a turn. Unlike Allison, who gave up when she was ignored, Kyle isn't willing to cede his teacher's attention. He begins to bounce in his chair and chant, *"Prime! Prime! Prime!"* Then, when he turns out to be right, he rebukes the teacher, saying, *"See,* I told you."

When the girls in Mrs. Richter's class do speak, they follow the rules. When Allison has another question, she raises her hand again and waits her turn; this time, the teacher responds. When Amy volunteers her sole answer of the period, she raises her hand, too. She gives the wrong answer to an easy multiplication problem, turns crimson, and flips her head forward so her hair falls over her face.

Occasionally, the girls shout out answers, but generally they are to the easiest, lowest-risk questions, such as the factors of four or six. And their stabs at public recognition depend on the boys' largesse: when the girls venture responses to more complex questions the boys quickly become territorial, shouting them down with their own answers. Nate and Kyle are particularly adept at overpowering Renee, who, I've been told by the teacher, is the brightest girl in the class. (On a subsequent visit, I will see her lay her head on her desk when Nate overwhelms her and mutter, "I hate this class.")

Mrs. Richter doesn't say anything to condone the boys' aggressiveness, but she doesn't have to: they insist on—and receive—her attention even when she consciously tries to shift it elsewhere in order to make the class more equitable.

After the previous day's homework is corrected, Mrs. Richter begins a new lesson, on the use of exponents.

"What does three to the third power mean?" she asks the class.

"I know!" shouts Kyle.

Instead of calling on Kyle, who has already answered more than his share of questions, the teacher turns to Dawn, a somewhat more voluble girl who has plucked her eyebrows down to a few hairs.

"Do you know, Dawn?"

Dawn hesitates, and begins "Well, you count the number of threes and . . ."

"But I know!" interrupts Kyle. *"I know!"*

Mrs. Richter deliberately ignores him, but Dawn is rattled: she never finishes her sentence, she just stops.

"I know! ME!" Kyle shouts again, and then before Dawn recovers herself he blurts, *"It's three times three times three!"*

At this point, Mrs. Richter gives in. She turns away from Dawn, who is staring blankly, and nods at Kyle. "Yes," she says. "Three times three times three. Does everyone get it?"

"YES!" shouts Kyle; Dawn says nothing.

Mrs. Richter picks up the chalk. "Let's do some others," she says.

"Let me!" says Kyle.

"I'll pick on whoever raises their hand," she tells him.

Nate, Kyle, and two other boys immediately shoot up their hands, fingers squeezed tight and straight in what looks like a salute.

"Don't you want to wait and hear the problem first?" she asks, laughing.

They drop their hands briefly. She writes 8^4 on the board. "Okay, what would that look like written out?"

Although a third of the class raises their hands to answer—

including a number of students who haven't yet said a word—
she calls on Kyle anyway.

"Eight times eight times eight times eight," he says triumphantly, as the other students drop their hands.

When the bell rings, I ask Amy about the mistake she made
in class and the embarrassment it caused her. She blushes again.

"Oh yeah," she says. "That's about the only time I ever
talked in there. I'll never do that again."

▪

Voice and Silence

▪

I had chosen Amy, along with two of her friends, Evie
DiLeo and Becca Holbrook, as three of the subjects for this
book partly because, within minutes of our first meeting—and
months before I ever saw them in a classroom—they announced
to me that they were not like other girls at Weston: they were,
they proudly announced, feminists. Amy explained that to them
"feminism" meant that as adults they plan to be economically
independent of men. Until that time, though, it means "knowing
that boys aren't all they're cracked up to be."

I had hoped that these girls, with their bold credo, would
defy the statistics in the AAUW survey *Shortchanging Girls,
Shortchanging America*. Yet although they spoke of themselves
in terms of grit and independence, those qualities were rarely on
display in the classroom. Whereas their male classmates yelled
out or snapped the fingers of their raised hands when they
wanted to speak, these girls seemed, for the most part, to recede
from class proceedings, a charge they didn't deny.

"I don't raise my hand in my classes because I'm afraid I
have the wrong answer and I'll be embarrassed," Becca, who is

gangly and soft-spoken, explains one day during lunch. "My self-confidence will be taken away, so I don't want to raise my hand even if I really do know."

"I hate when teachers correct you," says Evie, who, dark-haired and serious, is enrolled in Weston's gifted students' program. "And it's worse when they say it's okay to do things wrong in that voice like 'It's okay, honey.' I can't handle it. I get really red and I start crying and I feel stupid."

"I think," Amy says slowly, "I think girls just worry about what people will say more than boys do, so they don't want to talk so much."

I mention to Amy that the boys freely volunteer in the math and science classes I've observed, even though their answers are often wrong. They seem to think it's okay to say "I think," to be unsure of a response.

Amy nods in agreement. "Boys never care if they're wrong. They can say totally off-the-wall things, things that have nothing to do with class sometimes. They're not afraid to get in trouble or anything. I'm not shy. But it's like, when I get into class, I just . . ." She shrugs her shoulders helplessly. "I just can't talk. I don't know why."

Girls' hesitance to speak out relative to boys is not mere stylistic difference; speaking out in class—and being acknowledged for it—is a constant reinforcement of a student's right to be heard, to take academic risks. Students who talk in class have more opportunity to enhance self-esteem through exposure to praise; they have the luxury of learning from mistakes and they develop the perspective to see failure as an educational tool. Boys such as Kyle and Nate feel internal permission to speak out whether they are bright or not, whether they are right or wrong, whether their comments are insightful, corrosive, combative, or utterly ridiculous. The important thing is to be recognized, to assert the "I am."

"I think my opinions are important, so I yell them out," Nate tells me one day after Mrs. Richter's math class. "The teacher'll tell you not to do it, but they answer your question before the people who raise their hands. Girls will sit there until the bell rings with their hands up and never get their question answered." He waves his hand in the air as if brushing the girls aside and says contemptuously, "Forget that."

According to gender equity specialists Myra and David Sadker, students who participate in class hold more positive attitudes toward school, and those attitudes enhance learning. Yet they also found that, in the typical classroom, boys overwhelmingly dominate the proceedings: they consistently command more of the teacher's time and energy than girls, receiving more positive reinforcement, more remediation, and more criticism. Nor is the difference just one of quantity: in the Sadkers' observations of one hundred classrooms in four states, they found that the boys were routinely asked more complex questions than girls, and were commended for their academic acumen, while girls were commended for social skills and docility.[1]

In every class I visit at Weston there is at least one boy like Nate or Kyle, a boy who demands constant and inappropriate attention and to whom the teacher succumbs: if she doesn't, after all, she won't get much done during that period. In a straight count of who talks in Weston classrooms—who yells out answers, who is called on by the teacher, who commands the most interaction—the ratio hovers roughly around five boys to one girl. Compared to other schools, however, this constitutes progress: the Sadkers placed the rate at eight to one.[2] Even in English class, traditionally girls' turf, Weston boys received roughly three times the recognition of their female classmates.

The argument can be made that boys as well as girls suffer

from the hidden curriculum. Boys such as Nate may be learning an unfortunate self-centeredness along with a lack of respect for their female classmates. Yet they still profit from the attention they receive. Ignored by their teachers and belittled by their male peers, girls lose heart: they may become reluctant to participate at all in class, unable to withstand the small failures necessary for long-term academic success. Even girls such as Amy, Evie, and Becca, who frequently proclaim that "guys are *so* obnoxious," have absorbed the hidden lessons of deference to them in the classroom, and, along with it, a powerful lesson in self-abnegation.

Several days after joining Amy in her math class, I visit Ms. Kelly's English class. Ms. Kelly is a second-year teacher: freckle-faced and snub-nosed, dressed in a T-shirt and khaki skirt, she barely looks older than her students. The class has been studying Greek mythology; today Ms. Kelly, who has placed the desks in clusters of six, instructs the students to write out the discussion they imagine took place between Zeus and Hera when she discovered he had fathered an illegitimate child.

"Any questions?" she asks, after explaining the assignment.

Two girls, Kathy and Amanda, raise their hands and she calls on Amanda. Amanda glances at Kathy, who sits in the group of desks next to hers. "Well, can you help me when you've answered her question?" she says politely. The teacher tends to Kathy, and then to a boy in another group who is misbehaving; she never returns to Amanda, who becomes frustrated.

"What are we supposed to do?" she mutters. "I don't get it." She puts her pencil down and looks over the shoulder of the girl sitting next to her. After a few minutes, she sighs wearily and begins to write.

I walk around the room, asking the students if I can read

their works-in-progress. Amanda, who will eventually get an A on her paper, covers hers when I ask to see it.

"Oh," she says, "mine's so stupid you wouldn't want to read it."

Kathy reluctantly hands me her work. As I skim through it, one of the boys shoves his paper at me.

"Don't you want to read mine?" he asks.

I smile politely, as unwilling as the teachers to chastise him for interrupting, and take his paper. The dialogue he's written is almost incoherent and laced with misuses of the archaic forms of "you," as in "Hera, I'll whip thou butt for that."

He smirks as I read.

"Good, huh?" he says, then takes the paper back to read to his seatmates.

During an earlier lesson, the students have composed their own original myths, and have voted on the one they think is the best in the class. At the end of today's period, Ms. Kelly reads the winner, written by a wiry, sharp-featured Latina girl named Amber. The tale is surprisingly artful, the story of a young boy's search for the answers to questions that his father says are unsolvable. His quest takes him through enchanted woods, where he encounters talking animals who help him unlock the secret of a magic waterfall. He attains wisdom through risk and adventure, and, in the end, brings insight as well as treasure home to lay before his father.

After class I ask Amber why she chose to make a boy, not a girl, the central character in her story. She shrugs. "I used a boy because little girls don't go into creepy places and explore things," she says. "And it was an adventure; it wouldn't be right if you used a girl."

I ask Ms. Kelly to lend me the students' stories from all of her class periods and flip through the stack. Although many girls chose men and boys as the embodiments of bravery, strength, and wisdom, it did not surprise me to find that not a single boy had imagined a female hero.

Certainly some girls at Weston act out, demand attention, clown in class, but when they try those tactics, using disruption as a tool to gain individual attention and instruction, they are not met with the same reward as boys.

In mid-November, Mrs. Richter is giving out grades to Amy's class. The teacher sits at her desk in the back corner of the room, and the students come up one by one, in reverse alphabetical order; their faces are tense on the way up, then pleased or disappointed on the way back.

When Dawn's turn comes, Mrs. Richter speaks sharply to her.

"You're getting a B," the teacher says, "but for citizenship, you're getting 'disruptive.' You've been talking a lot and there have been some outbursts."

Dawn scrunches her mouth over to one side of her face, lowers her eyes, and returns to her seat.

"Disruptive?" yells Nate from across the room where the teacher's voice has carried. *"She's* not disruptive, *I'm* disruptive."

Mrs. Richter laughs. "You've got that right," she says.

When his turn comes, Nate gets a B plus. "It would've been an A minus if you turned in your last homework assignment," Mrs. Richter says. As predicted, his citizenship comment is also 'disruptive,' but the bad news isn't delivered with the same sting as it was to Dawn—it's conferred with an indulgent smile. There is a tacit acceptance of a disruptive boy, because boys *are* disruptive. Girls are too, sometimes, as Dawn illustrates, but with different consequences.

So along with fractions and exponents, Dawn has learned that she has to tamp down assertive behavior, that she has to diminish herself both to please the teacher and to appease the boys, with whom she cannot compete. Meanwhile, Nate has learned that monopolizing the class period and defying the teacher gets him in trouble, but he also garners individual attention, praise, and answers to his questions.

Over the course of the semester, Dawn slowly stops disrupting; she stops participating too. At the semester break, when I check with Mrs. Richter on the classes' progress, she tells me, "Dawn hardly talks at all now because she's overpowered by the boys. She can't get the attention in class, so she's calmed down."

Nate, however, hasn't changed a bit, but whereas Dawn's behavior is viewed as containable, the teacher sees Nate's as inevitable. "I'll go through two weeks of torture before I'll give him detention," Mrs. Richter says. "But you have to tolerate that behavior to a certain extent or he won't want to be there at all, he'll get himself kicked out.

"I know his behavior works for him, though," she continues. "He talks more, he gets more answers out there, and he does well because of it. I try to tell him that we need to let others talk so they can understand too. But when I do, I begin and end with positive things about his behavior and sandwich the bad stuff in the middle. I'm never sure which part he really hears."

■

Unbalanced Equations:
Girls, Math, and the Confidence Gap

■

Although the skewed equations of voice and silence are not the exclusive province of math or science, they are arguably the most damaging in those classes, where the tradition of male dominance is most entrenched. *Shortchanging Girls, Shortchanging America* showed that girls and boys who like math and science have higher levels of self-esteem than other children (and, for that matter, that children with high self-esteem tend to like math and science). For girls in particular, those subjects are also tied to ambition: girls who like math and science—who are, perhaps, more resistant to traditional gender roles—are more likely to aspire to careers as professionals. As adults, women who have taken more than two math courses in college are the only ones who subsequently achieve pay equity and even earn more than their male counterparts.[3]

Unfortunately, girls are far less likely than boys to retain their affection for math and science. As they move through school, their confidence in their mathematical abilities falters and their competence soon follows suit.[4] It's important to note that the confidence drop often *precedes* the competence drop: even in early adolescence, girls who perform as well as boys often evaluate their skills as lesser. By their senior year, convinced of their ineptitude, they become less persistent in solving problems than their male peers and less likely than boys with poorer grades in the same class to believe they can pursue a math-related career.[5]

Amy is one of those girls who have little faith in her math

skills, although her performance is well above average. "School is important to me," she says during lunch one day, when I catch her struggling with a homework assignment. "I want to do good in school and be proud of myself. I don't want to be a lazy bum. And I'll need math when I'm older. There's math in everything, no matter what, so it's important to learn. So I know I should have a better attitude, but I just want to give up. It's not that I don't try, it's just that I don't believe in myself and I don't get it. I'm just so *slow.*" She glares down at her paper.

Amy goes on to say that a person has to be smarter to do well at math than at English. She also believes that girls—herself included—have a natural bent toward English and boys toward math, which, by her logic, would make girls less intelligent than boys. When I point this out, she begins to backtrack, but then stops, leans forward, and drops her voice, continuing in a solemn, confidential tone. "Boys do better in math, believe me, they do. Girls, we have other things on our minds, I guess."

Yet in spite of this purported genetic disadvantage, during the same class in which Dawn receives her disappointing citizenship mark, Amy receives an A in math, which clinches her spot on the school honor roll. The news doesn't change her assumptions one whit.

"It's not hard to get an A in here," she says. "Basically you just have to show up. And I still think I've done it wrong every day. I'll probably be in, like, special ed. math next year."

From her vantage point in the front of the class, Mrs. Richter says she can see the girls' waning interest in her subject, and it frustrates her. She is especially disturbed by a trend she's recently noticed: the boys in her class tend to improve over the course of the school year—some even jump from D's to B's or A's—while girls stay exactly where they were in September: the good students remain good students, the poor students remain poor. She worries that, for the girls, the holding pattern is simply temporary. Next year, perhaps the year after, even the good students may begin to slide; they simply don't trust their ability.

"The boys see math as something that shows they're brainy and they like being able to show off that way," Mrs. Richter explains. "And they're more risk-taking than the girls, so they'll do better on tests every time, even if the girls turn in all their work and the boys don't. It's like the girls set themselves up to fail. They do the work. I see them practice one kind of problem over and over because I've told them it'll be on a test. But then the test comes and they miss it anyway. I've heard them say, 'Oh no, I got that kind of problem wrong last time.' So even though they practiced it, they go and get it wrong again. Amy does that. She'll look at a problem and say, 'There's no way I can do this,' and give up, even though I know she has the skills. But the boys are different: they can get all the homework wrong, but they don't care as long as they tried. And then they figure out *why* it's wrong instead of being embarrassed about it. That makes them more confident."

Mrs. Richter considers parents, more than teachers, to be responsible for girls' confidence gap. Every year, she says, her female students tell her, "My mother said she couldn't do math either," as if math skills are genetic, which, the teacher hastens to add, they are not.[6] Still, she admits, the classroom culture can further undercut the girls. "I try to teach them the same; I try to call on them the same. But I know I don't always hold them accountable the same way. I let the girls off the hook because they get so embarrassed when they're wrong. And the boys want control of the class, so sometimes they get it . . ." She trails off, shaking her head. "I don't know," she says. "We try, but somehow we're still not getting to the girls, and we're going to lose them."

■

Bad Chemistry: "Guys Like It When You Act All Helpless"

■

It is another late-fall morning under the oak tree at Weston. Amy, Becca, and Evie huddle together slightly apart from the other students, the intimate turn to their shoulders making it clear that they're exchanging the juiciest gossip. A squadron of seventh-grade boys on bicycles zips by and the girls look up, annoyed, sidling to the left to avoid being hit.

A few seconds later, Becca, usually the most reserved of her friends, shrieks.

"Get that away from me!"

The bikers are forgotten as the girls scatter, screaming, their faces flushed, revealing Carl Ross, a boy from Evie's math class, whose feet are firmly planted where the girls once stood. An uncapped jar labeled "Felicia" dangles from his left hand. Until a minute ago, it held a large spider he'd captured for extra credit in science class. Felicia is currently hanging from a dead pine needle in his other hand, her legs tucked in and body contracted in fear.

Becca runs about ten feet and turns around. When she smiles, she reveals a mouth full of braces. "I'm *deathly* afraid of spiders," she says, her eyes shining as she looks back at her tormentor.

The other two girls run up to her. "God, me too!" Amy says breathlessly, clutching her friend's arms. "When I saw *Arachnophobia* my dad had to go check my room for me. He had to look under the bed!"

Evie's cheeks are pink and her dark hair is falling from its

21

bun. She tucks the wayward wisps back in place as a second boy lets the bug drop from his finger by a lengthening strand of web. "Yuck, how disgusting," she says, widening her eyes. "I hope he doesn't come near me with that."

As a woman standing among these girls, I wasn't sure how to react. I desperately wanted them to stand up to the boys who increasingly joined in the game. I wanted them to be brave, to marvel at the spider's jewel-green body, to ask for a turn at holding it and watching it try to spin its escape. But I felt the pressure too: a real girl, a girl who wants a boy to like her, runs screaming from spiders. The more she likes a boy, the more she allows him to terrorize her, and the more helpless she pretends to be. Showing any real interest in spiders would've been imprudent for the girls, a denial of their newly important femininity. During my year at Weston, I saw girls run from spiders innumerable times; with each flight toward traditional femininity, I thought about who has permission, who has the right in our culture, to explore the natural world, to get dirty and muddy, to think spiders and worms and frogs are neat, to bring them in for extra credit in science. In fact, to be engaged in science at all.

"I'm not *really* afraid of that stuff, except snakes and blood," Amy admits later, after the hoopla. "But guys like it if you act all helpless and girly, so you do."

As with math, there is a circular relationship among girls' affection for science, their self-esteem, and their career plans. But unlike in math, the achievement gap between girls and boys in science is actually widening: the National Assessment of Educational Progress found that, for thirteen-year-olds, gender differences in all areas of science performance except biology actually increased during the 1980s, with boys' skills improving and girls' slipping during that time.[7] This is particularly disturbing when one considers that today's young people are growing up in an era of rapid technological change; without a solid grounding in science, girls will not only be unable to participate in shaping that change, they will be helpless in the face of it.

Certainly, the culture outside the classroom discourages scientific competence in girls. Boys still have more casual exposure to science—whether it's light meters, chemistry sets, or, like Carl and his friends, spiders—and they're more likely to have computers at home.[8] Science toys are still marketed almost exclusively toward boys, with boys featured on packages (or, worse still, girls *watching* boys) and the world of video games seems constructed with an entirely male audience in mind.[9]

In school, girls opt out—or are pushed out—of science at every stage of advancement. In high school, boys and girls take introductory biology and chemistry in similar numbers, but far more boys go on to physics or advanced chemistry, while girls, if they take science at all, continue with biology.[10] And although the numbers of women who pursue the sciences has skyrocketed, there were formerly so few that even huge jumps yield small results: for instance, the number of female engineers grew 131 percent during the 1980s, but women still make up only 8 percent of that field. In fact, a scant 16 percent of currently employed scientists are female, and that figure may well have peaked: by the late 1980s, the numbers of women pursuing degrees in science and engineering (excluding the social sciences) had leveled off and was dropping, especially in advanced physics and computer science.[11]

Nonetheless, in spite of the achievement gap, today's girls believe that they can excel in science; the trouble is, boys (perhaps prejudiced by the overreaction to spiders and snakes) do not share that belief about their female classmates.[12] Because of that disparity, science laboratory groups—in which boys grab equipment from girls, perform experiments for them, and ridi-

23

cule girls' contributions—can become less an opportunity for partnership than a microcosm of unintended lessons about gender.[13]

Amy's science class is taught by Mr. Sinclair, a mustachioed fellow with a receding hairline, who chose teaching as a profession during what he describes as his idealistic youth in the late 1960s. He periodically considers changing careers, mostly for financial reasons, but he enjoys his work too much to quit. Instead, he stays sharp by attending conferences on science instruction, subscribing to newsletters, seeking out new ways to teach. He tries hard to be creative because, he says, the kids tend not to like physical science very much. But judging from what happens in his classroom, it's really the girls who don't like it.

Like Mrs. Richter, Mr. Sinclair never intentionally discriminates against the girls in his class; both he and the other eighth-grade science teacher at Weston—who is also male—are quick to point out the few girls who do participate (although in further conversation I found that many of those girls felt neither affection nor affinity for the subject). What I saw instead, even more than in the math classes I observed, was a kind of passive resistance to participation by the girls that went unquestioned by the teacher. Call it gender bias by omission. When, week after week, boys raised their hands to ask or answer questions in far greater numbers than girls, when only boys shouted out responses, when boys enthusiastically offered up extra-credit demonstrations, the teacher simply didn't notice.

The very morning that Amy flees shrieking from Felicia the spider, Mr. Sinclair invites me to observe as her section of his physical science class performs an easy, fun experiment called "The Cartesian Diver." Each group of three students is given an empty dishwashing liquid bottle, an eyedropper, and a beaker of water. The idea is to fill the bottle with water, drop in the dropper, and, through some magical process that the students must determine (which turns out to be placing a little water in the dropper in advance, then squeezing the bottle to cause mass displacement), make the dropper sink and float at will.

In Amy's lab group there is another girl, Donna, and a boy, Liam, who sits between them. Liam performs the experiment as the two girls watch, occasionally offering encouragement, but no criticism. When he is successful, Amy squeals and pats him on the arm. Eventually Liam lets Donna and Amy each try the diver exactly once; then he recovers it and continues to play.

In another group of two girls and one boy directly behind Amy, Roger stands behind the girls, supervising . . . sort of.

"You're doing it wrong, ha-ha," he taunts in a singsong voice. Roger has a long rattail and a pierced ear; he wears an oversized tie-dyed T-shirt. The girls, who have styled their long blond hair identically, huddle together, trying to ignore him, and continue to attempt the experiment. Roger watches them a moment longer, then grabs the bottle from them, pours the water into the beaker and walks away with the dropper. The girls do not protest. When he comes back a few minutes later, the girls have refilled the bottle, but, still uncertain about how to proceed, have decided to empty it again and start over.

"Oh, smart," Roger says sarcastically. "*Real* smart." He grabs the bottle again. "*I'll* do it." He refills the bottle, puts the dropper in, and completes the experiment while the girls watch in silence.

I wander to the far corner of the room, where Allison, from Amy's math class, and Karla, a round-faced Latina girl with deep dimples and black hair pulled into a topknot, are having trouble with their diver. There are several girls sitting around them, yet they have asked a boy for help.

"I told him he could do it for us because he has man's hands," Karla, who once told me she wants to be an astronaut, tells me, smiling.

A second boy is watching the scene. When his friend completes the experiment, he pumps his fist in the air. "Yes!" he says. "A *man* had to do it!"

"But *how* did you do it?" Allison asks.

"I have magic hands," the first boy answers. *"Man* hands," and he laughs.

The girls laugh too—acting appropriately "helpless and girly"—but they never learn how to do the experiment. Instead, like the girls in the other groups, they have become outsiders in the learning process, passive observers rather than competent participants. In truth, "man hands" do complete most of the experiments in the room.

Later, Mr. Sinclair tells me that his classroom is free of gender bias. "I try to emphasize the subject for both," he tells me. "I never tell girls they can't do something." But there was much that he didn't see. When I ask whether he's noticed that boys speak out more—sometimes exclusively—in his class, and are more eager to perform extra-credit demonstrations, he looks up at the ceiling and squints thoughtfully. "Yeah," he says, "that's true. I'm guessing they're more mechanical, doing stuff with machines outside of school. Boys probably do have that, and it's probably true that gives them an advantage I hadn't thought of."

We discuss the marketing of science toys and again he slowly nods his head. "I didn't think about that either," he says. "Yeah, that's probably true, the toys are geared toward boys; that would give them an advantage too."

Finally, I tell him what I've seen in lab groups.

"Man hands," he says, looking bemused. "Really? Well, hopefully they picked up that it's the level of water and not gender that does it."

▪

You Can Say "I Think" in There

▪

Teachers at Weston varied tremendously in their reactions to boys' dominance in their classroom. Some, like Mr. Sinclair, simply didn't see it. Others fought the boys for control: one eighth-grade history teacher—who proudly told me that his wife had founded the local NOW chapter—would break into class discussions to say, "We haven't heard from any of the girls in the room. What do *you* think?" The girls seemed to be uncomfortable with such attention at first, but, as the year progressed, they became increasingly vocal. During a lesson on England's debtor's prisons one girl even yelled out, "What about the women? What happened to them?"

Another teacher, Liz Muney, who runs the district's gifted program and teaches sixth grade at Weston, told me that when *Shortchanging Girls, Shortchanging America* was first released, she discussed its findings with her class. She explained that, from now on, she was going to call equally on girls and boys, and, just to make sure that she did, she held her attendance roster during class.

"After two days the boys blew up," she told me one afternoon during a break between classes. "They started complaining and saying that I was calling on the girls more than them. I showed them it wasn't true and they had to back down. I kept on doing it, but for the boys, equality was hard to get used to; they perceived it as a big loss."

Like the teachers, the girls I interviewed were not always aware that they were being ignored in class (in some classes, such as math, they even preferred it), but their favorite teachers just happened to be the ones who actively wrestled with the hidden curriculum. For Amy, Evie, and Becca that teacher is Ms. Nellas, with whom they study American history.

"She teaches good," Becca assures me one day during lunch.

"Yeah," Evie says. "She makes you want to strive to be better. She'll do 'the power clap' and say how good you're do-ing . . ."

"Even if your work sucks," interrupts Amy, whose work rarely "sucks." "So you try really hard. And you can say what you want in there and no one ever says you're wrong; it's like, you're not afraid to say 'I think.' "

Becca returns to her original assessment: "She teaches good," she says, nodding her head.

Amy's demeanor in Ms. Nellas' class is utterly different than it is in math, science, or even English: she uncrosses her legs and plants both feet on the floor. She sits up straight, leans forward, and thrusts her hand in the air. Once, she even gives an impatient (and uncharacteristic) little wave for attention.

This is election year, and when I first visit Ms. Nellas' class in late October, she is discussing the electoral college. She stands at the front of the room, a craggy-faced woman with an easy smile, and offers a blunt explanation of that esoteric organiza-tion: "The reason there's an electoral college is that people who wrote the constitution—who were all men—*didn't* really want everyone to participate in electing officials," she says. "They only trusted people like themselves, so they said, 'We don't want the common people to vote. They can't read or write and we can't trust them to elect leaders.' And they certainly didn't trust *women,* so they weren't about to let *them* vote."

During the lesson, boys raise their hands roughly twice as often as girls, but Ms. Nellas has a trick for making sure that girls who do volunteer are recognized: after she asks a question she looks around the room to see whose hands are up, then says, "Okay, first Randy, then Jeffrey, then Amy." If she inadvertently continues without exhausting the list, the slighted students are quick to protest. She also promotes a more tolerant culture through her classroom decor: among the encouraging messages she has posted on the classroom walls are "You Have a *Duty to Assist* Anyone Who Asks for Help" and the somewhat convoluted "Everybody Is Good at *Some* of the Abilities." Under the clock, in the most strategic spot in the room, there is a yellowed poster depicting a teacher in Renaissance garb saying to his student, "Columbus, will yer [sic] sit down and stop asking all those dumb questions?" Beneath it a caption reads: " 'Dumb' questions lead to learning. Don't be afraid to ask."

Amy's class meets just before Ms. Nellas' free period, so, one afternoon after the bell rings, I linger behind to chat. Ms. Nellas invites me to sit at one of the students' recently vacated desks and settles in opposite me. As a veteran teacher—she's been in the profession for over twenty years—Ms. Nellas is comfortable discussing both her strengths and her weaknesses. She looks pleased when I tell her that girls seem to feel the most comfortable in her class, but adamantly denies that she's solved the gender dilemma.

"I definitely play to the boys," she says, shaking her head. "I know I do. The squeaky wheel gets the grease and they're louder."

She mentions Andrew, a curly-haired, slightly pudgy boy in Amy's class who shoots his hand up—sometimes snapping his fingers for attention—whenever she asks a question. When called on, he tends not only to answer but to offer up an additional mini-lecture of his own.

"Andrew's into history," Ms. Nellas says. "He knows a lot

and he teaches the class things with what he has to say, so he's a good resource and I like that. But on the other hand he's loud, and, like a lot of boys, he pulls my attention. I know that means they walk out of here with greater self-esteem, they feel more valued. For the girls, it seems more important that they feel a personal bond, that makes them feel valued. I have that with Amy, Evie, and Becca, but I don't have that with all of them. I try to make it up some by encouraging girls to talk, by stressing that a question is a question and every question is worthwhile"—Ms. Nellas gestures to her Columbus poster—"but I know some girls end up feeling bad, they feel reduced by the experience of my class."

Like many teachers at Weston, Ms. Nellas is an advocate of cooperative learning: students collaborating on projects in groups, each with an assigned role. Cooperative learning—in which success is not contingent on quick response time or a loud voice—is said to be especially beneficial for girls and has become somewhat voguish in progressive schools. But, as with lab groups, the interactions, if not effectively monitored, can merely reinforce the students' stereotypes. "I've noticed that when they do group work, the boys want to be the leader," Ms. Nellas says, "and the girls always take the recorder role and that's a problem. I suppose I let it happen, too, but I don't want to assign them the roles in groups because I'm afraid of my own prejudices. I think I'd pick the quick students to lead the group, and so I might end up with the boys too, although I think I'd pick more girls than they do.

"The dynamics are already in place when they get here," she continues, "and they don't improve as they get older: when I teach high school, boys put their arm around me, pat my head like I'm a pet or something because I'm a woman. It can be funny, but it's still a power play. It's all about control, about who's in charge. When they really act out, though, I'll just stop the class and wait, even if it takes thirty seconds and it's driving me crazy. That sounds like a long time, but it's less of a waste, in the end, than sending them to the principal or yelling at the student. That way, they don't get the power, they don't get the attention, and they don't get the control. And *maybe* you can make it a little more equal."

2

Toeing the Line: Schoolgirls

■

■

■

In algebra class, Lindsay Sutter sits toward the back of the room with her friend Suzy Maynard. Neither girl likes math, and they hope their physical distance from the teacher will give them some measure of anonymity, as well as the opportunity for a furtive chat. Lindsay is a slender, graceful girl with hips that she thinks of as fat rather than merely wide-set, and pale blond hair that reaches midway down her back. Her face is round and her eyes wide and blue; with her green T-shirt, faded jeans, and scuffed Keds, Lindsay would be the image of the 1960s California Girl except for a slight flatness at the tip of her nose. That and what one of her teachers called a "piercing intelligence": Lindsay is in the gifted program at Weston and on the advanced math track. Her seventh-grade history teacher describes her as a "dynamo," and this year, when a shy new student arrived from Mexico, it was Lindsay who was asked by her English teacher to mentor the girl, helping her to adapt both academically and socially to Weston.

Like Lindsay, Suzy is a gifted student. She has a head full of light brown curls, coffee-colored eyes, and a somewhat prim expression. Suzy often laughs after she speaks—a nervous, high-pitched giggle—as if she's trying to disassociate herself from her own ideas; when she isn't talking, she looks down demurely.

The girls have scoped out their territory accurately: discipline is loose during most of the algebra lesson, and they quickly abandon their assignment, although they leave their books open in case the teacher looks their way. Since it's the last week in October, they fall into a discussion about Halloween costumes. Suzy is planning to dress as a black cat; Lindsay says she's going to be "a bunny," adding, "Doesn't that fit my personality?" They go on to talk about an English assignment, and, after a few guilty minutes devoted to their math lesson, drift into a conversation about their future career plans.

"I'd like to be an interior decorator or a teacher," says Lindsay, who has also expressed interest in being a stay-at-home mom, like her own mother. "I like putting colors together and making them look right, but I think it might be kind of a waste. I want to help people, and I don't know if it's helping someone to tell them where the couch goes."

"My parents would be proud if I were a surgeon," says Suzy, who is an only child. "But it's too gross—whenever I think about it I think about the shower scene in *Psycho*. . . . I think maybe a lawyer."

Lindsay snorts at this notion, which she seems to view as ludicrous, and swings her hair over her shoulders. Suzy laughs, too, a little anxiously.

"I'm trying to imagine this sweet girl questioning someone on the witness stand," Lindsay says, still laughing. "She'd be in a cold sweat."

"It's true," Suzy says sheepishly. "I'm too cute to be a lawyer."

"Yeah," says Lindsay. "You'd be like: 'Did you kill him?

No? Oh, okay, sorry.' " She ducks her head shyly, still playing Suzy-the-lawyer, and pretends to turn and slink away.

"It might be interesting, though," Suzy says, still trying to be taken seriously.

"Interesting?" Lindsay exclaims. "Well, that's one way of putting it. You'd meet some characters, all right."

Suzy capitulates and joins the game. "Yeah, all the guys you'd meet would be murderers. Can you imagine? 'Hi, Mom, this is my husband—no, he didn't do it.' " Both girls crack up.

As used by Lindsay and Suzy, "sweet" and "cute" are interchangeable with "deferential," "polite," or "passive." They are code words for that time-honored notion of the good girl: the girl who is nice before she is anything else—before she is vigorous, bright, even before she is honest. As the girls talk, Suzy tries to put forth an alternative vision of herself, imagining all the opportunity her sharp intellect could provide, but in the end she betrays both her intelligence and her ability to agree with Lindsay: she is too cute to be competent. This in spite of the fact that law is now an acceptable field for bright women to enter. This in spite of the fact that Suzy's own aunt is a judge.

■

Too Cute to Be Competent

■

The lessons of the hidden curriculum teach girls to value silence and compliance, to view those qualities as a virtue. In fact, students tend to believe that, although they pay more attention to boys, teachers actually like girls better: as one Weston girl once told me, ticking the list off on her fingers, "teachers like us because we're nicer, quieter, and better behaved."[1] And the girls are right: teachers *are* more likely to describe girls as "ideal" pupils.[2] Yet since, in practice, educators reward assertiveness and aggression over docility, the very behavior that is prized in girls becomes an obstacle to their success. Furthermore, the praise girls earn for their exemplary passivity discourages them from experimenting with the more active, risk-taking learning styles that would serve them better in the long run.[3] As the author of one study put it, by adolescence, girls have learned to get along, while boys have learned to get ahead.[4]

Girls like Lindsay and Suzy are the biggest losers: gifted girls, who best combine tractability with superior performance, receive less attention from their teachers, and often their talents are overlooked entirely. When Liz Muney, who directs the gifted program in the Weston school district, reviewed her files in the late 1980s, she discovered that boys were referred to her twice as often as girls for special testing, precisely because giftedness is seen as aberrant, and girls strive to conform. Since she alerted teachers to her findings, she says, the ratio in the district has improved.

Although they're ignored in the classroom, smart girls are singled out by their peers for stigmatization.[5] Asked directly, most of the girls at Weston will say that it is acceptable for a girl to excel, to get good grades. Yet behind their backs, girls like Lindsay and Suzy are referred to as "schoolgirls," an insult so great that, once tipped off, I never revealed the title of this book. The social pressure, Liz Muney says, has prompted innumerable Weston girls to repudiate their intelligence (as well as their self-esteem) and drop out of the district's gifted program.

As they proceed through school—and, in the case of Lindsay and Suzy, as they consider career options—gifted girls who remain academically engaged must negotiate between the independence necessary to fulfill their potential and the compliance which, although expected of them, is in direct conflict with standing out and shining bright. The task is daunting: how can they, after all, be both selfless and selfish, silent and outspoken, cooperative and competitive?

In their extensive work on girls' psychological development conducted in two private all-girls schools, psychologists Lyn Mikel Brown and Carol Gilligan found that, confounded by this irresolvable dilemma, their subjects invented a superior self who could solve it—"the perfect girl": "the girl who has no bad thoughts or feelings, the kind of person everyone wants to be with . . . [it is] the girl who speaks quietly, calmly, who is always nice and kind, never mean or bossy."[6] The "perfect girl" acts as an imaginary companion and a constant reproach. She reminds young women to silence themselves rather than speak their true feelings, which they come to consider "stupid," "selfish," "rude," or just plain irrelevant. To achieve the ideal that this exemplary creature represents, Brown and Gilligan's girls believed they must suppress the unruly self, with all of its nasty opinions and rebellious feelings; as Carolyn Heilbrun has written, they believed they must sacrifice "truth on the altar of niceness."[7]

In her relentless selflessness, the "perfect girl" is painfully reminiscent of the Victorian "angel in the house," the woman who, through saintlike virtue, conquers personal desire and lives only to enhance the lives of others. In that era, if women unleashed anger or rebelliousness they were deemed monsters; they were shut away, depicted, like Bertha in Charlotte Brontë's *Jane Eyre,* as the "madwoman in the attic."[8] Such renunciation of self inevitably caused ill health: the nineteenth century saw an upswing of emotional "hysteria" in upper-class women, as well as an epidemic of "fasting girls," who willfully refused food, sometimes unto death.[9]

But today's "perfect girl" doesn't just bludgeon young women into a bland silence: she wreaks havoc on their academic self-image as well. Girls like Lindsay and Suzy believe that, in addition to being perfectly nice, they must be perfectly smart. In his study of the effects of gender, race, and class on self-esteem, psychologist Charles L. Richman found that high-achieving white girls in particular are subject to unrealistic standards of success. When they fell short, they overgeneralized failures with an intense self-punitiveness; by late adolescence, their self-esteem had spiraled downward.[10]

■

"Good Enough" Isn't

■

Lindsay, especially, is in the grip of what writer Louise Bogan has called "the knife of the perfectionist attitude."[11] In conversation, she moves her neatly manicured hands nervously; sometimes they tremble, ever so slightly. I once asked her what she'd change to make her life happier, more relaxed: she said that she'd move to the country, where she'd be near more trees, and "no matter what I did, I'd get perfect grades every time, straight A's. It seems like no matter how hard I try, I'm always doing something wrong." During another conversation she said, "I pressure myself to do perfect; I can make myself sick doing it. I don't like to get below a B. If I'm honest, I don't like to get below an A. I just feel like I failed."

Lindsay's vision of excellence is so unattainable that she's left herself little room to maneuver, and little leeway for positive self-esteem. Like the girls in Richman's study, she inevitably falls short of her ideal and becomes self-recriminating. To hide her imagined flaws, she withdraws from taking risks and has developed a low threshold for humiliation, especially in math class, where she is slowly losing ground. "In math, I just keep my hand down because I'm always afraid," she explains. "The two times I raised my hand last year I made these stupid mistakes like nine plus nine is sixteen, that was one. It was embarrassing; everybody else would be getting it and then I'd be making these stupid, stupid mistakes. So I just stopped raising my hand."

Lindsay does not, however, fear risk when it is appropriate to her vision of femininity; in fact, where expressing affection is concerned, Lindsay is downright aggressive. When the bell rings for lunch, it takes Lindsay about ten minutes to walk the fifty feet from her locker to the schoolyard. Every few steps, she sees someone she knows—a girlfriend, a younger boy, someone from her church youth group—and she breaks off in mid-sentence to run toward them, flinging her arms around them and hugging them as if they're newly released hostages. Sometimes her friends respond in kind, sometimes they look a little startled. Mostly they hug back, a bit less exuberantly, and shrug. "Lindsay just attacks," Suzy explains, watching her friend engulf a tiny sixth-grade boy.

Yet it is in this display, and what immediately follows, that the cost of braiding the ideal girl with the ideal student becomes disturbingly clear. In between the emotional reunions with her friends—which reaffirm her essential "sweetness"—Lindsay pulls from her locker the brown-bag meal her mother has packed for her. She holds it in her right hand and extends her arm into the hallway behind her as if she is holding something foul; she doesn't even turn her head. One of her friends walks by and grabs the bag, laughing.

"What has Lindsay's mom made me today?" she asks.

Lindsay explains that she doesn't eat her lunch because she is too nervous. "I'm such an uptight person," she says. "I'm so worried about doing perfect in all my classes and everything that my stomach ties in knots and I can't eat. I can only really eat late at night, when I'm not awake so I don't really know what I'm doing."

Lindsay has been taught both to achieve and to minimize her success, to be self-determining and to value others over herself. She struggles with the specter of the perfect girl in the classroom, among her peers, even at home. Several weeks after the girls' conversation on careers, I grab Lindsay's lunch—as well as Lindsay and Suzy—and the three of us head to the school library. We settle in at a table in a corner of the room, surrounded by outdated textbooks and audiovisual equipment, breathing in the room's musty smell. While Suzy and I split both lunches, Lindsay talks about her schoolwork and her family, whom she loves very much, but, who, she believes, intensifies the pressure she already places on herself.

"The other day I brought home my report card and I got a B in science," she says. "I was kind of thrilled, because the class was so hard, but my mom said, 'Why didn't you get an A?' and she looked stricken. So I said, 'Mom, it's a really hard class, hardly anyone got A's.' She said, 'You have to get an A to get into biology next year.' I don't want to get into biology. I don't want to take advanced science. I already have to do geometry and that's bad enough."

It is hard to imagine Lindsay's mother, Alice, as so baldly critical of Lindsay's academic performance, especially in math or science. Whenever I've talked to her, Alice has spoken of her daughter with pride; she has described Lindsay as caring, bright, and, like herself, more verbal than mechanical. But since in Lindsay's world, there is only perfection and failure, even small criticisms become magnified and sting deeply; this is the first time in our conversation that Lindsay's eyes fill with tears.

Lindsay's eyes well up again when she talks about her brother Mark, who is two years older than she is. She is convinced that her parents favor her older brother, although she doesn't know why. *"He's* not perfect," she says. "He's obnoxious." Suzy bobs her head in corroboration.

As she discusses her brother, Lindsay slouches in her chair and looks increasingly despondent. "He cuts me down all the time and makes fun of me, and my mom never tells him to leave me alone. Maybe I'm not the perfect daughter, but I don't see that he's so perfect either.

"Like last week I brought home a B plus on my algebra test and I was excited, I thought it was good, for me." Here Suzy breaks in to explain why Lindsay finds this particular B plus acceptable. "And my brother brought home something he'd done in his drafting class. It was pretty and it was done on the computer and he'd gotten one of the highest grades in the class. So he's waving it around and saying, 'See how great it is, see how wonderful and how perfect it is,' and I'm trying to talk about my B plus in algebra, and my parents say, I swear to God, 'Hey, Mark, that's great, that's fantastic . . .' " She turns her head briefly to an imaginary person behind her and says in a flat, dismissive tone, " 'What did you say, Lindsay?' "

This makes her tear up a third time, and she runs a finger across her lower eyelid. "It makes me feel inferior. I don't know why they favor him. What do they expect from me? What's he doing that I'm not? I think maybe I should act more like Mark, but if I did, if I acted arrogant like him, then I wouldn't have any friends. Maybe I'm not perfect, maybe there's stuff I could do, but I really try. And I try harder and harder because I want them to notice, to tell me I did something better than he did. So it's like I have to build myself up, because they won't."

Lindsay in no way connects the difference in her parents' treatment of her and her brother to the different expectations we place on boys and girls. But what she's describing at home is akin to the dynamic that permeates both our culture and our classrooms: Mark is praised for aggressiveness; Lindsay knows she must balance drive with deference. Mark is allowed free play of the self; Lindsay believes she is only valued for her "perfect" qualities. She cannot understand why the very behavior that would disgrace her is rewarded in her brother.

I was surprised to find Lindsay so wounded by this, since in earlier conversations she had seemed to accept girls' second-class status: she is the girl who thinks her friend is too "sweet" to pursue a legal career and who once told me that she thinks women aren't "cut out" to be President because "they're a lot more sensitive. If a war broke out, I think it would really crush them." She is the only one among the girls who wants to be supported by a man so she can be a stay-at-home mom (although she is not the only one whose mother stays at home), and she has a certain contempt for some of the other girls I am interviewing, whom she calls "libbers." Yet, like the girls in Richman's study, Lindsay has not reconciled her traditional image of femininity with her desire to be recognized and celebrated; whichever way she turns, she loses.

Before the bell rings, Lindsay mentions that she's playing soccer on Saturday. The game will decide whether her team goes on to the regional play-offs, and she invites me to watch. Sports are supposed to be a gateway to self-esteem for girls: athletic young women are reputed to be less depressed than their peers, more positive in their body image, and more willing to take risks on and off the playing field.[12]

Lindsay puts it another way. "Soccer," she says dramatically, "is my life."

▪

Brothers and Sisters: The Big Game

▪

The Sutters live on the outskirts of Weston, in one of a series of suburban tract developments with names such as Oak Glen and Shady Trails. There are no sidewalks here. Children play in their yards or on dead-end streets; adults rarely go out without their cars. At midday on a Saturday there is no one in sight. The Sutters' house, at the end of a cul-de-sac, is small but cheery, landscaped with rose bushes and a large cherry tomato plant that Lindsay tends. Lindsay and Mark have been at the soccer field for hours. Their mother, Alice, was there too, but returned to escort me to the game in the family's minivan. Alice has dark hair, which is held back at the sides with barrettes, thinly chiseled lips, and large, pink-framed plastic glasses. Her eyes are the same pale blue as Lindsay's.

We drive through quiet, tree-lined streets, the red and gold leaves fluttering in the breeze. In late November, California looks like Middle America in September, luxuriously autumnal. Alice concentrates on the road, checking for turns and talking intermittently in a bright, staccato voice. Her style is self-conscious, like her daughter's, and she frequently apologizes for "rambling," once saying, "I hope you can make sense of this stuff, but I guess that's your job."

Alice has told me that the Sutters live by traditional family values: they go to church on Sundays and believe Christian tenets will guide them toward good, just lives. They don't own a television (Alice says it turns her husband, Larry, into a "zombie"), and they avoid movies that feature explicit sex or violence. As parents, they've divided their responsibilities along classic gender lines: Alice is a homemaker, and Larry, an accountant, supports the family economically.

"I don't begrudge other women their choices," Alice said, "but I know that my husband loves to come home, have dinner on the table, and have the evening free to spend time with the kids and read. That works for us." Alice isn't impressed by what she sees in her friends' two-career homes: the women are so busy that there's little time left for housework or child care. Babysitters—virtual strangers—raise the children during the day. In the evening, the husbands, who have also worked full days, have to help with dinner, help with the housework, help the kids with their homework, then help put the kids to bed. It's not long, Alice says, before the marriage falls apart. "If some women have the energy to have a career and raise a family, that's great," she says, "but I don't have the energy and I don't know where they get it either."

Alice thinks about Lindsay and Mark along traditional gender lines, too: Lindsay is verbal and creative, Mark is perceptual. She imagines Lindsay as a homemaker, or if she chooses to work, as a teacher or maybe a child psychologist. She hopes that Mark will be an engineer (Larry studied engineering in college before switching to accounting) or maybe an architect.

Although Lindsay believes her mother favors Mark, whenever Alice talks about her children, it seems to be Lindsay who garners the most respect. "Lindsay is a caring, giving person, which I hope she stays as an adult," Alice says. "Mark doesn't want to think about that kind of stuff, he just wants to play Nintendo . . . and he's so lazy. If he thought he could just open his mouth and have me drop in the food, he'd do it.

"I think the kids have good self-esteem," she continues. "Mark's got kind of an ego and we have to puncture that big head sometimes. But maybe that's because he's male. Sometimes I think I praise too much, especially Lindsay. She gets so upset if you criticize her, or if she does something wrong or doesn't do it perfectly. She gets really angry. I think I'm partly to blame for it. She doesn't think she should fail at anything."

We arrive at the field just before the game begins. The girls on Lindsay's team, the Screaming Yellow Zonkers, have put glitter in their hair and troll stickers on their faces to inspire esprit de corps. Sometimes they spray their hair blue and yellow to match their team uniforms. Mark's team has played an earlier game, so he's sitting on the sidelines with his and Lindsay's grandmother. I ask him if the boys decorate themselves before games, too, and he shakes his head, wrinkling his nose in disgust.

"They don't have any spirit," Lindsay says as she finishes her warm-up stretches.

"No, we're just not stupid," Mark snaps back.

When the whistle blows, the girls begin dashing back and forth, putting varying degrees of effort into their game. Under American Youth Soccer League rules for both boys and girls, anyone who signs up is put on a team, regardless of skill, and everyone on each team plays three quarters, so there's a real range in both ability and engagement among the players. To some of the girls, the game is fiercely competitive. They kick the ball expertly with the sides of their feet, they sprint across the field, they don't break stride when the ball catches them full in the face, chest, or stomach. Others, including Lindsay, pull back from the ball, shielding their faces from it, or hesitate between running and the kick.

Still, all of the girls seem to be having fun, and the spectacle is liberating. The fitness boom of the 1970s and 1980s often undercut women's self-image: instead of a trend toward health and well-being, the quest became one of perfection, for an image of beauty and body so tyrannically unobtainable that women starved and surgically altered themselves to achieve it.[13] In that version of women's athletics, women seemed to take no pleasure in the repetitive pumping of limbs in aerobics, the Sisyphean Stairmastering. But this is something else. This is not exercise but sport: a team effort with mothers, fathers, and grandparents cheering the girls on, encouraging them to feel their power and agility, to exert control, to try their hardest for the group, not just to flatten their stomachs.

Lindsay starts out as goalie and stands all quarter without ever needing to go near the ball. Meanwhile, her brother Mark, who looks like a blond Alfred E. Newman, talks nonstop about his own game, which ended in victory a few minutes earlier.

"Mom, Mom!" he says, pulling Alice's attention away from the game. "Did you see Brian and Alex? Did you see how that other guy plowed over them? Did you hear everyone yelling, 'Trip 'em! Trip 'em!' "

Larry Sutter walks up, having heard the last line of Mark's conversation. Larry is a ruddy-faced, cheerful man with a substantial potbelly straining against his T-shirt. He's spent the morning hauling furniture, helping the family pastor move into a new home. "Sometimes," he says to Mark, laughing, "I think you're not such a nice person."

Mark laughs, too. "*I* wasn't yelling, 'Trip 'em,' they were on my team!"

"Oh, my mistake," Larry says, still smiling, reaching down to take his wife's hand.

Mark is allowed (even expected) to be inconsiderate, and his rudeness is a source of amusement, although not to Lindsay. When she lopes off the field at half time, her face flushed and dripping, she asks if she can have some of the water from Mark's thermos bottle.

"I guess," Mark says, "but don't drink it all." As she lifts the bottle to her mouth, he adds, "I spit in it."

She turns to him and says, "I'll pretend I didn't hear that comment."

Over the course of the afternoon Mark makes several similar remarks to Lindsay, and interrupts both Lindsay and me during conversations with his mother. He is never reprimanded. Lindsay, however, is given soft but stern warnings several times to be a little quieter, a little less argumentative, a little more polite. While she is sitting on the sidelines, one of her teammates scores a goal; she screams and her mother says, "Lindsay! Not when someone is sitting next to you," and, subsequently, "My ears still hurt, Lindsay."

Later, Lindsay, who is nursing a cold, coughs as I'm asking Alice a question. I pat her on the back, and begin to say, "Poor Lindsay!" but before I can finish, she claps her hand to her mouth and says, "Oh! I'm sorry, I didn't mean to disturb you—I'll hold my breath if I have to cough again."

I start to protest, but she continues. "In algebra I had to cough but I knew if I did everyone would stare at me and think I was stupid, hacking away. So I held my breath until I turned red and tears ran down my face and finally I coughed anyway and everyone *really* noticed then. It was horrible."

This is a girl, I think to myself, who has taken the lessons of silence too far.

When her team wins, Lindsay runs onto the field. The Zonkers fling their arms around each other and squeal with joy; Lindsay is in her element. A few girls on the other team burst into tears at the realization of defeat. "That's too bad," says Lindsay, returning to the sidelines. "They played really well. It's too bad someone has to win."

I've never played a team sport, and when I ask Lindsay what it feels like to be out there participating, her answer disappoints, but, by now, does not surprise. "It's intense," she says, her breath coming fast and shallow, her face still flushed with victory. "It's very intense. It's fun but I feel like . . . it's like the whole time I'm out there I'm thinking how awful it would be if I made a mistake. If I make a mistake and we lose, I feel like it's all my fault, like I let everyone down, and I'd rather just never get near the ball than make a mistake."

■

The Pressure Cooker Explodes

■

Several months later, on a February afternoon, Lindsay stood by her locker preparing to leave school for the day. She leaned over to pick up her backpack, just as she always did, but suddenly her heart started beating too fast, her breath came short and hard, and everything began to spin. At the time, she thought she might be having a heart attack, but after a few minutes, the feeling passed. Or so it seemed; a few days later, apparently for no reason at all, it happened again. The episodes scared Lindsay, and at first she kept them to herself. But as the weeks rolled by, the "palpitations," as she called them, became more frequent—they would come on at lunch, in the hallways, in class—once she was so affected that she had to leave school and go home in the middle of the day. When the attacks became a daily occurrence, Lindsay told Alice, who rushed her to the family doctor. A physical turned up nothing; neither did an EKG, so the pediatrician just advised Alice to wait and watch her daughter closely.

It wasn't until spring quarter report cards were imminent that Lindsay connected her palpitations with her grades: the straight-A student was going to flunk math, and she was terrified that, as she put it, "my parents were going to slaughter me."

Of course, when Lindsay confessed her impending failure Alice and Larry weren't angry at all; they were, in fact, relieved that they'd discovered the source of what they now realized were anxiety attacks, and they assured their daughter that she wouldn't be punished for her low grade. The palpitations immediately subsided.

A few weeks after Lindsay's panic attacks had ceased, I visit Alice at home. Mark is outside shooting baskets, and Lindsay is in her room, chatting on the phone. We decide to talk in the living room, and, at first, Alice takes the chair furthest from the flowered couch where I sit; when I laugh and ask her to move closer, she joins me, still a little nervous. To Alice's mind, Lindsay's palpitations were not so much an indication of perfectionism as they were a signal that she had been placed in a math class that was beyond her capabilities. "We were surprised that Lindsay was placed in algebra at all," she says. "The one thing Lindsay has consistently gotten B's in is math, so that's not her strong subject. I told the counselor I hope they consider this kind of thing before they do this to another student."

I ask Alice whether the panic attacks could possibly be construed as a warning; perhaps Lindsay was routinely placing herself under too much pressure. "I guess we never see it," Alice says, "because Lindsay always gets the A's she's trying for, so she never seems like she's struggling. This whole thing was really strange. . . . I think the panic was just from not knowing what was going to happen if she brought home an F. We didn't kill her, and I think she was surprised." She laughs and shakes her head. "But I said, 'Now, if there's any other class where you *should* be doing well and you get an F—*then* you'll be killed for sure.' "

3

Fear of Falling: Sluts

■

■

■

There is only one label worse than "schoolgirl" at Weston, and that's her inverse, the fallen girl, or in student parlance, the slut. A "slut" is not merely a girl who "does it," but any girl who—through her clothes, her makeup, her hairstyle, or her speech—seems as if she *might*. Girls may protest the prudish connotations of "schoolgirl," but they fear the prurience of "slut": in order to find the middle ground between the two, a place from which they can function safely and with approval, girls have to monitor both their expressions of intelligence and their budding sexual desire. They must keep vigilant watch, over each other and over themselves.

■

The Danger of Desire

■

On a warm day, Evie DiLeo and I buy a couple of Cokes after school and walk to a park near downtown Weston. Evie is wearing a loose red T-shirt with a clavicle-high neck, blue-jean shorts, and broken-down huaraches. Her dark hair is in a ponytail, and when she smiles, she displays a mouthful of braces with rubber bands that match her shirt. She'd like to wear sexier clothes, Evie tells me, regarding her current outfit with disapproval, but she had to battle her mother just to get to wear lipstick, and even then, she was the last among her friends to be allowed.

Evie is a fast-talking, matter-of-fact young woman, the daughter of a lawyer mother and a computer programmer father who have been divorced for eight years. Like Lindsay, she is enrolled in Weston's gifted program. Evie has a thoughtful, analytical gaze, and from our first meeting was unusually forthcoming in her observations. She rarely pauses before answering my questions, and follows every assertion with a deepening "because" clause. Sometimes she's so eager to get her opinions out that she doesn't wait to understand my question. Once, she told me she thought girls had an advantage: since more was expected of boys, they had to play by the rules, while girls could be more creative. Yes, I said, but boys still end up ahead. She nodded her head emphatically, said "Yeah," and then went on for a sentence or two before pausing and saying, "What do you mean by that?"

Although she frequently declares herself "a feminist" and "independent," Evie's self-confidence is held in check by the rules she is learning about female sexuality. She is keenly conscious of which girls at Weston are sluts, and she readily points them out to her friends and to me. Sometimes she does so casually, saying, "She's kind of a slut," when I mention a particular girl I've been interviewing. Other times, she has grabbed my arm and pointed sluts out to me. I wonder, as the year progresses, whether her point isn't so much to help me distinguish the characteristics that comprise "slut" as to reassure herself of the safe distance between her and them.

Evie tells me she was in love with a boy named Bradley Davis all through sixth and seventh grade. When she described Bradley, it took a moment for me to place him. Bradley is not a boy an adult would take much notice of: average height, average grades, average looks. But Evie says she would've done anything to secure Bradley's affection and that, apparently, was what he hoped: starting in sixth grade, in math class, Bradley began asking Evie if she would have sex with him.

"At first I wanted to say 'yes,' " she admits. "I wanted to do it—I didn't know what it would feel like. It was sort of like a mystery, something that I wanted to know about. But then I thought, 'My dad would kill me,' so I just said 'no.' 'No, Bradley!' and he'd say, 'Why not?' I'd just say, 'No!' "

When Evie refused to relent, Bradley shut her out. He ignored her for the remainder of sixth grade and the first semester of seventh, although her own feelings remained strong. "He didn't talk to me, he didn't want to be around me, he didn't need me," she says bitterly. So when she regained Bradley's affections in the spring of seventh grade, and he propositioned her again, she knew the price of saying 'no.' This time, she says, "I said 'yes.' I was ready to do it. I was convinced I'd made a mistake and it would be all right this time. And I was just curious. I mean, why not?"

In truth, Evie didn't exactly say "yes" to Bradley; when he

asked her over the phone if she would "have sex" with him she was silent, and both of them interpreted her silence as consent. "It was like I said 'yes,' because I didn't say 'no,'" she explains now. Bradley began to make plans: a date, a time, a place. But as the moment grew near, Evie began to worry: what if she had sex with Bradley and then became a slut?

Evie begins to pick nervously at the grass where we sit.

"After I said 'yes,'" she says, "I started having these dreams about this friend of mine. She started having sex in sixth grade. This guy told her he loved her so she'd have sex with him, then he dropped her. Then he did the same thing again, and she'd run to him every time. Now she's in a special school for troublemakers.

"I had thought girls like that were bad and terrible and they didn't give it a second thought," she continues. "But now I feel like I understand what she was going through. I think you're more pulled into it. It's not like you just decide to have sex: it's like you don't have a choice. You're so emotionally torn, you just say, 'Do it, get it over with, nothing will happen.' But so-cially, mentally, physically, something does happen. You change. Even your hairstyle changes. That girl, she'd had her hair back and pinned up and a happy face. Then suddenly it was down and across her face, over her eye. She started dressing in tight clothes, a tank top pulled down so it's low in front and high in back—one of those cropped tops. She'd lay on the grass on her belly and put her chin on her hand so the guys could see her breasts. It was dramatic: her whole opinion of herself changed, and everyone else's opinion of her changed, too. The guy told all of the other guys and some of the girls knew. So everyone thought she was a slut and she thought so, too. *Her* life changed, but the guy, he's still in school. He's popular. It didn't damage his image, just hers. And he just forgot about her, used her until she left. In my dreams, that's what happens to me."

Just before their agreed-upon date, Bradley telephoned Evie to confirm their plans; this time, she made her feelings clear. "I said, 'No, Bradley.' And he said, 'No to what?' I said, 'No to *everything.*' He said his dad was coming and he hung up. Now he ignores me again."

Evie looks down at the ground when she finishes her story. Although the incident is over, it still haunts her. "I feel scummy," she says, softly, fluffing the grass with her fingers. "Even though I didn't actually do it, I feel like a total slut inside. I feel like a slut for considering it. It damaged my personality and my opinion of myself. And if people knew, nothing would happen to him, but it would damage the way *I* was treated. That transformation that happened to my friend would happen to me. Not the clothes—my parents wouldn't let me even look at a crop top—but inside. Inside, my attitude would change.

"I wish I could just forget it," she says, rolling over on her back. "It makes me feel so bad about myself. I'm ashamed of myself. I wish I could wipe the glass clean. Like if I had Windex for my soul."

Evie's story is typical of Weston girls' encounters with sex. It is the story of male aggression and female defense; it is the story of innuendo serving as consent; of a fixation, much too young, on intercourse as the fulcrum of sex; and it is a story, most of all, of shame. Evie's shame, articulated several times in our conversation, comes not from actually having sex, but from *thinking* about it: from admitting desire. At thirteen, just as she is awakening to her own sexuality, she has learned she must suppress it immediately; she has learned, in fact, to convert it into feelings of disgust, and to make girls who express sexuality into untouchables—"sluts." Evie knows that desire is dangerous: a girl who explores it, like the girl in her cautionary dream, forfeits respect, integrity, and intelligence. "I don't know why," Evie says during one conversation, "but usually the slut girls aren't very smart."

Sexual entitlement—a sense of autonomy over one's body and desires—is an essential component of a healthy adult self. Even Sigmund Freud, before yielding to the conventions of his time, once recognized the importance of voicing female desire.[1] More recently, Germaine Greer wrote that women's freedom is contingent on a positive definition of female sexuality.[2] But the harsh either-or dichotomy imposed by "slut" precludes self-determination. Just as, at adolescence, girls learn to disconnect from their "bad" feelings, they must also disengage from their "bad" bodies. Quite suddenly, as Simone de Beauvoir has written, "it seems to [a girl] that she has been doubled; instead of coinciding exactly with herself, she now begins to exist *out-side.*"[3] Evie's own mother, Margaret, has advocated the duality —for her daughter's own good—during what Evie calls "the sex talk." "Your body wants one thing and your mind says another and you'll always feel that way," Margaret told her. It is the girl, she warned, who is "in the driver's seat and she has to make the decisions and it's difficult because your body is telling you, 'Yes, yes, yes, yes, yes, yes, yes! I want to do this, it feels wonderful.' " But the conventional assumption, one that Evie believes, is that a boy cannot be expected to stop, so a girl must listen to her "mind" and say no.

It is difficult to consider allowing girls to unleash their sexuality. Like Evie's mother, many parents and educators believe that we protect our daughters by exacerbating their vulnerability, by instilling them with what we know are the perils of sex: the fears of victimization, of pregnancy, of disease. Those fears are, of course, all too real, but so is desire, and we do not teach girls that. We do not, as a culture, give girls clues as to how to navigate between the two toward a healthy, joyous eroticism, to what Audre Lorde has called "the *yes* within ourselves."[4] Instead we consciously infuse girls with a sense of shame.

Boys have far fewer constraints. At Weston, girls may be "sluts," but boys are "players." Girls are "whores"; boys are "studs." Sex "ruins" girls; it enhances boys.[5] In their youth, they may be snips and snails and puppy dogs' tails, but by adolescence, boys learn that they are "made of" nothing but desire, that, as Naomi Wolf has written, their "sexuality simply *is*": a natural force that girls don't possess.[6] Girls are, in fact, supposed to provide the moral inertia that (temporarily) slows that force. Just as in the classroom, just as in the family, girls' sexual behavior is seen as containable; boys' as inevitable. The Weston girls themselves participate in this dynamic, shunning sexually active girls, but excusing male behavior by saying, "Boys only think with their dicks." But what would ensue if we whispered the truth to girls, if we admitted that their desire could be as powerful as boys'?

In her groundbreaking work on girls' sexuality, psychologist Deborah Tolman points out that encouraging girls to disengage from their appetites not only does them a disservice but is an ineffective strategy for lowering the rates of teen pregnancy and transmission of disease. Banishing sexual feelings dissuades girls from considering the numerous ways *other* than intercourse in which they might explore their desire, ways that might be more appropriate, more fun, and certainly less risky to their health. Evie, for instance, does not suggest to Bradley that, at the age of twelve, they might want to try kissing or even touching before proceeding to intercourse; in the good girl/bad girl construct, sex to Evie means only one thing, "going all the way," and only a slut does it. What's more, Tolman notes that, although negative attitudes toward sexuality rarely deter sexual activity, they do discourage contraceptive use: responsible preparation for intercourse requires an active admission of desire, something girls have little incentive to make.[7] In fact, if a girl fears that by saying "yes" she may subsequently become a pariah, consent itself becomes a murky issue. Evie, for instance, believes she said "yes" to Bradley, when, in fact, not a word was uttered. Absent a language of female desire, boys like Bradley learn that they may interpret silence and passivity (perhaps even "no") as consent.[8] Sometimes it is; sometimes they intuit incorrectly, and sex becomes coercion or straight-out rape. Yet as long as girls feel they cannot say "yes," boys will continue—unwittingly and willfully—to misconstrue "no." As Tolman says, "I'm uncomfortable with this, but I know in my heart of hearts that 'no' cannot always mean 'no.' How can 'no' always mean 'no' if you're not allowed to say 'yes'?"[9]

■

Sex Education: Don't Ask, Don't Tell

■

Desire and the dynamics of power embedded in it are rarely broached in sex education curricula, especially as it pertains to girls. Educator Michelle Fine has written that boys' desire is included in classrooms, intrinsic to the biological lessons of erections, ejaculation, and wet dreams. Girls' pleasure, however, is evaded, and their sexuality is discussed primarily through the veil of reproduction: the onset of menstruation, the identification of ovaries and the uterus. Desire, as it relates to girls, is reduced in most classrooms to one element: whether to say "yes" or "no"—not even to themselves, but to boys.[10] By emphasizing refusal and ignoring desire, Fine argues, schools contribute to the repression of girls' sexual selves. The "official" version of sexuality that is taught, she says, becomes a discourse "based on the male in search of desire and the female in search of protection."[11]

At Weston Middle School, as in many schools, the community dictates what children may or may not learn in sex education classes. Principal Andrea Murray estimates that 25 percent of the students at Weston are already sexually active. And if "sexually active" is measured solely by engaging in intercourse, that's probably about right: the average age of sexual initiation dropped steadily in the 1980s, and some studies have found that up to 53 percent of middle and junior high school students have had sexual intercourse at least once.[12] If national statistics hold, one out of five of those sexually active girls at Weston will become pregnant before she graduates high school.[13] Yet the sex education curriculum endorsed by the community forbids a discussion of contraception until tenth grade, precisely because of the fear that contraceptive knowledge will promote desire.[14]

Maureen Webster, a young, maternal woman with a throaty voice, teaches the middle school's sex education course, which students take as seventh graders. During the course, she may not mention birth control in class—she is even prohibited from informing her students that condoms are a source of protection against HIV, lest the information in some way sanction homosexuality (activity which, free from the possibility of procreation, is necessarily based on desire).

"It's got to change," she tells me when I visit her classroom one day. "But right now some parents think that if you talk about contraception you're giving the kids a license." Ms. Webster says that if a student specifically asks about condoms, or some other taboo topic, she may answer the question, saying, for instance, "a condom is a sheath that fits over the penis," without revealing its purpose or in any way detailing its proper use. Essentially, though, if Weston's students want to know how to prevent unwanted pregnancy or sexually transmitted diseases, she says, "they have to find it out elsewhere." Ms. Webster says that the Weston community even bridles at her clinical explanation of masturbation, an activity that provides plenty of entertainment without the side effects of either pregnancy or disease. "I try to answer as correctly as I can," she says, "but I know that the parents are concerned. So when some boy asks, 'How do girls masturbate?' I'll say, 'Just as boys can fondle their private areas, likewise a girl can,' and leave it at that."

The curriculum Ms. Webster uses includes a month's worth of lessons, but since the course falls within a larger, quarter-long health class, and time is limited, she usually condenses it into a week or two, which is still somewhat longer than most sex education classes.[15] That leaves one class period each for male and female anatomy and one class period devoted to a lecture on how sexually transmitted diseases are spread (but not how they can be prevented). Given both communal and temporal constraints, a useful discussion of sexual desire—or any talk of sexual activity that isn't grounded in "consequences"—would be unthinkable. Yet although issues of sexual entitlement are never overtly addressed in Ms. Webster's class, when the bell rings, the power dynamics of "slut" and "stud" are firmly in place.

Ms. Webster had invited me to visit on the fourth day of the sex education unit. The students have already zipped through male and female anatomy, which included a lecture on the female reproductive system but—because there wasn't time for the more comprehensive film Ms. Webster had planned to show—no identification of the clitoris or even the labia. Today, Ms. Webster is trying to illustrate the effect of sleeping with multiple partners on disease transmission. She has passed out a photocopied work sheet which summarizes the symptoms of eight STDs and now stands at the front of the room.

"We'll use a woman," she says, drawing the Greek symbol for woman on the blackboard. "Let's say she is infected, but she hasn't really noticed yet, so she has sex with three men."

Ms. Webster draws four symbols for man on the board, and as she does, a heavyset boy in a Chicago Bulls cap stage-whispers, "What a slut," and the class titters.

"Okay," says Ms. Webster, who doesn't hear the comment. "Now the first guy has three sexual encounters in six months." She turns to draw three more women's signs, her back to the class, and several of the boys point at themselves proudly, striking exaggerated macho poses.

"The second guy was very active, he had intercourse with five women." As she turns to the diagram again, two boys stand and take bows.

"Now the third guy was smart—he didn't sleep with *any-one*." She draws a happy face and the boys point at each other derisively, mouthing, "You! You!"

During the entire diagramming process, the girls in the class remain silent.

This drama is played out without the teacher's noticing. She goes on to explain the remaining diseases, allotting several minutes to each and ten minutes to AIDS. When the bell rings, the students shove the handout into their backpacks. I doubt whether, in this short time, they've truly learned the risks of disease; but they certainly have been reminded of the rules of desire.

■

Objects of Desire

■

In late October, four sections of Weston's eighth-grade social studies classes are learning about the creation of history by making their own time capsules. Each student contributes a one-page description of an object that she or he thinks will best represent contemporary culture to people in the year 3000. Some of the essays are on neutral topics (since it's almost Halloween, Lindsay, for instance, writes about candy); others describe the scourges of our era, such as AIDS, violence, and drugs. Overwhelmingly, though, the boys in each class have chosen computers, CD players, VCRs, guns, and sports equipment to epitomize the twentieth century. The girls, meanwhile, have chosen clothing, hair-care products, and makeup. One girl even details which colors of which brands are appropriate for specific skin types: "Now for an example, I will tell you what colors will look good on a person such as me, fair complected," she writes, listing products for eyes, cheeks, and lips.

Whether their chosen objects are beneficial or destructive to society, in their essays boys are engaged by action: technology, sports, weapons, musical instruments. The girls take a more passive stance. Their message to the people of the future is that appearance supersedes all else. The symbols of the culture that are the most valuable to them are those that assist in the quest to please others: the objects that will help girls themselves become perfect objects. In the language of the hidden curriculum, the time capsule essays show that, as much as girls repress desire, they embrace desirability. From an early age, girls learn to stand outside of themselves, to disconnect and evaluate themselves as others might. As they mature, then, the question they begin to ask themselves is not whether they *desire* (a notion they quickly suppress) but whether or not someone would desire *them*.[16] The idea, as articulated in the time capsules, is to look sexy, but say "no"; to be feminine, but not sexual; to attract boys' desire, but never to respond to one's own.

When being desirable supplants desiring, sexual activity takes on a frightening dimension: it becomes an attempt to confirm one's self-worth, one's lovability, through someone else. This confused motive only intensifies the conundrum of the "slut": she earns her peers' contempt by engaging in the very activity she believes will bolster her self-respect. It may also, in part, explain why girls who have sex as young teenagers regret their decision at twice the rate of boys, and why, although sexually active girls have lower self-esteem than their nonactive counterparts, boys show no such difference.[17]

Girls emphasize being lovable when they lose faith in their competence.[18] Yet according to *Shortchanging Girls, Shortchanging America,* girls' evaluation of their overall abilities drops sharply in adolescence: the young women surveyed were about half as likely as boys to cite their talents as "the thing I like most about myself," while they were twice as likely as boys to cite an aspect of their appearance.[19] The biggest exception, again, comes among girls who continue to enjoy math and science. Without that fundamental faith in her ability, desirability becomes the central component of a girl's self-image;[20] and the more she invests in her desirability, the more vulnerable she becomes to sexual manipulation.[21]

■

Midnight Confessions

■

It turns out that Evie isn't the only one with a Bradley Davis story. In mid-October, Amy, Evie, their chum Becca, and a newer friend, Jennifer, attend a slumber party at another girl's house. In the middle of the night, after the prank phone calls, the pizza, the popcorn, and the séances, the girls dim the lights and their talk turns intimate and confessional. Evie confides the secret she's been carrying about her encounters with Bradley, and her friends do not condemn her as she feared. Instead, Amy and Jennifer—who have both had long-term crushes on Bradley —admit that he has approached them too.

After a rehearsal of a school play, Amy says, Bradley came into the area where she was changing. He approached her from behind and slid one hand languorously up her leg, lifting the hem of her slip. Then, he began to slide his other hand under her shirt toward her breast. "I didn't know what to do," she tells me later, "I just stood there. I couldn't even say anything. I didn't want him to do it, but it's like I couldn't talk. Finally I told him to go away and he did, and he didn't speak to me for the rest of the year. And he said that if I told anyone what he'd done, he'd ruin my reputation."

Jennifer is a small, nearly silent girl, the daughter of a Caucasian father and a Chinese American mother who are in the throes of a bitter divorce. Her hair is light brown and falls across one eye like a veil. She says that Bradley calls her when everyone else turns him down. Although she knows she shouldn't, she goes to his house and, as she puts it, lets him "do things to me," which she doesn't enjoy much but thinks will keep his affection. Once, she says, "he put his hand up my shirt, and I said 'no,' but he kept doing it and I was too afraid to stop him because I liked him so much and I wanted him to like me. I thought it would make him like me more if I let him."

Evie and Amy have been "best friends" since sixth grade, but because both have been attracted to Bradley, there has been an undercurrent of jealousy in their relationship. They occasionally spread gossip about each other, or pass cruel notes; more than once during the year they refuse to speak to one another because of conflicts over boys. But that night, their disclosures brought them closer together. They hugged and cried when they finished their tales, and they hugged Jennifer, too, because, as Amy later said, "we all felt so used." They swore to one another that they were through with Bradley, and vowed to engage in a sort of conspiracy of silence: they will neither confront Bradley nor tell anyone else (even other girls whom he's pursuing) about their experiences with him. The fear of the fallen girl is so strong that every time I ask the girls, individually or together, why they don't challenge Bradley, they react violently: they can't, they say, because, even though they refused him, *their* reputations, not his, are in jeopardy. "The thing is, we don't have control," Evie explains. "He could just say we were asking for it or that we wanted it. Then everyone will think we're sluts."

The girls aren't just guarding their reputations. Secretly, they're also hedging their bets: since, to varying degrees, male approval determines their self-esteem, none of them is willing to destroy the possibility of a future relationship with Bradley. Later, when we're alone, Amy adds, "I don't know. I still like him." She holds her thumb and forefinger apart, indicating that her feelings are still there, a little bit. "He's really nice when you know him; he's got a cute personality. I can't help it, I still sort of love him."

65

■

A few days after her friends' slumber party confessions, Evie and I walk to the park again. The days are beginning to shorten, and it's almost dusk as we settle in to talk. A beat-up brown Camaro pulls up to the curb, some thirty feet away, and continues along at a crawl. The two young men inside, half hidden in shadows, laugh loudly, but we don't turn. Then one yells, "Fucking cunts!" and the car peels out.

"Gross," Evie says, staring blankly after them.

Evie informs me that, since the slumber party, she has made a decision: she is going to remain a virgin until marriage. Sex and what she calls "guys' hormones" are just too volatile, too much "can happen." Yet even with that brave thought, Evie cannot fully insulate herself against desire. Immediately after making her announcement, she adds, "Bradley asked me to have sex with him again. This time I left it at a maybe. I don't know why, I feel ashamed of it. I kept the most control I have so far, but eventually"—she lowers her voice in a husky imitation of Bradley's—"he got into my head and I just said what he wanted me to say." She pauses, and her voice returns to its customary timbre. "He just starts talking, I can't explain it, and your face starts getting hot and you just don't think about what you're saying anymore. My hands start shaking . . . it really bugs me, but I can't stop it. It's not like you're even thinking you should say 'no'; you just automatically say 'yes.'"

4

Confronting
Vulnerability:
The Sensitive Girl

■

■

■

Becca Holbrook is a portrait in hesitance. When she meets me at the door of her family's home—an ample, two-story house in the newer section of Weston—she stands with her shoulders curved forward, her head hung slightly, her thin legs poking out beneath rolled denim shorts; when we sit down to talk in the Holbrooks' terraced garden, her posture becomes further exaggerated and she seems to be shaped like the letter C. Becca's hair, home-streaked with Sun-In, falls across her face when she speaks, hiding what is often a slightly anxious expression. The face itself is locked in the transition between girlhood and womanhood. From some angles, Becca looks surprisingly mature; but straight on, the full, womanly lips, aquiline nose, and large eyes seem unnatural on a child's face, giving her an awkward look.

Becca is the third of the trio that also includes Evie and Amy. Since the other girls are often at odds over boys, Becca, who is less socially adept, tends to take on the role of the peacekeeper. "I'm the kind of person who listens to people," she explains. "I listen to people and I can kind of understand how they feel, I can't explain it exactly, I'm just very sensitive and people know that about me. I guess I'm a good friend."

Over the course of the school year, I notice that Becca sometimes seems to anticipate the needs of those she cares about before they are aware of those needs themselves. She studies her friends and parents for small signals of mood in the same way she scrutinizes me now, frequently glancing up to check my reactions to what she is saying, to make sure that her smiles are accepted and her critique of friends and family understood in the spirit offered. Becca views her sensitivity primarily as a virtue and, in particular, as a uniquely female trait. Like Lindsay, Becca believes that girls "express their feelings" more than boys and are innately more emotional. Neither has ever considered that girls are only encouraged to express *certain* feelings, and that their emotionalism might, in part, compensate for what girls are denied: feelings of independence, competence, control.

■

The Nature of Caring

■

Becca's naming of "sensitivity" as the defining aspect of her self recalls the controversy over the model of female development put forth by a school of psychologists (sometimes called "cultural feminists") that includes Nancy Chodorow, Jean Baker Miller, and Carol Gilligan.[1] Their work, popularized in Gilligan's 1982 book, *In a Different Voice*, was initiated as a much-needed corrective to classic psychological theories which either regard women's development as inferior to men's or ignore it entirely. Gilligan and her colleagues argue that women are not, in fact, stunted, as such authorities as Sigmund Freud and Erik Erikson would have us believe, merely different. Chodorow traces this difference to the psychodynamics of motherhood: since girls grow up in a society where their same-sex parent cares for and nurtures them, they strive to remain in a relationship with their mothers as they form their identity, and so learn to cherish intimacy. Boys, on the other hand, follow the more familiar developmental pattern: to become men, they separate from their mothers as they move through adolescence, and, therefore, they learn to value autonomy.[2]

Chodorow and Gilligan considered these patterns of development to be socially constructed, based on a division of economic and familial labor that began during the industrial revolution and still persists today.[3] Yet, as their work has entered the public discourse, women's "difference" has been transformed into a function of biology. In a familiar set of stereotypes, weirdly reconstituted as "feminist," the psychologists' work has been used to support the notion that women are not just different, but actually morally superior to men—more caring, more connected, and more empathic simply by dint of being women. Portraying a "caring nature" as a chromosome-linked characteristic rather than a universal human trait not only catapults us back into a nineteenth-century gender ideology but, as psychologist Carol Tavris has pointed out, it encourages a dangerous disregard for those qualities in men—it even absolves men of responsibility for them.[4] Conversely, glorifying empathy in women and girls ignores both the capacity and the necessity for female autonomy as well as the gray area where sensitivity ends and victimization begins. Tavris notes that "women's intuition" might more rightly be called "subordinate's intuition," since it is not so much a female trait as a self-protective skill: women learn to understand and predict the behavior of men for their own safety and security, much as servants develop an uncanny knack for "reading" their masters. Men in general, Tavris argues, can quickly develop a sixth sense when, for example, faced with the moods of a temperamental boss.[5]

For girls, especially white middle-class girls, the expectation of "sensitivity," the willful canonizing of it as inevitably feminine, can blind us to the fragility it may signal, to the powerlessness and reduced sense of self it may express. Indeed, in Becca's case, I was to learn that hers truly was "subordinate's intuition" developed in response to the lessons she was learning about female victimization and vulnerability in our culture, lessons she was learning in the crucible of her own family.

■

My Daughter, Myself

■

Ellen Holbrook is a tall, long-limbed forty-four-year-old, with sun-roughened skin and, like her daughter, newly blond hair (although hers is professionally tinted). She meets me at the front door of their home, just as Becca did, but whereas Becca's gaze is circumspect, Ellen's is direct; whereas Becca draws back, Ellen's handshake is firm. She wears jeans and a black embroidered blouse, silver earrings coil into lizards just below her lobes, and her red-painted toenails peek out of sling-backed espadrilles. Ellen, as it happens, is the only teacher among the mothers; she has recently returned to the classroom after fifteen years as a reluctant stay-at-home mom, taking care of Becca and Jason, the Holbrooks' seventeen-year-old disabled son.

Because Jason is still sleeping, Ellen leads me to the terraced garden, which she has landscaped herself with an array of poppies, roses, and wildflowers. It is the cool of the morning when we settle into a pair of lawn chairs, but as we talk, the sun arcs toward the middle of the sky and the heat rises with it. By the time our conversation winds down, hours have passed: our arms are beginning to burn, and Ellen has fine beads of sweat on her forehead.

Ellen talks briefly and lovingly of her daughter, but quickly segues into the story of her embattled marriage, a story which, since she has few friends, she has shared mainly with the pages of her copious journals. She tells me that she dates the disintegration of her relationship with her husband, Tom, a government administrator, to Jason's birth and Tom's realization that this would not be the son he had hoped for. But as she continues, it seems clear that the seeds of the couple's division were present from the start.

Ellen began seeing Tom when she was a nineteen-year-old college student, pregnant and abandoned by her previous boyfriend. "My self-image was so low then," she says, "I never even told that guy I was pregnant. He had wanted me to get breast implants, and I wonder if I would've if he had stayed. Luckily he didn't; he probably found some woman with bigger boobs."

Since abortion was illegal at the time, Ellen carried the fetus to term—Tom nursing her through the pregnancy and birth—then gave the baby girl up for adoption. Difficult as it was, the experience could have forged a bond between the couple, but instead it became a guilty secret; although they were subsequently married, Ellen and Tom never mentioned the pregnancy again. Seven years later, when Ellen went into labor with Jason, she told the nurses in the delivery room that this was her first birth. Tom, who was present at the time, said nothing.

Jason was born with an unusable right arm and several less serious physical disabilities, but over the next two years, as it became apparent that he was also severely developmentally disabled, the well of unspoken feelings between Ellen and her husband only grew. "I was in total denial when I had Jason," Ellen says. "When he didn't sit up, the pediatrician told me that he should be tested. I knew something was wrong, but I didn't want to accept it. So I got angry with the doctor and I didn't go back for two years, not until he didn't walk. Jason was the firstborn son of two firstborns—the firstborn grandson. I thought, 'Well, I really blew it.' I was going crazy—and the *guilt!*" The force of the memory pushes Ellen forward in her chair, and she clasps her hands. "It was awful. Tom was in denial as long as I stayed in denial, obviously. He could've taken the kid and said, 'Something's not right—I'm taking him to a doctor,' but he didn't. I think that he had an affair at that time. I had that suspicion, and I think I was right."

According to Ellen, Tom's disappointment with Jason led him to withdraw from both children, leaving her not only with the responsibility for their son's doctors and special schools but with all the child rearing. "Maybe if Tom hadn't had his hopes and expectations dashed when we found out about Jason," she says, "but they were dashed, and I think because of that, he left me to raise both children. He wouldn't admit it, that he's done that. And it's by choice that I've stayed at home and done this, but then, it's not by choice, because someone had to do it. I've stayed home because Jason's needs have to come first. But it's me who made that choice, who decided those needs come before mine."

Ellen doesn't exactly hide her bitterness from her husband, but neither does she voice it; instead, she records her feelings almost daily in a series of detailed journals, which she's been keeping throughout their marriage. She invites Tom to read the entries, she says, but he never does, and so her resentment only deepens. She seeks solace in her collection of crystals and in her library of books on healing and women's spirituality.

"There's love between Tom and me in a way," she says. "I'm used to him—but for me it's not an impassioned love. For him it is." She draws a breath, then continues in a matter-of-fact voice. "Tom is a physical man—he needs sex daily, even when I was pregnant, even when I have my period. It's something I have to give in to. Sometimes I try to spend a long time straightening up downstairs or writing—anything—and hope he'll fall asleep and forget about it. But when he says lights out, it's lights out. The only thing I can do in the dark is exercise, so sometimes I do yoga and he might fall asleep, but it's rare. I used to think I was frigid," she continues, "but I read up on it and now I know that's not true. It's just another thing I have to cope with."

I ask Ellen how, with the physical demands compounding so much unspoken bile, she can remain married to her husband. "Believe me, there's been some times when I've thought about leaving," she says, her voice hardening, "but I can't because of my economic status. I want to be able to write, to be able to travel in later life. I'll put up with the relationship for that. I learned from my mom's divorce: she walked off, left my dad without a plan. She's never been economically stable since, and she has to live with my sister now. She says it's not worth it— she says work on it. What she means is that a *couple* should work on it, but in our case it's just me. I admit I have to do it, though, I'm not in denial about this relationship." She stops and looks squarely at me. "And it's darned hard work."

Ellen took her teaching job, to a large degree, to try to offset the example she was setting for her daughter. She wants to instill Becca with messages of possibility, of hope, of emotional and intellectual fulfillment for women; within the bounds she's set for herself, she is trying to be a role model, and she speaks optimistically about her progress. "Becca and I are kind of on a parallel course," she says. "We're both learning who we are together. I know the messages I got when I was her age, and that's not what I want for her. I want her to be more of an individual, not be defined by her relationship with boys. I try to tell her that responsibility and commitment are important and you have to work on them, but not lose yourself."

Ellen takes a breath; her shoulders droop slightly, and her smile grows rueful. "I say that to her, but I felt like a hypocrite. I mean, I tell you I want her to get the message to be independent, to be strong, but what I tell her is one thing—look at who's the nurturing one in the family, who left off her career to put the family's needs first, who takes care of everything, who's the teacher, who doesn't earn the money.

"So I've tried to be more assertive, not about the sex, but about work. But when I told Tom that I couldn't sort American Greeting Cards at home anymore just so I could be here when Jason's bus rolls in at three P.M. I thought, 'Well, what will I do? Who will hire me without experience, and where will I get the experience?' So I went to work doing special education for the county. It's not what I wanted, but it's a start."

■

Woman = Victim

■

It is not until late November that Becca chooses to discuss her family with me. We sit after school, on the bleachers at the edge of the PE field, watching a group of boys playing football, stopping our confidential conversation when they come too near. It is a cold day, fragrant with wood smoke and drifting leaves, suffused with the sharply defining light of a California autumn. Becca is wearing jeans and a cotton-knit cropped top that slides across her shoulders when she moves and occasionally exposes her flat midriff. She wears more makeup than the other girls—lipstick and eye shadow as well as face powder—and she's plucked her eyebrows into a fine line, similar to her mother's. Today, as they were the last few times I've seen her, Becca's eyes are red-rimmed. At first, she says the pinkness is caused by her contact lenses, but later admits it's more often from crying.

She turns to me suddenly. "Do you want to get into my parents' relationship? My mom and my dad?"

"Sure," I say, caught off guard.

"A while ago, my mom came in to my room and she sat on my bed and said, 'Good night, I love you,' and that motherly kind of stuff, but she was in tears. It's not like she was bawling or anything, just these tears on her face, and I don't know what's going on. So I say, 'Okay, good night, Mom,' and she closes the door. The next day, she told me it was 'fear crying.' She told me that she's scared of my dad and that she can't stand sleeping with him anymore. He wants to have sex every night and she doesn't enjoy it at all. She said it's like rape for her every night." Becca says all of this in a soft voice, with just a touch of urgency in the last phrase. But as she proceeds, she wraps her arms around her waist, and seems to shrink even further into herself than usual. "She said that if she didn't do it, though, she'd be out of there like the speed of light. So it's like she has to give in to him for, like, an insurance policy or something."

Becca has yet to kiss a boy or even hold hands, but at thirteen, she is already grappling with female victimization based on her mother's experience. She is privy, as it turns out, not only to knowledge of the nightly sexual capitulation but to the existence of the never-mentioned first child. Becca hastens to add that Ellen is always careful to tell her that *she* should enjoy sex. Nonetheless, she looks apprehensively toward her own future relationships, and, as much as she wants a boyfriend, her brow furrows when she considers the possible hazards: "It makes me scared and I guess I feel powerless," she says. "I'm afraid something like that could happen to me, that some guy

75

would be obsessed with me and not let me go or kill me if I tried to leave. That could happen."

As she allies with her mother, absorbs her pain, Becca's relationship with her father has grown overtly hostile. In fact, she very much imitates Ellen's dynamic in her own interactions with Tom: his attempts to win over her affection, usually undertaken after a few drinks, merely increase her revulsion, and although she dismisses her father as a physical threat, Becca worries that "emotionally he could scar me for life. Like once when I was doing something in the garage, I kept slamming the door when I went into the house, because I'd forget. He told me to stop slamming the door, and when I did it again, he came out and said, 'You slam that door one more time and you're out of here, I mean it.' I was just shattered, I just fell into pieces on the floor. I know my dad, and when he talks like that he means it. He really would kick me out of the house."

More than once, Becca tells me that she feels older than her friends because of what she knows about "life and relationships and stuff," and, given that unique understanding, she feels only she can offer her mother true succor. The two of them are best friends, she explains; they are like "the eyes of a hurricane."[6]

"When my mom first started telling me those things, I felt suffocated in a way," Becca says, "but I realize I'm the only normal thing in her life, I'm the only one who can really comfort her. She needs me and I can be there for her."

Today is the only time I hear Becca question whether the economic trade-off her mother has made is worth the burdens of an abusive marriage. "She told me that we can't move, because she doesn't have a good job and we'd have to live in a crummy apartment," she says. "I don't think it would be that bad, though, not if this is the way she has to live, practically having nervous breakdowns all the time. We wouldn't have to spend much, I have enough clothes and we don't need to buy fancy food. Jason and I don't care." She drifts off for a moment as the football players tromp by us, their game over. "I think sometimes it would be easier for my mom if my parents didn't have kids and I feel bad. But, then, she needs to get things off her chest and so she needs me and I can be there for her. I just don't like to think of her doing this in twenty years, being forced to do something she doesn't want."

Using her parents' relationship as a powerful leitmotif, Becca begins to see all male-female relationships in an aggressor-victim dichotomy. At home, she sees her father as the ogre, her mother as the victim. Among her peers, who use the term "slut" to punish and suppress girls' sexuality, she sees Bradley Davis as the predator and her friends Evie, Amy, and Jennifer as prey; like them, she believes girls' and women's vulnerability is inevitable because "all guys think with their dicks."

Although all of the girls at Weston fear sexual victimization, Becca sees the potential for violence everywhere. She tells me about an episode of *A Current Affair* in which a man blackmails a beauty pageant contestant by threatening to expose her abortion, then she makes connections between the television program, her own father, and Bradley Davis. One day at lunch, Becca comments that Bradley's current girlfriend is passive, and in a flat voice adds, "She looks like the kind of girl who lets men beat her up."

When, during a trip to a drugstore near her house, Becca is sexually harassed by a group of older boys, her sense of helplessness engulfs her. Up until that moment, she had been a child in the eyes of adults; if a man commented on her body, if he tried to "pick her up," he would be a pervert. Now that she's developed a woman's figure, she believes such public invasions are inescapable. Her mouth twists down in anguish when she dis-

77

cusses the incident, and she plays with her fingers nervously. "It was like I hit a brick wall—BAM!" she says. "Or like a hurricane that happens inside you and you just can't say anything. What really scares me is that it'll happen again—it freaks me out, the idea of having that brick wall smashed into me again, that I'm being portrayed as just my body like that."

Becca's feelings were not assuaged by *Girls and Sex*, the popular book on sexuality for teenagers that she consulted when the incident happened. In it, Wardell Pomeroy, a co-author of Alfred Kinsey's renowned report on male sexual behavior, writes, "Much as feminists may deplore it, appreciative whistles from strangers on the street or from passing truck drivers are trivial. The feminists argue that such behavior degrades women by making them sex objects, but this has been so through recorded history."[7]

The explanation, which equates entrenched behavior with acceptable behavior and all but encourages girls to regard harassment as a compliment, incenses Becca. "That's not right," she says. "It's different than if a cute guy says 'hi' to you—then your stomach drops straight down but it's a kind of good feeling; the other feeling is mortifying. It makes me feel like I don't want to grow up."

■

There's No Perfect Family

■

By the time I meet Tom Holbrook, he has become a mythic, frightening figure. I expect a fierce man, and am startled to find instead a mild-mannered balding fellow with a goatee, wearing jeans, a T-shirt, and old deck shoes, who slouches much like his daughter.

Tom is not about to discuss his sexual habits, which is no surprise: since Ellen suppresses her feelings, he may well be unaware of the depths of her rage. To that extent, her confiding in a journalist is a kind of passive-aggressive gesture, a demand that, if her husband will not reckon with her anger writ small in her journals, he will reckon with it writ irredeemably large.

Tom *is* aware, however, of his daughter's increasing moodiness, but he casts about for its source in vain. "It doesn't make sense," he says, stroking the family cat, which has jumped into his lap. "She's got two parents, we're college-educated, we have all these neat things, she has anything she wants, we don't speak with foreign accents—what's the problem? I think Becca looks for things to get mad about."

When I suggest that his liquor consumption might, in part, explain Becca's petulance toward him, Tom seems genuinely shocked. Although Ellen has described him as a "pattern drinker," and possibly alcoholic, Tom insists, "I don't drink to excess, I'm never out of control. But maybe Becca sees things she doesn't care for. We've never debated the issue, she's never been negative about it to me."

Tom also briskly dismisses Ellen's theory that his disappointment in his son has placed a wedge in his relationship with Becca. "I didn't expect to live my life through Jason," he says. "It's not like we called him Tom Jr. or anything. When you have kids, you have to accept that all bets are off. That *Father Knows Best* thing is only on TV. I don't know that Becca understands that. We're not perfect—there is no perfect family. I think she has this image of a father that's like Alistair Cooke."

Having rejected other alternatives, Tom attributes his daughter's withdrawal to a natural teenage phase, carried to an extreme by a coddled child. He considers Becca overwrought and hyperbolic in her emotions, but then he blames himself and Ellen for that: perhaps, he says, their indulgence of her moods encouraged Becca's hypersensitivity. Since it's too late for what he calls "behavior modification," Tom feels the best course of action for him is to steer clear of his daughter, to communicate through Ellen, and to appreciate the rare moments when Becca and he are at ease in each other's company. In the end, though, he feels that a rift between fathers and daughters is inevitable and, interestingly enough, invokes the current ideology of male-female difference to justify his position. "It's harder to be a father to a daughter, than a son," he explains. "I subscribe to that theory that women are from Venus and men are from Mars, and we can't understand certain things about each other because of that. Daughters are female and fathers are male, so I guess that would be true for us, too."

■

The Limits of Insight

■

Under the weight of her family burdens, Becca's academic confidence has begun to falter. Like Lindsay, Becca fears humiliation and holds herself to unrealistic standards (Ellen says Becca's perfectionism sometimes "paralyzes her"), but whereas Lindsay's anxiety drives her toward excellence, Becca, like many bright girls, uses her "sensitivity" as an excuse to shrink from challenge and avoid risk. In sixth grade, Becca was an A student; at the end of seventh grade, she asked to be removed from the advanced math class; and by the middle of eighth grade, her grades in all of her classes were drifting to low C's.

As a quiet girl, Becca says she has never spoken much in class ("unless I'm really, really sure of an answer, and sometimes not even then"), but with her self-esteem flagging, she stops volunteering entirely. She even begins to see her silence as an advantage: as long as she's perceived as shy, her teachers won't notice that she has, in truth, disengaged from school. At the same time, though, Becca complains that teachers make her feel invisible on the few occasions when she does try to participate. After attempting, and failing, to get her English teacher's attention one day, Becca observed sadly, "You know how some people have charisma? I have, like, *negative* charisma. I feel like I can be talking and people can be looking right at me and they don't even see me."

In a sense, Becca *is* invisible. Her teachers don't see her as someone in need of counseling or special help, because, although her grades have dropped, she is never combustible: she never, for instance, yells in class, pounds desks, fights with other children, conspicuously challenges authority. Becca's is a passive resistance—a typically feminine resistance.[8] By opting out rather than acting out, Becca still conforms to the image of the ideal female student—quiet, compliant, obedient; as such she is easily overlooked, or seen as "making choices" rather than expressing psychological distress. "Becca is so quiet," her math teacher admits, "she gets lost in the crowd. I don't like that to happen, but it has happened with her. She doesn't disrupt. She always looks like she's paying attention, but maybe she's not, I don't know."

"Maybe she thinks she'll be more cool as a C student," her history teacher says. "But she doesn't even get it together after she gets the bad grade. I'll say, 'Becca, you have a D, you may fail,' but then she doesn't turn in the next homework assignment, which is really easy. But I think of her as someone who's responsible for her own grade, and I let her be responsible for that."

Becca has "chosen" to let her grades drop, but not out of laziness. Her disengagement is actually an academic strike, an expression of anger, a statement of hopelessness that she willingly acknowledges. "Lately I've been thinking I don't care about anything," she tells me in February. "I don't see why I should care about my grades, you know? It's just a letter. What's the difference? Why do I need to learn anything in these classes?" She pauses, weighing the gravity of her statement. "It's not like I really mean that," she says, "I know it's important, but I have to get my anger out."

By making Becca her confidante, Ellen only deepens her daughter's anxiety. Nonetheless, Ellen badly wants Becca to rise above her environment; she wants it so badly that she, too, ignores Becca's retreat from her potential, saying that, because of Becca's "sensitivity," she "doesn't want to pressure her in school." So several years back, when Becca decided against enrolling in the district's gifted program, saying she didn't want to be seen as a "schoolgirl," Ellen supported that choice. Last year, when Becca asked to drop advanced math (although her grade was a B), Ellen agreed, hoping it would boost her daughter's confidence in the subject; it did, temporarily, but by the third quarter of eighth grade, her grade had slid to a D. More recently, Becca has begun to express anxiety about college (where she would have "the pressure of midterms and stuff and it would be really hard") and Ellen does not question her timidity: instead, she alleviated her daughter's worry by telling her she could delay the option as long as she wants. "Becca wants to blend in, be part of the crowd," Ellen explained to me. "She doesn't want to be smart. She's a very sensitive person, and if it's easier for her to be average, then that's okay with me."

The emphasis on Becca's vulnerability—as opposed to her rage and despair—further reinforces her helplessness. With the adults in her life unwilling to confront her pain, Becca's efforts to gain their attention escalate. During a visit to the Holbrooks' home just after Election Day, Ellen tells me Becca, who is twig-thin (and is, in fact, sometimes called "Twig" by her friends), just asked her what it means to die of starvation. "I told her people don't actually die of starvation," Ellen says. "Their organs malfunction; I told her that Karen Carpenter died of a heart attack, not actual starvation. And she thought about that and said, 'Well, maybe I can get my appetite back.' I didn't say anything to her. But I've noticed that sometimes her mirror is out of her closet. She brings it out to look at herself, and she does it a lot. And some days she comes down and says, 'I can't go to school today, I'm too fat.' Then a few minutes later she'll say, 'Okay, I found something to wear that hides it, but I've got to lose weight.' "

Echoing Becca's history teacher, Ellen says that, as with academics, developing a body image is Becca's responsibility, so she won't "pick up the rope" and interfere. "I don't say anything," says Ellen. "I see that she doesn't eat for a day or so and then suddenly a whole box of Nutri-Grain bars are gone. Or the tater skins I was saving for Tom's lunches will disappear. Or all the leftover Halloween candy. Or a bag of doughnuts. I know she doesn't binge and purge, but she does have this very erratic way of eating. Becca doesn't have an eating disorder, but she's messing with the choices, with the possibilities of it. But I'm not going to give her attention on that topic. I don't want food to be a battleground." Ellen adds that she "lets Becca's eating slide like Tom's drinking," although, to her mind, Tom's drinking is part of what's destroying their family.

Like Becca's teachers, Ellen downplays her daughter's behavior, although she herself once spoke to me of the perils of misreading girls' passivity. "When boys have problems," she said, "they act out and get in trouble. But with girls, they aren't supposed to get in trouble, and often they just turn it in. So you don't hear about the problem until they try to commit suicide."[9] It didn't occur to her, at that time, to apply that wise insight to her own daughter.

■

Becca Turns It In

■

When I first began talking to the Weston girls, we agreed that, so they would feel free to speak candidly, I would not discuss our conversations with their parents or teachers. To reassure them further, I explained the journalistic notion of protecting your source, an idea which they met with much enthusiasm. But in the spring of the year, Becca asked me to read her journal, and I realized that my promise of confidentiality had to be broken.

Early in the second semester, Amy and Evie decided they no longer wanted to be friends with Becca. Although the rift began with a seemingly inconsequential spat, Amy realized she was sick of Becca's "putting herself down," and Evie said, "You have to reassure her fifty times a day that she's not fat, that she's pretty. She's so sensitive; I know I should be more understanding, but it's kind of a relief not to have to worry about that anymore." In truth, Evie and Amy were drifting apart, too, and were beginning to spend their lunch periods in different groups with newer friends. As girls will in their middle school years, they shifted alliances. But when the new cliques were formed, Becca was left alone.

With few emotional reserves to fall back on, Becca panicked. She began spending her lunch periods in the school library so she wouldn't have to be alone on the schoolyard; when her mother would allow it, she took "mental health days," staying at home in bed. As her social isolation increased, she began confiding in her journal (with an eye toward a reader), trying to sort out her anger with her friends from her own culpability. "I never really felt that I was that good," she writes in one entry. "It felt like no matter what I did it wasn't good enough . . . Putting myself down kind of reassured me that I was okay"; later, she muses, "I lack self-esteem and confidence." But when her anxiety doesn't abate (and her friends don't return), Becca begins to conflate her distress over her parents and friends with her dissatisfaction over her weight: "I need therapy and diet pills *soon*," she writes in March, as if both were needed to effect a true cure.

Then, on March 23, Becca writes, "I downed eight Tylenol P.M. Good. I hope I end up in a coma then die!! . . . Why am I suicidal? . . . I don't even want Peggy to read this entry. She's an adult and would call a drug or suicide hotline."

After finishing Becca's journal, which was permeated with suicidal feelings, I sat alone for a long time, thinking. I considered myself to be an observer of these girls' lives, not a participant in them. Yet I felt I couldn't ignore the significance of Becca's gesture. So on my next visit to Weston, I sat Becca down for a talk. That day, she was feeling better, and was more interested in discussing some recent prank phone calls she'd made to boys rather than her journal entries. I told her that her instincts were right: I did have to talk to an adult about what she'd written, and we agreed I would talk to her mother. Becca just asked that I not tell anyone at school.

A week later, Ellen and I sat on the Holbrooks' front steps—she in her gardening gear, sunglasses covering her eyes—talking about the breach between Becca and her friends. Ellen had tried to intercede, calling Evie "friend to friend" to discuss

85

the situation, but that didn't seem to patch things up for long. In the meantime, Ellen's own relationship with Becca has grown strained. "Becca's gotten sullen," she says. "Our relationship isn't as intimate or consistent as before. She's been pulling back; sometimes we don't talk at all."

She turns to me, confidentially. "A week ago Monday, I could hardly wake her," she admits. "I came in and her lips were kind of stiff and I thought, 'Oh, my God, can I do CPR? How do I revive her? Do I call 911?' I was scared she'd done something. I shook her and she was okay, but she was sort of stumbling down the stairs, really groggy." Ellen kept Becca home from school that day and arranged an appointment with the school counselor. She also broke one of her own rules and snooped around her daughter's room while Becca was out. "All I found was Bayer headache formula, and that wouldn't account for it. She's being deceptive. She's never been deceptive before." Ellen pauses. "But she seems okay now, and it hasn't come up again, so I let it go."

I tell Ellen what I read in her daughter's journal. She rubs her palms against her thighs; her dark glasses hide her eyes, but her lips and the muscles in her cheeks tighten. "Well," she says and lets out a breath, "I'm not surprised." She pauses. "Oh, dear." Another deep breath, "Well, I'm not surprised. I guess I'll have to find out what's in her drawers and talk to her about it."

Ellen continues to rub her legs, looking grim. "I guess she's been asking for more help than I've been giving," she says. "Maybe I should've paid attention a long time ago.

"I'd decided already to put her in therapy," she continues, "but I thought we'd do it this summer, because I didn't have time now, so I guess I have that tinge of mother-guilt. I know she needs to get her self-image into some perspective. I can't keep her home for mental health days in high school. And she needs to get her thoughts on relationships with boys and men in order."

Ellen sits for a moment, staring straight ahead, then says, "Becca really needs a boyfriend, it defines her so much."

I ask if she really thinks that's the solution.

"Well, it has so much to do with her self-image right now. But I guess, if they broke up . . ." She trails off; the sentence need not be completed.

"I know that when she goes into therapy, she may get angry with me as well as Tom," Ellen says. "I'm prepared for that. She may get angry at the role model I've been, tolerating what I've been tolerating. But she's experiencing anger now, obviously. I'd like to see it come out in a more healthy way. I'm not sure I'm prepared for what Tom has to deal with, though. I don't know what he'll do with the issues as they come up. But it will be this summer, so we'll see. I think it's going to be, and I apologize to Mr. Shakespeare for this, the summer of our discontent."

5

Bodily Harm:
Purging, Gorging, and
"Delicate Self-Cutting"

■

■

■

"I don't know why it started," Evie says.

We are sitting in the DiLeos' living room on a quiet morning during a school vacation. No one else is in the house; Evie's mother, Margaret, won't be home for hours—she bustled off to work amid a barrage of reminders and instructions to her daughter along with a quick kiss and an affectionate "love you" —and Evie is an only child. After Margaret left, Evie made us tea and brought cups and saucers out to the living room on a tray. Now she's curled up on a navy-blue love seat, stirring her drink thoughtfully.

Evie and I have been talking about parents, friends, her cats, and what she plans to wear to an upcoming school dance. She is brimming with bold assertions and big plans for the future; but each dream, each statement, has been shadowed by uncertainty. She would like to follow her mother's lead and become a career woman, although she's not at all sure whether those plans are compatible with a stable marriage. She's boasted about her independence—which she considers a positive by-product of what she calls "our divorce" from her father—but she has also conceded, "I guess I'm going to get over not willing to be submissive someday, when I find the perfect guy."

Mostly I have listened while Evie has talked, sometimes addressing the topic at hand, sometimes veering off into something she's been thinking about that leaves me far behind. At one point, she suddenly leapt up to demonstrate the self-defense moves her father taught her when she visited him in Southern California this summer. She fractured an imaginary assailant's kneecap, kneed another in the groin, then looked up at me triumphantly; the sunlight, streaming through a window behind her, turned her hair a fiery auburn, and deepened the hazel of her eyes. "My dad says he wants me to be a 'man's woman,' " she said, sitting back on the couch and picking up her teacup. "He wants me to be able to stand up for myself."

Throughout our conversation, Evie has looked directly at me when she's spoken, but now I bring up something she mentioned months ago, when we first met, and suddenly her gaze drops. She puts down her cup and slips from the couch to the floor fiddling with her striped T-shirt, tucking it meticulously into her shorts. She picks at a wicker magazine rack next to the sofa, bending and breaking small strands of the wood, pointing out the destruction and saying, "My mom will kill me for this."

I wonder, since we're discussing her bout with bulimia, about which her mother knows nothing, whether the wicker is really Evie's main concern.

■

An Easy Way to Lose

■

This is an uncomfortable topic for Evie, who usually seems so assured and opinionated. Even her voice changes, becoming slow and flat, its usual sparkle utterly gone.

Reluctantly, Evie tells me that she learned how to throw up in school, in fact in health class, from a one-day lesson designed to discourage eating disorders. "They were telling us not to do it," she says, "but I thought it would be an easy way to lose weight." I remember that, in a conversation with Weston's health teacher, Ms. Webster told me she worried about just such repercussions: every year, she confided, there were certain girls who asked too many questions during that lesson, whose bodies seemed, soon after, to grow thinner and markedly peaked. It was the danger, she told me, of covering such sensitive topics in a mere forty-eight minutes, of tackling social issues without adequate curricular guidance.

Evie says she vomited after dinner three to five times a week off and on for almost a year. She didn't do it over the summer, she says, just when school was in session; and never during lunch—only after dinner, especially when her mother's boyfriend, a frequent guest at the table, urged her on to extra helpings of Tater Tots or dessert. On those nights, she'd wait until the dishes were done, then, a little while later, she'd mosey into the kitchen and pilfer a spoon.

"I didn't rush to the bathroom after dinner," she explains. "That would be too obvious. And you can't exactly sneak a spoon straight from the table to the bathroom—what would be the excuse? I'd wait a little while, sneak the spoon, then all of a sudden I'd be in the bathroom. I knew I shouldn't do it, I knew it was wrong, I had all these excuses about why it was okay. I figured it wasn't hurting me, and I was looking better even though I didn't feel good. And it helped me control my life. It really did, for a while."

Eventually, Evie says, she recognized that purging *was* hurting her—her weight began to swing erratically, she was often fatigued, her skin took on a yellowish tinge—and through rigid discipline she gave the habit up. "I tried to go cold turkey, but I couldn't," she says. "But I would do it five times a week, then four times, then three, two, one. I was really hard on myself about it. And I tried not to let it feel like a good thing, or like I needed to do it."

She pauses momentarily, smoothing over the damage she's done to the magazine rack with the flat of her hand. "Maybe I *was* overweight," she says thoughtfully, "maybe that's why I did it, but it was more I was compelled to do it. Like how some people go up to the mountains to live for a while, but this was for evil, not for good."

She looks up at me. "Of course, I wasn't losing in my thighs." She laughs and slaps her legs, which, clad in jean shorts, are of perfectly normal proportion. "I wish I would. I still do."

■

The Hunger Strike

■

Not all teenage girls develop negative body images or eating disorders. Personal psychology, physiology, family dynamics, and culture all play a role in an individual girl's vulnerability.[1] But the girls who are at the highest risk fall squarely into the Weston demographic: girls who are white and middle- or upper-middle-class, girls who are most likely to receive the conflicting messages of silence and assertiveness at home, at school, from boys.[2] Among these girls, negative body image is rampant: a Gallup poll found that as many as one million teenage girls are afflicted with eating disorders; other studies have estimated that 10 percent of American women—and 20 percent of women on college campuses—are anorexic or bulimic and nearly two-thirds of young girls have distorted body images.[3] The recent economic, educational, and legal gains that have been made by women of privilege are tempered by these sobering statistics, and by the fact that, if anything, the future looks more grim: during the late 1980s, one prominent treatment center reported a doubling in the number of female patients under the age of twelve seeking help for severe eating disorders.[4] Girls as young as seven have internalized society's slender ideal of beauty, and some studies have shown that up to 50 percent of nine-year-olds are dieting, starving themselves before the natural heft and roundness of womanhood can even begin.[5]

It is tempting, when regarding such widespread aberrance, to begin to view it as normal, part of an indulgent teenage phase that girls will outgrow. But a distorted body image is integrally linked with a dangerously disturbed self-image. Girls who despise their bodies are not only more likely to become anorexic or bulimic but are more vulnerable to depression and thoughts of suicide.[6] Eating disorders themselves can have harrowing long-term consequences, including anemia, liver and kidney damage, infertility, and a loss of bone mass that may contribute to osteoporosis in later life. Half of anorexics never fully recover and approximately 20 percent eventually die from their disease—a figure which includes adult women who, as anorexic teenagers, unwittingly weakened their hearts.[7]

Study after study shows that girls know, in spite of the overt messages of success and achievement proffered them, that their body is their most valuable commodity; indeed, they believe it defines them. In *Shortchanging Girls, Shortchanging America,* for instance, confidence in "the way I look" was the single most important determinant of self-worth for white middle school girls. Boys, meanwhile, were more likely to cite their abilities, which may, in part, be why when they do have a negative body image, the repercussions are less severe.[8]

Privileged girls have long been taught to look outward for the confirmation of self, and, especially, for substantiation of their crucial desirability. Simone de Beauvoir writes that an adolescent girl is "led to make an object of her whole self, to set herself up as Other."[9] And Anaïs Nin romanticizes narcissistic alienation, writing, "Every girl of fifteen has put the same question to a mirror: 'Am I beautiful?' . . . there is always the question. The mirror is not going to answer it. She will have to look for the answer in the eyes and faces of the boys who dance with her . . ."[10]

Yet although appearance has been the sum of women's worth for generations, that has not inevitably led to pathology. Like other diseases, eating disorders can only thrive in a hospitable culture—which, with today's soup of conflicting messages to young women, we generously provide. We live in a society that associates thinness with success, self-control, strength, and, most significantly, masculinity; we see fat as synonymous with failure, sloth, weakness, and feminine fecundity. We boldly encourage girls to leave behind the limits of tradition—to leave behind the stove and the apron and the soft heft that comes from nurturing many children—to join the world of men. But, at every turn, we remind them that their abilities alone will not ensure a place at the table of success: in order to "have it all" they must also conform to an impossible, media-driven standard of beauty which holds that "you can never be too thin."[11] To achieve it, they must diet rigorously in the name of health; they must even, if need be, sacrifice their health to their diets.

In *Fasting Girls,* a historical perspective on eating disorders, Joan Jacobs Brumberg views the current epidemic of anorexia as almost inevitable, the "perfect psychopathology" for the Superwoman culture we expect privileged girls to enter. "The kind of personal control required to become the new Superwoman parallels the single-mindedness that characterizes the anorectic," she writes.[12] As Brumberg wisely recognizes, eating disorders are, in part, an assertion of control (Evie admits that, more than merely keeping her slim, her bulimia helped her "control my life. It really did, for a while"), an attempt to navigate between the simultaneous valuing and devaluation of female bodies, a response to the whirl of conflicting expectations these girls face.

Yet as much as they are *generated* by the impossible standards we place on girls, eating disorders may also be seen as a protest against them. By refusing the most basic sustenance, the most fundamental of needs, girls don't merely try to sculpt themselves into Christy Turlington or Cindy Crawford: they engage in a kind of unconscious hunger strike. They express anger, defiance, and despair with their bodies—the most visible aspect of the self and, to them, the one that matters most. Through their hypercompliance with contemporary expectations, girls show us just how hypocritical our messages to them are. They arrest their development to tell us that, if this is what womanhood means, they want no part of it.

Notions of "femininity" and "body" are deeply entwined with sexuality;[13] and, indeed, for the girls at Weston, the militaristic control exerted over hunger is inextricable from that which they exert over sexual desire. It was "control over my life" Evie sought when, alone in the bathroom, she shoved a spoon down her own throat; it is "control" over her desire that she struggles for when she hears Bradley Davis' seductive voice proposition her on the phone. To the Weston girls, "fat" represents falling as much as "slut": either label, the girls believe, will render them social outcasts, will obliterate them. If they have sex, they believe they will become only sex. If they are fat, they believe they will become only fat. To avoid the devastation of either reduction, these girls not only suppress their sexual appetites, they deny and demonize the sensual pleasures of eating as well: of savoring, of wanting, of indulging their "sinful" urges. They learn to guard against their lust for food just as they learn to contain other "inappropriate" desires, including the desire to speak, to act out, to be heard. Such wholesale denial of hunger may be a logical end result of women's being told they should not need or want anything.

■

Lunch at Weston

■

During lunchtime, the students at Weston eat in shifts in the school's undersized cafeteria. While the younger students eat, the eighth graders lounge against a wall across the schoolyard, under a concrete overhang that acts as a windbreak in the fall and a shelter from the heat that pounds the asphalt playground in the spring. The girls stand in small groups, hugging their books to their chests, heads bent together, always aware of what the boys are doing. The boys stand together too, talking about sports or music, occasionally responding to the girls. Sometimes the groups are mixed, and thick with flirtation: a few couples lean against the wall holding hands, or stand with arms wrapped around each other's waists, palms wedged into each other's back pockets. Twenty minutes into the period, the sixth and seventh graders trundle out to the playground and the eighth graders move closer to the cafeteria (which they seldom actually enter) and continue their conversations.

The girls at Weston rarely eat during "lunch." Lindsay gives her lovingly packed brown bag away; Becca claims that she doesn't like "all that fatty food." Evie, who, true to her word, has stopped purging, says that she has developed a new diet strategy for eighth grade: "I try to always be a little hungry," she explains one day, after asking me to break a five-dollar bill so that, when she gives her mother the change, Margaret will think she's eaten something. "I try never to eat lunch, I leave the dinner table a little hungry, then I'm a little hungry all night and I eat just enough for breakfast so that I'm still a little hungry all day."

Only Amy buys the occasional cellophane-wrapped burrito from the fast-food window; when she does, Becca and Evie "take bites," which means that, by the time they're through, they've eaten about half of her lunch for her. More often, though, the girls eat nothing at all.

Yet while the actual food intake is low at Weston, fear of fat still runs high. Part of the role of a girl's lunchtime chums is to reassure her that she is "so skinny," even if it isn't true. And although they frequently chafe at the standard of beauty that the media foists upon them (this was the year that Calvin Klein model Kate Moss made anemia into a fashion statement), the girls also treat their own eating disorders with nonchalance, even, on several occasions, bragging about them.

One mid-fall afternoon, Lindsay offers her home-packed lunch to a group of girls standing near the cafeteria. Evie, who says she is starving, accepts a cheese sandwich, but before she can eat it, Lindsay grabs it back.

"I have to take one bite or she gets mad," Lindsay says.

For a moment, I think she is talking about her mother and wonder how Alice can confirm the truth, but then Lindsay turns to a friend named Kelly.

"Eat *two* bites," Kelly commands, and then tells me, "Lindsay is anorexic."

"Are you?" I ask.

Lindsay shrugs.

"She thinks she's fat all the time and she doesn't eat," Kelly says. "That's anorexic."

"I'm kind of anorexic," Lindsay admits, taking her requisite two (infinitesimal) bites, then returning the sandwich to Evie. "I mean, I'm sort of borderline, I guess. I know I was anorexic last year."

Evie jumps into the conversation. "I was anorexic last year," she says with a touch of pride. "No, not anorexic, what do you call it?" She looks away for a second. "Bulimic, yeah, I was bulimic." The girls nod, unimpressed. It is as if eating disorders are an expected female rite of passage, the words "anorexic" and "bulimic" a comfort rather than a threat. After all, as long as, through the magic of those words, a girl can safely be classified as too thin, she can't possibly be too fat, or can she?

On another day, late in the first semester, a thin blond girl accuses Becca—who is standing near an empty potato chip wrapper—of littering; Becca's defense is a haughty "It's not mine; *I* don't eat."

"You don't eat?" the blond girl says. "Neither do I." They give each other the thumbs-up sign. "I never eat," the blond girl continues. "You know what I did today? I ate breakfast; it was the first time this year."

She laughs and someone asks her, more curious than concerned, "Are you anorexic? You're so skinny!"

"I weigh more than you think I do," she answers.

The talk drifts away from the girl and back to gossip about boys, but although no one is listening, she repeats her final phrase twice more before walking away. The half-approving moniker of "anorexic" was apparently not enough, no more reassuring to her than her actual body, which was nearly prepubescent in its thinness. She continued to express her fear to her friends, insisting that, in spite of appearances, she *was* still fat, but they were so used to such expressions of dread—so enmeshed in them themselves—that they didn't even notice.

▪

"Fat" and "Dumb"

▪

The Weston girls' fears of what "fat" augurs may seem exaggerated, but in fact they aren't far off. When a girl among them *is* truly fat, just as when a girl has been deemed "slut," the stigma can be crippling: girls who are severely overweight, for instance, are 20 percent less likely to attend college than their thinner counterparts.[14] It is almost as if they believe that, since our culture equates "fat" with "dumb," then dumb they must become.

Lisa Duffy is the only one of the Weston girls I meet whose claims of being overweight are actually accurate. Lisa is a fat girl. Her weight particularly shows in her face, where the roundness seems to overwhelm her features. The first time we talk, just before school starts, Lisa wears tight pink leggings and an oversized jungle-print shirt, her blond hair pulled into a jaunty ponytail on one side of her head. We sit at a picnic table on her family's back deck, a cat in her lap, a cup of coffee in mine. Lisa's mother, Beth, an assistant warehouse manager at a discount outlet, is at work; her stepfather, Ed Richards, a retired MBA who now has his own real estate franchise, reads the newspaper in the living room.

Unlike the other Weston girls, Lisa never looks me in the eye as we talk. She doesn't learn my name either; during a break in our conversation, I hear her refer to me as "the lady" to her stepfather. When she speaks, in a soft, flatly suburban voice, Lisa plays with her fingers, twirls her hair, shifts her eyes, and seems to retract into her body. Still, in spite of her apparent discomfort, she carefully assembles her thoughts and fully answers all of my questions, saying that she finds the interview process "intriguing."

Lisa tells me that she was new to Weston last year, and from the very first, she believes her fatness determined—even predetermined—all of her social and academic interactions.

"My first day of seventh grade I was scared," she says, kicking the picnic table. "I thought, 'Oh God, I hope I don't mess up, I hope I don't say something or do something that makes me different.' But before school even started, this boy comes up to me and says, 'Hi, Miss Piggy! Hi, Miss Piggy!' He thought it was okay to pick on me just because of how I look. Then I had to go to school. And nobody even gave me a chance. It was like they were afraid to talk to me because I was fat, like I had a disease."

Although Lisa's vocabulary exceeds that of many of Weston's "gifted" girls, and her standardized test scores place her in the upper twentieth percentile statewide in both English and math, her grades that year hovered in the D range. Like the other girls, Lisa equates thinness with success and intelligence; as a fat girl, then, she sees failure as inevitable. "At first I thought if I got good grades and tried to fit in it wouldn't matter how I looked. But I still got teased, it didn't make a difference. All the good things about me—like that I was smart—it was just, 'You don't fit. You don't look good. You're fat.' I felt like I was doing all the good things for no reason. So I just said, 'Fine, if it's going to be that way, then I don't care.' And I don't try at all anymore, I don't care about school."

When I ask Lisa about the future, about her dreams for herself as an adult woman, she blushes, and looks down. She tells me she'd like to marry "a man with blond hair" and adopt twins, because there are so many needy children who could use a good home. "And," she says in a rush of embarrassed enthusiasm, "I'd like to stay at home while they're little and be a famous poet or maybe a child psychologist and, like, work while they're napping or watching cartoons."

She pauses and her face turns sullen. She begins kicking the table again. "I don't think that'll happen, though. In the movies the guys go with these cute girls even though the guys are nerds and geeks, but you never see anything like that for girls. So I don't think anybody will ever want to marry me, because I'm fat, so I don't think I'll get married. That will make it hard for me to adopt kids, and I won't have enough money without a husband anyway. So I don't think anything I want will come true, really."

She puts on the defiant, bored expression that I have seen her adopt at school. "But it doesn't matter," she says, shrugging. "I mean, so what?"

As Lisa talks, I study her body. The equation she has drawn seems awfully neat: because she is fat she fails in school; because she is fat, she can make no friends; because she is fat, she will not find love. Yet I wonder how Lisa would cope with her academic and social challenges were she not fat. Would "thin" really have the talismanic effect on her life that she, like the slimmer girls, believes it would? If so, Lisa does little to pursue that possibility. She says that she rarely diets and doesn't like to exercise. Meanwhile, she hoards food in her room, consuming family-sized boxes of sweet cereal in an evening, then hiding the empty containers.

As much as she insists that it thwarts her—and the discrimination against fat girls and women is indeed real[15]—Lisa's weight may provide her with something as well. Psychologist Susie Orbach has pointed out that, as with girls who are severely underweight, "big girls' " body size places them outside the bounds of acceptable femininity, and beyond its attendant expectations.[16] In that respect, Lisa's body, like that of the anorexic, becomes a vehicle for protest, a challenge to the customary invisibility of the female self. But instead of embracing denial and wasting away, Lisa expresses her needs by gorging on them. With potato chips, ice cream, and burritos, she creates an armor of flesh that both flaunts her powerlessness and gives her an excuse for it—as well as for her failure at school, and the scorn she's been subjected to among her peers and at home.

■

Building the Armor

■

Lisa was always a chubby child, but it wasn't until she was seven, and her parents separated, that her weight truly began to ascend. At that time, Lisa and her older brother, Billy, became the center of a six-year custody battle. Or rather Billy did. Now fifteen, Billy nearly died of cancer as a young child; after his miraculous recovery, his father, Bill Sr., wasn't about to risk losing him again.

Bill, who was a journeyman mechanic, hadn't worked in five years when Beth filed for divorce; he quit his job when Billy became ill, spending all of his time with the boy but refusing to care for Lisa, whom Beth placed in day care. Even so, Bill argued in court that he had taken on the role of the custodial parent for both children. The judge agreed, and Bill remained in the family home with Lisa and Billy while Beth took a job in another suburb and contributed two thousand dollars a month in child and spousal support. The decision, which was made after two years of hearings and visits to a court psychologist, was supposed to be in the best interests of the children: it would be easier for them to contend with the trauma of divorce, the judge reasoned, in familiar surroundings and an accustomed school district.

In a less acrimonious parting, this may have been true, but over the next six years Bill repeatedly denied Beth her visitation rights—often even forbidding the children to speak with her on the phone—and the couple landed in court repeatedly without resolving anything. It wasn't until 1991, when the children both petitioned the judge and asked to be placed with Beth, that Lisa and Billy moved to Weston.

Through it all, Bill's interests lay primarily with Billy, whom he still sees often. Lisa, meanwhile, found ready consolation in food. But soon even that source of comfort betrayed her: other children began to tease her about her excess weight, her brother tormented her, and her father taunted her with the "affectionate" nickname "Little Chubs." The cruelty made Lisa feel worthless and angry. The more worthless she felt, the more she ate, and the more she ate, the more worthless she felt.

Lisa doesn't like to discuss her years with her father, who, she says, neglected and belittled her. When I ask her about that time, she says, haltingly, "I just don't think he . . . he . . . he . . . respects me. It's like I don't have any feelings and don't deserve to be treated nicely. He's chummy with my brother and always says to his friends, 'This is my son, Billy,' like he's real proud. Then it's like, 'Oh yeah, and this is Lisa.'

"I used to try so hard," she continues, "but now I don't

103

think I can do anything to make him care about me. He doesn't like women, I think. His mom was terrible to him and my mom divorced him. I think he deserved it, but he doesn't see it that way. I think maybe I remind him of my mom, I don't know."

■

Anything for Friends

■

Self-conscious about her weight and bruised by her father's rejection, Lisa entered Weston craving peer approval at any cost. In seventh grade, she allowed girls to steal from her, insult her, and make her the butt of jokes, as long as they claimed to be her "friends." By the middle of this year, she has drifted through several cliques and has found a niche among the "headbangers": students who smoke, take drugs, and listen to heavy-metal music. The girls in the group, whom other Weston students consider "sluts," favor black lipstick and avoid looking adults in the eye. It is rumored that some of the boys—who wear T-shirts bearing the logos of bands that use extraneous umlauts in the spelling of their names—have tried to form a secret white supremacist group on campus.

Along with these friends, Lisa begins to cut her first-period science class, going to the park for a smoke and racking up detention after detention for her absences. In December, she is suspended for carrying cigarettes in school. When I pull her aside during a lunch period in January, she grins broadly, saying she has something to tell me that "you're not gonna believe." We go into the school library, and, after looking around elaborately to ensure that we're alone, Lisa confesses that, shortly after her suspension, she began experimenting with marijuana, although she says she doesn't care much for it. Later she says that she has also watched while some of the boys in her new group have snorted methamphetamine, or "crank."

These transgressions thrill Lisa because, she explains, they prove that she has officially become "a loser," and, as such, she has finally found acceptance. The only hitch is that "losers," like fat girls, don't do well in school. Although she began the year with a slight academic push, volunteering in class and turning in her homework, when she fell in with her new friends, Lisa discarded achievement as a source of self-worth. Her grades have since dropped to D's and F's, but she's philosophical about her failure.

"I'm not supposed to do well in school anymore," she explains. "I'm not the type. You see, I hang out with certain people. They're known as flunkers, so I'm like that too. And no one expects it of me—not the teachers, not the other kids, no one. If I started doing well, people would think it was weird."

As she's embraced her new identity—that of a "loser," a "flunker," and a "dumb blonde"—Lisa has altered her dreams to match. I ask her how she plans to become a child psychologist if she doesn't improve her school performance.

"I don't want to be a child psychologist anymore, because I don't want to go to college anymore," she answers. "Even if I did, I couldn't do well enough to ever do that. Maybe I'll go to one of those schools that teach you how to do one thing, just a certain area for a job."

I ask whether she means vocational school and she nods her head. Then she shrugs.

"I don't know," she says, "I don't like to think about what will happen to me and my friends in the future anymore, because if we keep on like this, it might not be good."

■

Feeling the Pain

■

It is the spring of the year, and Lisa and I are sitting on the Richardses' back deck again. Her pink leggings and brightly patterned shirts have been replaced by baggy overalls with the apron unbuttoned, a green T-shirt, and a plaid shirt tied around her waist. Her hair is down, brushing her shoulders. She no longer kicks the table while she talks, but during our entire conversation she pokes her fingers with a medium-sized safety pin. Sometimes she pokes at her frayed cuticles; sometimes she threads the pin through the unfeeling upper layers of a finger; sometimes she pokes through her jeans; sometimes she jabs deeply enough to draw blood.

Lisa tells me that her parents have received a warning from the school that she might be held back in eighth grade. As she says this, she pushes the pin through the upper layer of skin on her thumb and snaps it shut. "The school won't do it, though," she tells me, wiggling the closed pin back and forth. "They'll just put me in the reject classes next year, and that's okay, because it'll be easy. I'll just be a retard." She laughs, adding, "I mean, not really. If I really was, I wouldn't say it."

She unclasps the pin and begins poking each of her fingertips in turn. "School isn't as important as your friends," she continues, "and you can't have a good social life and good grades. That's just the way it is." She pricks her left index finger a little deeper than the others, and puts it in her mouth to stanch the blood, which stops our conversation momentarily. It also unnerves me.

When she takes her finger out of her mouth to scrutinize it, I ask if she jabs herself often.

"I do it a lot, yeah," she answers. "Sometimes I put pins through my tongue, too." She laughs at my look of revulsion.

As Lisa drops her hand, I notice a series of welts that resemble two eyes and a smiling mouth in the space between her thumb and forefinger. She turns the scar toward her and smiles at it fondly, explaining that she created the effect herself with the metal wheels at the top of a disposable cigarette lighter.

"I was just sitting in my room and I was bored, so I just did it," she says. "You make metal real hot, then you just put it on your hand. I left it there until my pinkie started to tingle, then I pulled it up. There were big red blisters, and it started to bleed. Later when I picked off the scab, I had the smiley face."

Lisa giggles, as if she's done something merely naughty rather than blatantly self-destructive. But in spite of her levity, I know that what she's doing may be as serious as hoarding food in her room for late-night solace, as meaningful as other girls' binging and purging. Self-mutilation, or "delicate self-cutting" —which most commonly involves burning the skin or cutting oneself with razor blades—is a widely practiced but seldom discussed phenomenon often found among the same demographic as girls who develop eating disorders. In fact, the afflictions often appear in tandem: nearly two-thirds of the women in one study of mutilators were or had once been anorexic, bulimic, or obese.[17]

Girls slice and burn themselves for much the same reasons that they deny themselves food: to alleviate anxiety and depression, to express powerlessness, and to restore a sense of control. They slice themselves because, as girls, they are disallowed the luxury of turning their anger outward; the only outlet they have for their rage is their own bodies. But, as with binging and purging, the relief is merely temporary and the circumstances that give rise to the behavior remain unaltered. So the urge returns, uncontrollably, again and again.[18]

A little nervously, I ask Lisa if she ever cuts herself.

She nods her head. "Sometimes I cut myself with a razor in the shape of a letter," she says, "like the initial of a guy that I like, or the anarchy sign. Then I spray it with hair spray because the alcohol makes it scar more."

Lisa rolls up her sleeves and then her pant leg to show me the results of her handiwork.

"I don't know why I do it," she says, gazing at the anarchy symbol she's carved on her leg. "Sometimes you're bored, I guess. And I know this sounds weird, but it feels kind of good. It feels like . . . it doesn't hurt, it's just . . . feeling the razor cut your skin feels good. And sometimes . . . sometimes you like the pain, you like how it hurts."

Lisa insists that her cutting and burning are not motivated by anger. And by some standards her behavior could be considered more fashionable than deviant: increasingly, today's young people pierce their noses, lips, or eyebrows as an expression of generational rebellion, similar to (although more permanent than) the long hair and love beads of the 1960s and 1970s. Like them, Lisa claims she is just trying to be different, to impress her friends, to be cool. That's especially crucial for Lisa, because if she's not cool, if she loses the "losers" as friends, she's back to just being the fat girl. And that would hurt a lot more than a few strokes with a razor blade.

"I know I have no self-esteem," she says, beginning to prick her fingers again. "My friends always hit me when I say something bad about myself. I cut myself down all the time, I don't know why. I guess because if I say it first, it's not as bad as if someone else does. But I can take everything—being stupid, being a dumb blonde—just not people saying stuff about my weight, I can't take that. All my life I've been teased about being fat, and you just believe it after a while, that you're fat and ugly. I mean, I know I'm fat. And you can only be uppity and all when you're skinny and pretty."

Lisa jabs the pin through the left leg of her overalls, hurting herself before someone else can. "Skinny and pretty," she says with finality, repeating a phrase I've heard from so many Weston girls. "That's just the way to be."

6

Striking Back:
Sexual Harassment
at Weston

■

■

■

Principal Andrea Murray is on the phone when I enter her office. She motions me into a battered oversized chair and swivels away from me to continue her conversation, tapping the long, red-painted nails of one hand impatiently against her cluttered desk. Ms. Murray's office is small and, on this January day, overheated; there's barely room in it for her file cabinets, her computer terminal, and the two empty chairs that lay in wait for errant children. The walls are an unforgiving shade of institutional green, but on the corner of her desk nearest me, Ms. Murray has placed an enormous jar of hard candy, a gesture of warmth and approachability from the person whose position usually fills students with dread.

Ms. Murray completes her call and turns toward me. A small, amiable woman with carefully styled brown hair wearing a flower-sprigged dress and sensible shoes, she folds her hands in her lap and looks at me expectantly.

An eighth-grade girl, she informs me, is being sexually harassed.

■

Laying Down the New Law

■

Jeanie Mayes, a quiet, somewhat mousy girl, has lodged a formal complaint against a group of boys in her gym class who have been taunting her about the size of her breasts. The gym teacher, who is male, has largely ignored the remarks, although he has occasionally punished the most insolent boys by making them run a lap around the school track. For the most part, though, Jeanie silently endured the heckling until last week, when a new, more physically developed girl moved to Weston and the harassment escalated. The boys began to walk by Jeanie, their hands cupped a few inches away from their chests, smirking, saying, "You've got competition, Jeanie. Connie is bigger than you are, but we'll always remember that you're second!" A few days later, one of the boys reached out and grabbed Jeanie's breasts.

"The thing is," says Ms. Murray, "this girl is actually not large-chested, this isn't happening because she's Dolly Parton. I suspect it's because they know they're getting to her. She doesn't have a lot of friends, and she's very nonassertive. She wouldn't even come in here on her own. Her mother told me what was going on and asked me to call her out of class."

Ms. Murray tells me she has been concerned about the level of sexual harassment on campus since she arrived at Weston last year. She describes incidences of boys insulting girls; boys restraining girls; boys grabbing girls' breasts, buttocks, and crotches. She's been mystified and frankly exasperated over why, in the face of such ill-treatment, the girls remain silent.

They even remain deferential to some of the harassers who are "popular" boys.

"They won't see this as something boys do to girls as one group to another, like racism," Ms. Murray says. "If they could just see themselves as a group, as powerful, if they just agreed to look at those boys as if they had leprosy, the boys would correct their behavior immediately."

But January 1, 1993, brought an opportunity for change at Weston, and that's why Ms. Murray has called me in here, that's why she looks oddly energized by this unhappy situation. On that day a new, innovative law took effect in California. Every school in the state is now required to develop a written sexual harassment policy for staff and students, to display it prominently on campus, and to distribute a copy to each teacher and parent. More to the point, a principal may suspend or even expel students as young as fourth graders who engage in sexual harassment.

Ms. Murray informed the students of the new law at a school-wide assembly just after winter break, in which she also discussed a number of other issues, such as the dates for upcoming standardized tests and the rising incidents of spitting on campus. The message was reinforced several days later in the school bulletin, which is read aloud in each class during first period.

Jeanie Mayes's complaint, Ms. Murray says, will be Weston's first test of the new law.

Ms. Murray has already transferred Jeanie to another gym class, and her science class has been switched as well, since most of the boys who harass her go directly there with her after gym, where they continue their behavior. The next challenge is to confirm her allegations, so it won't be just her word against the boys'. At Ms. Murray's request, Jeanie has compiled a list of girls who have witnessed the harassment; one of the school counselors has been assigned to convene that group after lunch today. The hope is that the girls will not only identify the perpetrators but begin to build a sense of cohesion and power among themselves.

"I'd like Jeanie to see that she's not the sole victim of abusive talk," Ms. Murray says. "That's part of why she's been so distressed. I even want her to see, maybe, why other kids don't take it as hard." Ms. Murray also suggested to the counselor that the girls might want to write an anonymous open letter to the Weston boys about harassment that would be placed in the school bulletin.

Once she's built her case, Ms. Murray plans to suspend the instigators of the harassment, using the new law—there will be no expulsions unless the boys persist—then she'll call their *fathers* with the news. "No man wants to hear from a woman that his parenting hasn't been too good," Ms. Murray explains. "Let alone hear it in graphic terms. I'll just say, 'It's not my job to train your child to be civil in public. You need to take him home and tell him not to make references to girls' bouncing boobs at school.'" She smiles impishly. "If I were a man I'd be so mad at my son for getting me in this humiliating situation!"

If she meets with any resistance, Ms. Murray says, she'll take her crusade into the community. "It's one thing for *me* to say I find it despicable when boys call girls 'ho's' and 'sluts,'" she says, "but it's not as meaningful as if our PTA supports the idea that certain behavior—including certain comments and language used consistently on campus—has adverse effects on the psyche of the girls and affects their academic performance.

"I see this as an evolution of standards," she continues. "We used to tolerate people saying nigger, we used to tolerate physical abuse of children, we used to tolerate slaves at one point if you go back far enough. We've evolved. We don't tolerate those things anymore, and now we won't tolerate sexual harassment."

▪

Sexual Harassment: Who Decides?

▪

Ms. Murray's fervor on this issue is unusual among school principals, to say the least. Technically speaking, students have been protected from sexual harassment since 1972, when Title IX of the Education Amendments banned discrimination based on sex and required school districts to designate an employee to handle complaints.[1] Up until recently, few administrators have enforced those regulations and students have remained ignorant of their rights.[2] But just about the time that the Anita Hill–Clarence Thomas hearings riveted national attention on sexual harassment among adults, a series of lawsuits brought it roiling to the surface in public schools. In 1991, in what may be the most celebrated of those cases, nineteen-year-old Katy Lyle won a $15,000 settlement from the Duluth, Minnesota, school district, which, while she was a high school student there, had failed to remove explicit graffiti about her from the walls of a boys' bathroom even after her parents' numerous complaints. The following year, in Petaluma, California, Tawnya Brawdy won a $20,000 out-of-court settlement from Kenilworth Junior High School, which did not stop boys who mooed at her and jeered about the size of her breasts. In a third significant case, Christine Franklin took her $6 million claim against the Gwinnett County, Georgia, school district all the way to the Supreme Court after a lower court held that Title IX violations were not subject to suit for punitive damages. In February 1992, the Justices unanimously sided with Franklin—even Clarence Thomas agreed.[3] By the spring of 1993, nearly half of the forty sexual harassment cases that were being investigated by the U.S. Department of Education's Office of Civil Rights involved elementary and secondary schools.[4]

In spite of the Supreme Court verdict, it has remained contentious to suggest that sexual harassment is possible—even has its behavioral roots—among young children. Media outlets from the daily papers to the afternoon television gab shows to such *éminences grises* as *60 Minutes* have served up reports on sexual harassment among schoolchildren. Yet, oddly, no matter how many times the issue is raised, and regardless of the growing hostility toward girls exhibited in such disparate incidents as Lakewood, California's "Spur Posse" sex-for-points scandal and the recent mob assaults on girls in New York City swimming pools, the media remain piously skeptical, hinting that this "teasing," this normal adolescent rite of passage, is being taken too seriously.

Perhaps if sexual harassment—which includes unwelcome sexual remarks that create a hostile learning environment[5]—happened in equal measure between boys and girls (or men and women) that argument might have merit. But it doesn't: overwhelmingly boys harass and girls (or other boys) are harassed, indicating that the behavior is less a statement about sexuality than an assertion of dominance. The prevalence of sexual harassment reminds us that boys learn at a very young age to see girls as less capable and less worthy of respect. One need only consider that the most shameful insult that one boy can hurl at another is still *"girl!"* (or "pussy" or "faggot," which have similar connotations) to understand how aware children are of female powerlessness, how important it is for boys to distance themselves from that weakness in order to feel like men.

Ms. Murray is right about the girls, too: middle-class and affluent girls in particular tend to accept sexual harassment as inevitable. And why not? The sexual teasing, stalking, and grabbing merely reinforces other, more subtle lessons: it reminds them that they are defined by their bodies; it underscores their lack of entitlement in the classroom (in fact, the harassment frequently *happens* in the classroom);[6] it confirms their belief that boys' sexuality is uncontrollable while their own must remain in check. Without encouragement and proper information, these girls, who already feel diminished, have little reason to believe that they could have recourse against boys' ridicule.

Certainly, middle school children are exploring their sexual identity; but, as we've seen, from the outset those explorations are mired in inequity, and that, too, serves to silence girls when they are harassed. If boys wield the power to ruin girls' reputations, speaking out against boys who offend becomes too risky. Meanwhile, since girls look to boys for confirmation of their desirability (which they've learned is central to their self-esteem), they are left in a muddle: like adult women, they are expected to draw the line between flattery and harassment. Like adult women, they judge one another by where and how they draw that line.

Ideally, the new California law would help redress the power inequities between boys and girls. And the legislation does take a step in that direction: by requiring a sexual harassment policy it admits to the existence of a problem. By stipulating a punishment, it offers girls a measure of the institutional support that they've been sorely lacking, and puts the burden of change squarely on boys. Those shifts in perception alone could have a profound impact on girls' self-esteem. Yet in spite of its good intentions, the law, which may well become a model nationwide, is essentially toothless. Gender equity specialist Nan Stein has pointed out that the state offers no guidance for the development of these new sexual harassment policies and, more importantly, its approach is solely punitive: there are no provisions either for staff training or for a curriculum that would help students define the boundaries of appropriate behavior and dissect power relations.[7] In fact, since the state has no means of enforcing the law, principals are free to soft-pedal it. Those administrators who are concerned about sexual harassment, such as Ms. Murray, are forced to improvise their own plans. They are also left with the fallout if those plans fail.

■

Strength in Numbers: The Girl Group

■

Just after lunch, Edie Deloria, a half-time counselor at Weston, convenes the group of girls whose names Jeanie Mayes submitted on her list. Mrs. Deloria is a heavyset woman in her late forties, with heavily moussed hair and bright pink nails; she wears olive stretch pants with a matching sequined shirt and suede ankle boots. As we wait in her office for the girls to assemble, she confides, "I've never done anything like this before, so I don't really know what I'm supposed to do. Andrea kind of booted this onto me."

Seven girls file in and perch uncomfortably on the chairs that Mrs. Deloria has arranged in a circle. Some of them look familiar: I recognize Emily and Samantha from Evie's math class. Amanda is in Becca's English class. Jeanie is among the last to arrive, trailing on the heels of her best friend, a compact girl with flowing red hair named Angie. Jeanie has ruddy skin with a patch of acne on one cheek. She's wearing a baggy sweatshirt that makes her upper body appear formless, and she lets her blond hair, which is limp and a little dirty, hang across her eyes. She looks around nervously and takes a seat under a poster that reads: "Make It Happen!"

The group gets off to a crashingly slow start.

"There've been some things happening in gym class," Mrs. Deloria begins. "Some boys saying some sexual things to girls, and some of you know about it and some of you don't."

A few of the girls stare straight ahead; others look baffled. Jeanie blushes deeply.

"How many of you are aware of this problem?"

There is no response for several seconds, then, one by one, five of the girls raise their hands. Mrs. Deloria looks heartened.

"You may have some feelings about this," she says, "Would anyone like to comment?"

Several of the girls shrug. Some study the ground.

Mrs. Deloria glances at me, then tries another tack. "We want to make the school safe," she says. "We want you to be free from remarks and other things that keep you from feeling comfortable learning here. Do you agree that this needs to be stopped?"

The girls shift in their seats. Jeanie darts her eyes back and forth. Seeing only disinterest, she sinks back into her chair. The meeting appears to be a flop. Then Emily, who is tiny and brooding, winces and says, "Sometimes guys say to other people that they're sluts."

At that, Samantha, who has been staring resolutely at the linoleum while wrapping her hair into a bun, begins to speak. "Something happened today in another class," she says reluctantly. "This guy called this girl a slut and . . . things like that . . ." She trails off and the other girls appear even more uneasy.

"That was my brother," Emily says. Emily, it turns out, skipped a year in elementary school; she is now in the same grade as her older brother Sid, who is a ringleader among the boys.

"And sometimes guys say to girls that they're half guy if

119

they like sports," Samantha continues, then adds, squirming, "but they don't use those words . . . exactly."

"Jeanie's too scared to talk," says Angie, who wears a floppy T-shirt and oversized jeans. Jeanie drops her eyes. "But boys talk about her breasts. And today when we were playing hockey, they'd take the stick and make this motion." She holds her hand near her crotch and pumps it up and down.

"Like masturbating?" Mrs. Deloria asks.

Several of the girls nod.

"Who does that?"

Angie names several names, then adds, "But a lot of the guys do it."

"Guys are just immature," says Samantha.

"It doesn't bother me," says Angie. "But it bothers Jeanie. They come up to her and say, 'Can I have some skim milk?' and stare at her breasts."

Amanda, who has been chewing her fingernails assiduously since the meeting began, snaps her head up. "Are you talking about all our classes?" she asks. "Because Robbie Jordan says he had sex with my mom and that . . . and other stuff."

"Can you say it?" Mrs. Deloria asks.

"Well, that my mom gave him a blow job."

The girls are loosening up now, and a tone of exasperation is replacing their initial reluctance. They begin recounting boys' remarks in detail: they talk about boys who say, "Suck my fat Peter, you slut," who call them "skank" and "ho' " (a variation on "whore" popularized by male rap artists). They talk about boys who pinch their bottoms in the hallways, or grab their breasts and shout, "Let me tune in Tokyo!" They insist that it isn't just "bad" boys who badger them: it's boys with good grades, boys who are athletes, boys who are paragons of the school. And, they all agree, their fear of reprisal is much too acute to allow them to confront their harassers.

Nonetheless, here in the safety of the counselor's office, the girls do name names, many of which are familiar to me: they are the same boys who interrupt and belittle girls in the classroom. They are often the very same boys whom I've seen demand— and get—the most teacher attention in the least productive ways.

During a brief pause in the girls' litany, Mrs. Deloria breaks in. "Girls think that guys 'just say these things,'" she says. "And after a while you think that this is the way that guys are supposed to talk to girls. But it doesn't have to be that way. Your feelings are important and you have to remember that. If you girls want them to stop, you have to tell them what's going to happen if they do it; and then you have to follow through. We take this very seriously at Weston."

"After assembly, the boys acted like it was a big joke," says Katie, a cherub-faced Asian girl. "Now they walk down the hall and touch you on the arm and say, 'Ooooh! Sexual harassment!' Like that's funny."

"I'm not saying it's easy," the counselor says. "But you have to be role models. I know it's just words, but you have to make it happen."

"Jeff Bellamy grabbed my breasts," Jeanie says softly, her eyes misting.

"How did you feel, Jeanie?" asks Mrs. Deloria.

"Jeanie was upset," Angie says. "I know, because I was sitting beside her and . . ."

"Let *Jeanie* finish," Mrs. Deloria interrupts.

"I'm finished," says Jeanie, who appears unaccustomed to speaking for herself.

Amanda, who has gone back to her fingernails, looks up thoughtfully. "I like guys who are your friends," she says. "Guys who talk to you for your personality, not just to get things from you."

The girls ponder this comment in silence; Jeanie looks morose.

"Would you girls like to meet again next week?" Mrs. Deloria asks. All seven girls raise their hands, as if they're in class; they decide, at that time, to work on a letter for the school bulletin.

As the girls get up to leave, Mrs. Deloria cautions, "This conversation is confidential, girls, it's between us. If anyone finds out about it, it was one of you who said something."

The girls nod solemnly; they won't tell a soul.

"Okay," the counselor continues, reaching for a jar of candy, "everyone have a piece of chocolate before you go. Like we need to add to our rear ends—that's where it goes on us!"

Mrs. Deloria shuts the door after the girls leave, leans back in her chair, and offers me the candy jar, apparently seeing no irony in her final remark. "I think that went pretty well," she says, relieved. "You know, a lot of these girls think they have to take this. They're taking it now, and by sixteen years old it will be so ingrained in them that they'll just accept it. Some of them, the girls who don't think they can fight back, they'll grow up and become depressed or battered, you can see it."

Mrs. Deloria's speech is cut short by Andrea Murray, who rushes into the room. "The group went very well," Mrs. Deloria begins to say, but Ms. Murray brushes her aside.

"You won't believe this," she says, turning to me. "Two eighth-grade girls just came into my office and they are livid about something that happened in *their* gym class—a different class. Sid Connelly called one of them a hooker, and another boy said, 'She can't be a hooker because she gives it away for free.' "

Ms. Murray shakes her head. "This girl was raped two years ago by a family member," she says, "so she's taking the remark pretty hard. Her friend brought her in to see me. I promised them I'd suspend Sid first thing tomorrow."

■

I Did It; So What?

■

At nine o'clock the next morning, Ms. Murray, wearing a "Distinguished California School" T-shirt, sits in her office with Gary Sanchez, the police officer who is assigned to work with her at the school.

"Are we going for tears here?" Officer Sanchez asks Ms. Murray. The principal nods.

Sid Connelly saunters in the door and, barely glancing at Officer Sanchez, sprawls in the chair next to Ms. Murray's desk. He's a tall, skeletal boy with dewy skin and crooked teeth. Like many boys at Weston, he's shaved the sides of his head and wears a baseball cap over the remaining thatch, giving the impression of total baldness. Since he's also wearing his jeans a fashionable three sizes too big and a huge T-shirt, the baldness makes him look vulnerable rather than tough, as fragile as an egg. He truly looks like a little boy dressed up in a bigger man's clothes, and the words he's been hurling at girls show just how important it is for him to convey that virile impression. Sid's eyes snap with defiance. He's been in here twice already this year for racial slurs and a number of times for other infractions, so he knows the drill.

Ms. Murray looks at him sharply. "We hear you've been talking about girls, Sid," she says.

"You mean Lisanne?"

"Yes, I mean Lisanne."

"So what, she calls me names and I called her one. I called her a hooker, so what?"

"What's a hooker, Sid?" Officer Sanchez asks. He's a big man, too big for the chairs in the office, which are the largest in the school. His graying hair is ridged around his head where his cap usually sits.

"A prostitute." Sid leans back in his chair and folds his arms.

"So you've been calling girls prostitutes," says Andrea.

"Sure," Sid says, shrugging. "She called *me* an asshole."

"Other girls say that's not all you call them."

Sid looks away. "I just did it once."

That's when Ms. Murray slips up, unwittingly identifying one of the girls. "Your sister and other girls say that's not true. They say you call them slut, ho', a lot of names. Are you calling them liars?"

"No," Sid says, kicking his feet against his chair.

Officer Sanchez turns to Sid, shaking his head. "Sid, Sid, Sid. Society doesn't accept boys calling girls sexual names anymore. It's illegal. You can be expelled for it. You can go to jail for it."

"Well, if they want people to know that, why don't they tell them," Sid says sullenly.

"We did, Sid," Ms. Murray says. "Weren't you at the assembly Friday?"

"I was absent."

"Well, didn't your first-period teacher read the note in the bulletin and discuss it this week?"

"I don't listen to him," Sid says.

The cop and Ms. Murray exchange a look.

"Expulsion means you're out of school for the rest of the year," Officer Sanchez continues. "You don't go on to high school next year either. And the parents of those girls? They can sue you, Sid. But since you're a minor . . . you live in . . ."

"Redwood Estates."

"Redwood Estates. There's a lot of nice homes up there," Officer Sanchez says, nodding appreciatively. He leans in toward the boy. "Since you're a minor," he says, "your mom could be sued by those girls' parents for what you did. And then you couldn't live in Redwood Estates anymore. Instead of your nice, comfortable house, you'd be down here in town living in a little apartment. Your mom wouldn't be too happy with you then, would she, Sid?"

Sid's eyes are getting a little glassy.

Ms. Murray interjects. "Do you see your dad on weekends?" she asks.

Sid nods.

"Do you live with him during the week at all?"

Sid shakes his head.

"Well, I'm going to call him right now and tell him to talk to you about how a man acts." She spins her chair around and places the call. "Will? This is Andrea Murray at the middle school. I have your son here. I'm calling you rather than his mother because we have a serious problem. I have girls complaining that he's making sexually harassing remarks to them." She recounts the incident. "I need your support in talking to him to say it's inappropriate to call girls sluts and hookers."

Sid's jaw tightens. He fights back tears as Ms. Murray goes on to explain the new law to his father.

"If you'd talk to him and explain how girls feel . . ."

She is interrupted as the father speaks. She tries to reiterate her point but is interrupted again. Sid looks, in addition to unhappy, uncomfortable. Something else is being exposed here.

"Well, the information really needs to come from you,

Will," Ms. Murray says. "He needs to hear it from a father figure, he needs to identify with your values, to learn his behavior from you. You can help him if you can have that conversation with him. If you tell him . . ."

There is another long pause.

"Yes, I'll notify her, but if you could talk to him from a male perspective maybe you can have a greater influence . . ."

By now, Ms. Murray is fairly begging Will Connelly to talk to his son, and the father is clearly refusing. Sid runs a finger under his eyes. His face is pink.

Ms. Murray hangs up the phone. "You know what your dad tells me, Sid?"

Sid shakes his head.

"He says this might not do any good. He says suspension might not get the message to you. He says he's surprised this hasn't happened before."

Sid looks rigidly ahead, his eyes brimming, his lips full and moist. Ms. Murray ceremoniously fills out a suspension form and hands it to him. He snatches it from her hand and runs out the door, just as the bell signals the end of second period.

After he leaves, Ms. Murray rolls her eyes. "Well, that's where he gets it. You can tell that vulgarity is that man's main way of communicating. He says that it's all his ex-wife's fault, that she doesn't know how to raise them. He probably usually uses those words that Sid used to describe his ex-wife." She lets out a long breath. "Well," she says grimly, "I can't fix his family, but I'm going to stop his behavior."

She begins to brief Officer Sanchez on the next boy who is coming in today, the one who said Lisanne "gives it away for free." This boy is a good student, from a solid family with a mother whom Ms. Murray describes as a feminist; the principal believes he was motivated less by malice than peer pressure, so she plans to go easy on him, just giving him a Saturday detention. But just as she locates his third-period class on the computer, the secretary slips in with a note from Sid's sister. Emily is panicked; she was promised anonymity in the counseling group, but suddenly Sid is blaming her for his suspension. He's told some of his friends, too, and they're starting to come up to her calling her "a big fat ho'." According to Emily, the other girls from the group are terrified; what if their names were used, too? What will the boys do to them?

"They are so scared," Ms. Murray says, shaking her head, "it's unreal."

Ms. Murray calls both Sid and Emily into her office. Emily sits in a chair and folds her hands in her lap. Sid stands next to her.

"Did you see your sister after we talked?" she asks. "Did you say anything to her?"

"Yeah," Sid says. "You said it was my sister who came in here and said I call girls hookers."

"I said what?" Ms. Murray sputters. "Sid, you don't listen too well. I said, 'Even your sister knows what you do.' "

Sid shifts from foot to foot, his lips tight and his eyes wet with anger.

"Your suspension is now *two* days," Ms. Murray says. "And if any girl comes in here and says you're harassing her, I'll just keep adding the days. And I'm calling your mother right now." Sid sniffles. Emily casts her eyes downward. Ms. Murray dials the phone.

When Ms. Murray reaches Sid's mother, Mrs. Connelly tries to dismiss her son's behavior, making excuses for it. Then Ms. Murray hands the phone to Emily, who tells her mother exactly what Sid has been doing. When she hears her own daughter's frightened voice, the excuses stop.

"She just said, 'I'll take care of it, and it *won't* happen again,' " Ms. Murray says after the children leave. "She became completely supportive. I wish every boy had a sister in the same grade."

■

The More Things Change . . .

■

Over the next several weeks, Ms. Murray suspends five boys for sexual harassment, including two of the boys who were hounding Jeanie Mayes. She gives several other boys, whom she views as "followers," detention or Saturday school. Her thoroughness buoys the Weston girls' spirits; they believe that Ms. Murray is on their side and will protect them from harm. But this seismic shift toward equality leaves the boys confused and hostile. For the first time, they cannot do or say anything they want. Some of the boys are philosophical about the change, but most are unsure of—or unwilling to consider—what, exactly, constitutes inappropriate behavior. A few of the boys suggest that sexual harassment is too subtle to define, but if girls let them know that they're being offensive, they'll stop. Others are like Carl Ross, who was suspended for making masturbatory motions at Jeanie Mayes and asserting that several other girls "suck dick," and now complains, "The principal says it's degrading gossip, but you can't even say a girl's fine anymore, and how's that degrading?" Rather than try to work through the dilemma, Carl has simply decided to avoid girls for the rest of the year. "I'll just wait until high school," he says, "and talk to the girls then."

Even Jeff Bellamy, the boy who grabbed Jeanie's breasts, seems to have difficulty understanding the charges against him. I stop to chat with him the day after his suspension, while he is running an errand for his math teacher. "I was puzzled by the punishment," he tells me, stroking the few downy hairs on his chin. "I don't remember doing it, but maybe I did. All the guys do that stuff, it's no big deal. The girls don't mind. I mean, they don't do anything about it. I'd beat the crap out of someone if they touched me like that. But girls are different, they don't really do anything, so I guess it's okay to do."

On February 4, less than a month since her campaign to eradicate sexual harassment at Weston began, Ms. Murray calls me back into her office. Her sexual harassment policy, she announces glumly, has "all turned to shit . . . It's come back to bite me."

First, she says the father of one of the girls in the counseling group called her. At home. He wanted to know why the word "masturbating" had been used in front of his daughter without his consent. Apparently, she had yet to learn what the word meant and he wasn't anxious to fill her in.

"I tried to explain that boys in this school are talking about girls' mothers giving them blow jobs," she says. "I told him there's no underestimating the depth of these kids' knowledge or their misinformation. But he wouldn't listen."

Worse still, Jeanie Mayes's case has collapsed. Ms. Murray had told Jeanie's mother in confidence that according to one of the other girls in the class (who happened to be Lisa Duffy), Jeanie was not forceful enough toward her harassers; Lisa said Jeanie sent "mixed signals," and that the boys as well as some of the girls thought she invited the problem. Mrs. Mayes did not find this well-intentioned critique illuminating. She informed her daughter that a girl was spreading rumors about her, and the next day Jeanie retaliated, persuading the other girls in her former gym class to ostracize Lisa (something she never tried against the boys). At that point, Jeanie stopped being the "victim" and Ms. Murray called home again, to request that the mother have a talk with the daughter about her aggressive behavior. Mrs. Mayes exploded.

"She was happy as long as I met the agenda, as long as I suspended boys who misbehaved," Ms. Murray says. "But when her own daughter was held accountable she didn't like it. Now she's pulled Jeanie out of the school."

Before she did, though, Mrs. Mayes called the district superintendent to complain about the principal's mismanagement of her daughter's case. The superintendent agreed that Ms. Murray had botched the proceedings, but not because she hadn't attended to Jeanie. Her complaint was that the principal had failed to protect the boys. "The superintendent was upset that Mrs. Mayes had the names of the boys who had perpetrated this," Ms. Murray says. "But if one kid was hitting another, the parent would know that so-and-so hit his kid, so why is this different? She was also concerned that I'd allowed a group of girls to discuss what had happened. She said the girls could spread it around and stigmatize the boys. But individually, girls are afraid to speak out, and I thought that the group empowered them. And part of the point was supposed to be that these girls would identify boys who were doing this and make them stop by not accepting the behavior.

"I guess I misread the situation," she says. "I thought I should be applauded for this, I thought I was doing something for girls, and that I was developing a culture where girls stood up for their rights. But I guess it's more important to keep a lid on it."

Ms. Murray says the superintendent's reprimand has made her feel "burned" and "gun-shy," so she's not going to confront the remaining boys on her list of chronic harassers. And since she's met with outrage from the parents of both boys and girls, she is dropping her initial plan to rally community support at a

PTA meeting. She has already told Edie Deloria to discontinue the girls' group, which, in spite of the counselor's promises, had yet to meet again anyway. That means the open letter for the school bulletin will be abandoned as well.

Maybe she folded without much of a fight, but, Ms. Murray claims, she can't effect broad-based change in her school without the backing of the superintendent. And, practically speaking, Ms. Murray says she has her own reputation to protect; if she crosses too many people, she could endanger her job. So instead of spearheading Weston's sexual harassment policy herself, Ms. Murray has decided to follow her boss's lead.

"There's still no procedure in place for dealing with this in the district," she says, "and no one seems to have any plans to develop one. There's been no discussion among the administrators, no talk about staff training, nothing. There's just the law, no way to carry it out . . . and I guess, looking back, I wouldn't try something like this again."

After leaving Ms. Murray's office that morning, I stop by the school gym. It is a rainy day, and the students are inside playing basketball. The boys dash back and forth, chiding one another for mistakes and slapping high fives over their triumphs. The girls, for the most part, hover on the periphery of the game, halfheartedly guarding one another. This is Lindsay's class, and at one point, when she is the only person on her team who is both near the basket and open, a boy passes her the ball. She purses her lips and shoots.

As the ball leaves her hands, I turn away. I don't want to know whether Lindsay makes the basket or not. I like to imagine that she does, that the ball arcs through the air and swishes perfectly through the hoop, that she embraces her friends, jumping up and down with glee. But perhaps that's not what happens. Perhaps the ball goes wild, and the boys in the class roll their eyes in disgust before continuing the game. Either way, I hope she tries again.

I leave the gym and walk through the rain to the parking lot. As I have on many days this year, I am splitting my time between Weston and another school. I slip into my car and turn it toward the freeway, toward Audubon Middle School, fifty miles and a whole world away.

Part II
Audubon Middle School

■

7

"You People Are
Animals":
Life in the Urban School

■

■

■

John J. Audubon Middle School sits at the precise juncture where a tidy residential neighborhood slides into the industrial gloom of a warehouse district in a Northern California city. It's a squat jailhouse of a building with concrete walls, sparsely placed narrow windows, and dull yellow doors. Back when Audubon was built, in the early 1970s, the brightly painted houses surrounding it were home to working-class families and artists seeking relief from high rents. But during the last two decades, the local population exploded, and real estate prices soon followed suit: a two-bedroom, one-bath house across from the school now costs well over a quarter-million dollars. But the children who attend Audubon don't come from those homes.

Like other urban schools, Audubon has been abandoned by the white and the wealthy, consigned to the children whose parents can't afford to buy them an education. Only about 10 percent of the students, most of whom are unhappily bused in from a nearby military base, are white. The rest are African American, Latino, Asian, or Filipino; they live in poor neighborhoods, barrios, or one of several public housing projects that are all a short city bus ride from the school. Many are first-generation U.S. citizens, who act as go-betweens for their non-English-speaking parents at the post office, the supermarket, even with school officials. A full two-thirds of Audubon's 650 students live in poverty. The school's test scores hover among the lowest in the city.

Audubon, however, is by no means the bleakest of urban schools: the hallways are clean and decorated with bright murals, painted by students in years past; the bathrooms are safe and the sinks and drinking fountains almost always work. There are no metal detectors at the gate: students do not bring guns here, although knives (as well as graffiti markers) are frequently confiscated. And there is a thriving after-school sports program. Since the majority of Audubon's students are considered "educationally disadvantaged," the district provides the school with extra funds to be used at the principal's discretion. Audubon's most recent administrator—the school's seventh in nine years—resigned over the summer, but before she left, she used that money to secure the kinds of social services that, these days, are considered a luxury: she hired a part-time social worker, a teacher to supervise an in-house detention room, as well as two part-time student advisers who identify learning-disabled pupils and oversee a peer tutoring program.

Yet whereas at Weston, the hidden curriculum teaches students that power is disproportionately conferred by gender, at Audubon—in spite of these recent efforts—the children learn a more comprehensive lesson: that, for them, power will not be conferred at all. Mired in discrimination by race and class and exacerbated by the statewide gutting of funds for education and the overburdening of teachers, Audubon's hidden (and often not so hidden) curriculum teaches these children that their minds and their potential are not worth as much as others'. In the classrooms at Audubon, issues of gender are often subsumed by issues of basic humanity, often secondary to enabling a student —any student—to go through a school day without feeling insulted, abused, or wronged by her peers or by her teachers.

■

When the Teacher "Don't Care"

■

Mr. Krieger, a pear-shaped white man with thin graying hair and a droop to his cheeks, teaches English to all of this year's eighth graders, and taught about half of them last year as well; he also teaches one section of eighth-grade social studies, so some students spend two periods a day under his care. His classroom is big—ample enough to seat thirty-five students— and unceasingly drab. The plastic chairs are gray, the cinderblock walls are gray, the linoleum floor is gray, even Mr. Krieger himself looks gray. There are a couple of fading basketball posters on the wall, one encouraging students to stay in school, but the dominant decor is a podium at the front of the room and a few textbooks scattered on the desks.

Before sitting in on a class at either Weston or Audubon, I always asked permission of the teacher, regardless of how many times I'd already visited. Today, a rainy January morning just after Christmas break, when I ask Mr. Krieger if I can join his third-period class, he shrugs. "Sure," he says. "I used to be embarrassed but I don't care anymore."

The students file in, laughing and gossiping with one another. Helen Ortiz, Carolina Castillo, and Marta Herrera take their seats on the left side of the room and promptly begin playing cards. Helen has a fair, freckled complexion and heavily made-up eyes. She smiles nervously when she talks, and since English is her second language—learned during the five years since she and her mother moved from Mexico—she winces when she mispronounces words. Carolina is round-faced and shy, and has tied her hair in an elaborate topknot; in jeans and a hooded sweatshirt, she looks closer to eleven than thirteen. Marta, a stocky girl whose home-permanented hair grazes her shoulders, tells me that she learned English from *Sesame Street;* her parents, who speak only Spanish, both work in industrial laundries. The girls discuss a disastrous party that Marta recently attended, a Quinceniera, or fifteenth-birthday party, which marks the passage into womanhood for Latina girls.

"So she told everyone to get out of the room, and her parents wasted three thousand dollars!" Marta says, abruptly switching to Spanish when she senses another student is eavesdropping on the conversation. Helen and Carolina shake their heads in rapt disbelief.

As class begins, Mr. Krieger looks up from his attendance book. "Damn it to hell, Helen, put those cards away."

"Why you always say, 'Damn it to hell'?" asks DeAndre, a minute African American boy with a small braid dangling from the nape of his shaved head. Mr. Krieger ignores him. "Damn it to hell, Carolina!" DeAndre repeats, shaking his finger at the girls.

It is a week before President Clinton's inauguration, and although he makes no mention of the connection, Mr. Krieger passes out "The Dentist," a short story by "On the Pulse of Morning" poet Maya Angelou, which he's photocopied from *Scholastic* magazine. The lesson looks promising: this is, after all, a story about a child's resilience in the face of racism, written by an African American woman who is the personification of the triumphant self. Yet when Mr. Krieger instructs them to read silently, the students appear nonplused.

"Excuse me, but we read this yesterday," says Crystal, an African American girl who had been exceptionally enthusiastic in the previous day's discussion of the story.

"We did?" asks the teacher. "Are you sure?"

The other students nod their heads. Helen and Carolina exchange a look.

"Oh, damn, I forgot," the teacher says.

Since he has nothing else prepared, Mr. Krieger begins flipping through the story again, asking questions such as "Who can tell me the name of the person who wrote this story?" and "How old was Ms. Angelou?" and "Carolina, what is that funny, squiggly type called?"

Within fifteen minutes, however, he has mined that vein to exhaustion, and the class degenerates into chaos: Crystal dashes across the room with another student's three-ring binder, which bursts open, spewing papers across the floor. DeAndre touches a girl's thigh and she tries, unsuccessfully, to push him away. Meanwhile, one of the boys is stuffing a friend into a supply closet with the assistance of roughly half the class, while Mr. Krieger sits at the front of the room chatting with a studious African American girl named Dashelle.

Helen and Carolina turn to me. "You see how he is?" Helen asks. "He's a terrible teacher, he doesn't teach you anything. Look at how everyone's running around and he doesn't do anything."

We survey the class in silence. Marta puts her head down on her desk.

"Yeah," adds Carolina. "And in social studies he gives us just a little work sheet and tells us to do it. That's it."

"I keep thinking," says Helen, furrowing her brow, "what happens when we get to high school? We won't know anything. We'll be all behind in ninth grade."

When the bell rings, Mr. Krieger motions me over to his

desk. In other brief asides during my visits he's said, "They're a rotten bunch of kids," or "A wise man once said, the only form of life lower than eighth graders is whale shit," an attitude which infuses his teaching. This time, he only smiles at me weakly.

"Well, that was a bad lesson plan," he says.

Immediately after Mr. Krieger's class, these eighth graders troop upstairs for science with Ms. Raynes, a large-bodied woman with fiery, red-dyed hair who is one of the school's few African American teachers. Ms. Raynes, who is nearing retirement age, teaches science to all of Audubon's eighth graders, save one class of thirty students. She considers herself to be a caring educator: when one of the students in this class, an African American girl named Tracey, ran away from home just before the winter break, Ms. Raynes was distraught.

"I have dreams that I see Tracey on the evening news and she's dead," she told me at the time. "I wake up crying. I've been asking the counselor about her, and I've made inquiries. I'm so worried."

But since last week, when Tracey returned unscathed, Ms. Raynes seems to have forgotten her concern.

"I tried with her, I honestly did," she told me after a class in which she called Tracey "tacky" in front of the other students. "I brought her in here and told her she had a bad attitude and that it makes her ugly. And I thought she was listening, but I guess she wasn't, because you can see she hasn't changed. I don't know what to do with her. I'd transfer her out of my class if I could."

Today, when I ask if I can sit in on a lesson on light and color, she gives me her stock response, not dissimilar to Mr. Krieger's: "Well, if you can stand it, I guess I can."

Ms. Raynes never gets through the lesson. The students continue talking and throwing paper well after the bell rings, until she stands in front of the class screaming for attention, her face contorted with rage and exasperation.

"I'm tired of spoon-feeding you people your lessons," she shouts. "Today, you open your book and do your lesson on your own time."

Perhaps three students open their books—which are six years old and haven't a single picture of women or girls engaged in scientific activity—and begin reading about the reflection and refraction of light. The rest of the class continues to misbehave.

Ms. Raynes raises her yardstick and cracks it hard against the blackboard. This gets the students' attention for a moment. "This is the stupidest class I've ever seen," she yells. "I don't know who's been raising you, but whoever it is has slipped up."

I sit at the back corner table with Marta and LaRhonda Johnson, an African American girl with an artificial ponytail of shoulder-length braids woven into her hair and gold hoop earrings. LaRhonda tells me she recently returned to school after two weeks spent in Juvenile Detention for shoplifting; on the advice of her probation officer, she's buckling down in class, trying to raise her grades. So far, she hasn't had much luck: like roughly a quarter of the class, LaRhonda is failing science. So is Marta. Both girls believe they might be doing better if someone would just teach them something.

"She doesn't teach nothing and everyone knows it," says Marta, who is resting her elbows on her closed textbook.

LaRhonda shakes her head, folding her arms across her chest. "This class is sorry," she says. "Look at this mess." She gestures with disgust at her classmates, who hoot, holler, and run about, then to Ms. Raynes, who never leaves her post behind a thick table at the front of the class.

"I will not spoon-feed you!" Ms. Raynes shouts again, slapping her yardstick for emphasis.

"I will not spoon-feed you," LaRhonda mimics, shaking her head again. "No one in here does the work. Maybe four of us."

LaRhonda frowns down at her tattered science book, dragging each finger across a line of text as she painstakingly mouths the words. She reads every sentence twice, once to sound it out and once to understand. "What's refection and what's reflection?" she asks, misreading the word "refraction." "Is refection when you look in a mirror? What is this?"

LaRhonda glances up as Ms. Raynes chews out Michael, who has just accused another boy of smelling like "last year's butt."

"She's like a substitute teacher," LaRhonda says. "No one listens. At least you know she's not prejudice, because she's black." She leans forward conspiratorially. "Some people say Mr. Krieger is prejudice. But I don't know—he's never gotten racial with me, so I can't say."

LaRhonda returns to her work and Marta begins doodling in her notebook.

"LaRhonda, stop talking!" Ms. Raynes yells.

LaRhonda, who wasn't talking, looks up at the teacher. "I wasn't," she says.

"Don't argue with me," Ms. Raynes snaps.

"She's crazy," LaRhonda says, *sotto voce,* to me.

Ms. Raynes emerges from behind her table and begins walking around the room, distributing work sheets.

"I don't understand this," LaRhonda says politely to her, pointing to a spot in the book.

"I'm not doing your work for you," Ms. Raynes answers.

"But I don't . . ."

"I tried to explain it to you, but you weren't listening, you were talking."

Marta looks at me and rolls her eyes meaningfully.

"I wasn't."

"You were too busy talking."

"I wasn't talking, I was . . ."

"Well, I'm not going to tell you now, it's too late."

Ms. Raynes walks away. "You see that?" LaRhonda says. "That's cold. That's why we don't be learning nothing."

A minute later she puts her paper down. "I ain't doing it. That's wrong, how she was. I ain't doing it now, man."

When the bell rings, Ms. Raynes, like Mr. Krieger, stops me before I can leave the room. "You see how it is?" she asks, echoing Helen's question from earlier in the day. "They're animals. No, animals are better behaved than that."

I nod my head. I see exactly how it is. These students, who are already considered by the school system to be educationally "at risk," go from Mr. Krieger to Ms. Raynes and then, for many of them, back to Mr. Krieger for social studies. During those three periods the class receives, by my watch, a total of forty minutes of instruction. The other hour and a half is spent on crowd control. The students are told that they're stupid, treated as if they're uneducable, and accorded no respect—then blamed for their behavior.

The next day, Ms. Raynes abandons an experiment she has planned for her students in the face of their continual disruption. The punishment for the class, she decides, will be to do no more experiments for the rest of the year—that is, the punishment is to deny them the opportunity to learn.

When Ms. Raynes makes the announcement, LaRhonda clucks her tongue. "It's too hard in here," she says. "It's too hard to do anything, because she don't care. You can't work when the teacher don't care."

■

Gender and Power

■

Indifferent instruction and demeaning educational environments combine to effectively stifle academic achievement among all low-income children. The gap in standardized test scores between the affluent and the poor is far greater than any gender gap between low-income boys and girls.[1] Low-income children, regardless of race, rarely score at the advanced levels in reading or math, while high-income students seldom fall below the basic skills level. Low-income students are also more likely than their middle-class peers to repeat a grade, and more likely to leave school without a diploma. Given the educational standards I often witnessed at Audubon, this comes as no surprise.

Yet devaluation by race or class does not preclude devaluation by gender. At Audubon, girls are far more likely than boys to attend school on a regular basis (a case, perhaps, of compliance working in girls' favor) and often comprise two-thirds of the students in a class. They also tend to earn higher grades than boys. But on those occasions when boys are equally represented (or when there are just *slightly* more girls in a class), the same patterns of interaction between teachers and male students arise as at Weston: boys grab the questions, boys are rewarded for aggressiveness, boys (who remain the key to control) get whatever limited attention the teachers may offer. This is particularly true of Audubon's honors classes, where the students are highly motivated and, not incidentally, the ratio of boys to girls abruptly shifts.[2] In other words, in classes where learning is most limited, the gender politics are most diffuse and may even favor girls; but where real knowledge—and real power—are at stake, boys quickly step to the fore. This may help explain why, although underclass girls outshine and outscore boys scholastically through middle school, by high school they lose that edge and the boys begin to make disproportional gains.[3]

There is one class at Audubon in which equity by both ethnicity and gender seems to be a priority: Ms. Leland's math class. Ms. Leland, a thin white woman in her mid-thirties with large glasses and a slight Boston accent, teaches math to all of the eighth grade, and taught many of the students in sixth and seventh grade as well. Even the lax standards of other classrooms can't fully undermine her efforts: although they have a long way to go, Audubon's eighth-grade statewide test scores will jump higher than any other school in the city this year. And just as the children know who "don't care," they also know who does: the students who throw paper in Ms. Raynes's room, who stuff themselves into the supply closet in Mr. Krieger's class, are quiet and serious with Ms. Leland, even when the class size is an unmanageable forty. And especially in the honors class, where boys tend to monopolize the proceedings, Ms. Leland refuses to let them dominate, no matter how hard they try.

On a late fall day, the honors students file into Ms. Leland's classroom and sit down at tables in their assigned learning groups. In the center of each table is a pile of large metal nuts and bolts, to help the class study what is, in truth, a "nuts and bolts" subject: addition and subtraction of positive and negative numbers. So for a problem that reads $5n + 2b$, the groups grab five nuts and two bolts from the pile; after screwing together two of the bolts and nuts, they are left with three extra nuts—so the answer is $5n + 2b = 3n$.

The physical representation is helpful, although nuts and bolts may be distant from girls' experience. To try to neutralize the gender difference, she sets the problem up this way: "Maria has a toolbox with five nuts and three bolts. She wants to have an even number, what are the two ways she can do this?" Maria, then, is a girl—quite possibly a Latina girl—with a toolbox, breaking down stereotypes in both hardware and equations.

As soon as they sit down, several boys begin vying for Ms. Leland's attention, waving their hands in the air, calling out questions, or needling a neighbor to force the teacher to intercede.

But Ms. Leland has her rules. She categorically refuses to answer a question unless an entire group raises its hands, which forces the children to use one another as resources rather than depending solely on her. If, when they are working out problems as a class, a student shouts out an answer, points are taken away from his entire group, especially if he has interrupted another student. The method foils the more aggressive boys, who cannot gain individual recognition.

"I need help!" yells one rambunctious boy early in the lesson. When he gets no response, he yells a little louder, "Ms. Leland, *I need help!*"

"You know how to handle it," she tosses back as she circles the room, checking in with each table, offering encouragement and advice. The boy continues to wave his hand in the air for a moment, then capitulates, turning to his fellow group members for assistance.

When she does quiz students from the front of the class, Ms. Leland alternates between girls and boys (although there are actually more boys in the room) and seems to reward and punish with an even hand. Ms. Leland's classes are also the ones I visit at Audubon where there are moments of absolute silence, during which the students are hard at work. Hers is, in fact, the closest I've seen to complete fairness in any math classroom. But Ms. Leland doesn't see it that way.

Several weeks after visiting her class, I join Ms. Leland in her classroom during her preparatory period. She has been reluctant to make time to talk to me, since she usually spends her lunch period as well as an hour or more after school tutoring students. Today, our conversation is interrupted several times: once she needs to call the parent of a truant student; a few minutes later, another student's social worker calls to discuss his depressed behavior in class; a third student's mother returns a call Ms. Leland put in to her to discuss her son's progress. Yet in spite of her obvious dedication, Ms. Leland says she feels inadequate to her task: she is the only teacher in either school to ask me to stop observing her class after the first semester, because, she says, her teaching is just not up to snuff.

"The class sizes are so big this year," she says in between phone calls. "Over thirty-five kids. I can't give the individual attention I'd like to and I feel guilty because it means I have to let some kids go. If a student is quiet, I can't check up on them. I have to deal with crises only."

And "crises only," she explains, usually means focusing on the boys. "There are some very aggressive girls in this school, very assertive girls," she says. "But still, when I look at the detention referrals I write, at the requests for special education testing, even at the phone calls home . . ." She breaks off. "Well, maybe not . . . No, even there it's more boys than girls every time. They definitely get more attention. I mean, it's all negative attention—detention, things like that—but it's *attention,* it signals who's more important. And with these kids, they want any kind of attention: a lot of times negative attention is the only kind they know how to get. If you don't get any attention at all, positive or negative, you stop producing."

Ms. Leland rests her chin on her palm. Her face is drawn and a little pinched; her mouth, in repose, turns down in a frown. "I see that a lot of the girls, especially the quiet girls, are not going to stick with it," she continues. "They won't keep producing. They give up on problems too easily. Or they look to the boys for answers. And sometimes the boys belittle them, abuse them."

She takes a bite of her sandwich, which she didn't have time to eat at lunch, and glances nervously at the clock. In five minutes the period will be over, and she hasn't finished grading papers for the next class. "I try to step in when that happens," she says, "when the boys abuse the girls. But with this many kids, that's really hard too: I know I don't always see it."

■

Bitches and "Ho's": Sexual Harassment at Audubon

■

Ms. Leland points out that, in large classes, it's difficult to monitor how students treat one another and that's certainly true. On the other hand, many teachers don't even try: during my visits to Audubon's classrooms—especially the ones in which discipline and respect for the students' intellects are scarce—I hear girls barraged by sexually explicit insults, and see boys grab girls' thighs, rears, and breasts. Presumably, if all of this is visible to me, a teacher could see it too.

Several days after the Maya Angelou fiasco, I join Carolina and Helen in Mr. Krieger's social studies class. The students are filling out a work sheet based on a chapter of American history they are studying; Mr. Krieger sits in the front of the room chatting with Crystal and Dashelle, who have finished their papers. Carolina and Helen work together, chatting quietly.

"Carolina! Carolina!" DeAndre calls out from several seats away. When Carolina turns, DeAndre licks the palm of his hand suggestively, as if he is in a Prince video, then rubs it across his face, ogling her all the while. When he's done, he wiggles the tip of his tongue at her lasciviously.

A minute later, he puts his hand on the thigh of the girl next to him and she punches his arm.

"Don't feel on me," she says.

"I wasn't," he responds, feigning innocence. "I just wanted to know how big your thigh was."

He looks back at Carolina, winks, and makes wet kissing sounds in her direction.

A few days later, when I visit the same students in their English class, DeAndre is still at it. In full view of the teacher, he leers at Carolina until she turns away. Then he turns to stare at Helen, who, exasperated, swats him lightly on the cheek.

"Slap me, Helen," DeAndre says. "Come on, slap me. Because I want to slap you."

Helen tries to turn away but DeAndre jumps in front of her.

"Now don't be talkin' about me," he says. "Just slap me."

A second boy walks up and genially pushes DeAndre aside, restraining him with one arm while asking Helen a question. As soon as the boy leaves, though, DeAndre begins pestering Helen again. Finally, he grows bored with the game and walks away, chuckling.

"I wish he'd die," Helen says to no one in particular.

There is one notable difference between the tenor of verbal harassment at Weston and that at Audubon: at Audubon, the behavior is more reciprocal, practiced by both boys and girls. In some respects, this could be viewed as a perverse kind of progress, an equal opportunity abusiveness.[4] At the very least, it is a break in the pattern of silence and shame I witnessed among girls at Weston. But the terms the Audubon girls use to heckle their male peers reveal that the locus of power remains unchanged. Absent a language that degrades men as colorfully and efficiently as it does women, the girls are forced to adopt the same terms boys hurl at them, terms such as "bitch" or "ho'," which equate weakness with femininity.[5] Yet while girls are expected to tolerate such humiliation, boys are not—at least not when the insults are dished out by a girl.

During a section of Ms. Raynes's science class, Barbette, a golden-skinned African American girl with pink rollers in her bangs, bursts into the room, irate over something a boy named Martin has said to her in the hallway.

"What the fuck you say, you punk?" she shouts, as Martin, a slightly built Latino, walks by her, looking smug. His silence enrages her. She stops in her tracks and plants her hands on her hips.

"You punk-nose, big-ass bitch!" she yells. "Why don't you come over here, niggah. I'll make you eat your words."

Martin sits down, smiling to himself. Meanwhile, Miguel, who sits across the aisle from Martin and is physically mature enough to pass for seventeen, eyes Barbette coolly.

"Don't let that bitch talk like that," he says to Martin, then flexes a bicep. *"You* need machismo lessons."

Although Miguel considers the insults a challenge to Martin's masculinity, it is the fact that Barbette is a girl, more than her choice of words, that provokes his response: neither boy seems to find it unusual that, to express the depth of her fury, a black girl could only think to call her adversary "nigger" and "bitch."

Some teachers dismiss sexual harassment at Audubon as a low priority, one they can't cope with when they're already so overburdened. "We have other things to think about here," a teacher snapped at me one day, "like hunger and poverty." Others' rationalization for allowing harassment within school walls is consistent with their attitude toward the students: when asked about the prevalence of taunts and touching in the classrooms and hallways, those teachers respond that the children's home environment makes their school behavior inevitable. In other words, instead of the hackneyed pretext that "boys will be boys," the unspoken implication is that "blacks will be blacks," "Latinos will be Latinos," or, perhaps, "poor people will be poor people." That assumption serves the school well: it conveniently blinds teachers to the large number of boys and girls who do not harass (or care to be harassed) while absolving them of responsibility for educating the ones who do.

Bob Pirelli is Audubon's acting principal, an affable middle-aged man with graying hair and a newly grown mustache who favors brown tweed sport coats. He's well aware of the climate of harassment and abuse at Audubon, but is of the belief that the fault does not lie with the school. "If it gets to be a real problem we deal with it," he explains to me one morning in his office, "but the students here are from a culture that talks a certain way, and there's nothing you can do. No teacher or principal can straighten that out. We can just try by example; the way we speak and talk to each other has an impact on the kids."

But, I point out, the children often are following the teachers' lead: I have heard a teacher call girls "toots," "child," and "lovely lady." I have seen a teacher break off in the middle of a sentence to peer at a girl in the back of a classroom and comment, "Gee, you have big eyes," which, although a far cry from "Get your period out of my face, bitch," nonetheless reduces a girl to the sum of her physical parts. Do the teachers also come from a culture that "just talks that way"?

He smiles wryly and nods, conceding the point. "Well, it's a slow process," he says. "The counselors, the administrators, we

151

have to model it for them, and show both the teachers and the students it's not acceptable: that's how people learn."

Despite the minimal administrative support, some of Audubon's teachers try to raise issues of harassment and abuse in the classroom. On one of my first visits to Audubon, I sit in on Ms. Alvarez' social studies class, which is reading a short play that centers on battering. The drama's villain is a high school baseball star who physically abuses his girlfriend. But, after a man-to-man chat with the school coach, the boy realizes the error of his ways and the problem is quickly solved.

In real life, resolutions are rarely so tidy, but Ms. Alvarez uses the story as the occasion for a little lecture of her own. She stands before the class, a thin woman with large eyes and short-cropped hair in a T-shirt and jeans, urging her female students to be on guard for abusive relationships. While she talks, several boys in the back of the room—unseen by the teacher—make fists and aim punches at their own jaws and faces, pantomiming what they would like to do to girls.

Over the course of the year, the boys' imaginary threats prove prophetic: in November, there is an attempted rape behind the stage in the auditorium and, soon after, there are two separate cases of male students exposing their genitals to female teachers. Late in the second semester, I speak with Liza, an eighth-grade Latina who is sitting outside the principal's office, obviously distressed, with a deep red mark on her cheek. She tells me that, earlier today, she became fed up with a particular boy who frequently manhandles her in the hall and in the stair-well.

"He always grabs me," she says angrily. "He touches me all over and I tell him not to. This time I told him to stop and he wouldn't, so I cussed him out. Then he slapped me."

It was only at that point, when harassment had crossed over into assault, that the school intervened, suspending the boy for the rest of the week. But in all of these incidents—the slapping, the exposures, the attempted rape—the boys had reason to believe they could get away with crimes *at school* that harm girls and women. The hidden curriculum had taught them that.

The new state law on sexual harassment applies as much at Audubon as elsewhere in California; the school district, in fact, already had a sexual harassment policy printed in its student handbook, which is given to each child at the beginning of the year. Yet although every girl in the school knows the rules which stipulate respect for authority—such as a dubious prohibition against wearing hats anywhere on campus—not a single one of the girls I spoke with knew about *this* rule, which demands that authority respect them. I tell Liza that the verbal and physical abuse she's been enduring is illegal and ask whether she told her teachers about it.

She makes a disdainful noise in the back of her throat. "I tell the teachers," she says bitterly, "but they don't do nothing. It's like"—she shrugs her shoulders—" 'Whatever.' "

Most of the girls at Audubon, like Liza, do not believe that the school authorities are concerned with students' rights; and when a girl who does believe in justice challenges a teacher, it turns out their skepticism is warranted. Shortly after my discussion with Liza about teachers' indifference to harassment, Mr. Krieger becomes annoyed with Carolina during social studies class and calls her "a little bitch." When Carolina brings Mr. Krieger before her counselor, a balding, bespectacled fellow named Mr. Morrissey, the teacher accuses her of lying. Mr. Morrissey accepts the teacher's word over the student's and declines to investigate further.

When I talk to Carolina after the confrontation, she is frustrated and disheartened by the betrayal. She thought that a girl with a good record would be a credible witness against a teacher, especially when there was a classful of witnesses to the incident. But she won't make that mistake again.

"I learned you can get in trouble if you tell on a teacher," she tells me. "And they don't listen to kids. They think you're young and you lie."

Later, I visit the counselor myself in his cramped, dimly lit office and ask why he didn't follow up on Carolina's complaint. At first, Mr. Morrissey stands by his official statement, that the student, rather than the teacher, lied.

"A lot of times kids fabricate things," he explains. "Once I was arguing with a kid in the yard, trying to get a basketball away from him, and he went home and said I called him a little nigger. That was a total fabrication. Or another time I touched a boy on the arm and he said I hit him."

But as we continue talking, Mr. Morrissey's excuses begin to unravel. "Mr. Krieger does tend to tease the kids and give them a taste of their own medicine," he admits. "He probably shouldn't do that. It encourages that kind of situation, that kind of behavior. And I guess"—he takes a breath and lets it out—"I guess I tend to think it probably happened. But he didn't really call her a bitch *directly;* he said it to the person next to her. He said to another student, 'Look at her sitting there, the little bitch,' so it wasn't really that direct . . ."

He pauses again, growing contemplative. "It put me in a position where I didn't want to . . ." He breaks off and tries to start again. "I told him to be careful, but I didn't want to . . ." He grimaces slightly and begins one last time. "I think Mr. Krieger's a good teacher," he concludes. "We're friends."

8

Split Loyalties:
Homegirl vs. Schoolgirl

∎
∎
∎

LaRhonda Johnson saunters down the hallway, hands shoved deep into her pockets, oversized Guess shorts sliding down her hips. It is late in the fall semester, and although the fourth-period bell rang several minutes ago, she is in no rush to get to her next class, which is science with Ms. Raynes; in fact, she probably won't go at all, and her reasoning is hard to dispute.

"We don't do nothin' in there anyway," she says.

LaRhonda is the oldest of six children. She was born when her mother was just thirteen, the same age LaRhonda is now. Her face is small, with prominent cheekbones and eyes that are large, liquid brown, and expressive: when she widens them in disbelief, she looks truly stunned; when she smiles, they shine; and when she drops her eyelids, veiling her pupils in anger, her gaze lands like a punch. It is that very combination—an easy warmth along with a grittiness she can back up with her fists— that has made LaRhonda a leader among the girls at Audubon.

Occasionally, LaRhonda wields her position to the benefit of the school: last year she planned, and partially choreographed, a school-wide talent show. This fall, when a local gang prevention program staged a teach-in in Audubon's auditorium, it was LaRhonda who raised her hand, strode up to the microphone, and spoke passionately to her peers about the importance of self-respect. "I was scared standing up there," she admitted afterward, "but I feel like I'm a leader in the school, and I can teach them littler kids how to act; if I tell people something, they'll do it."

Inside the classroom, however, LaRhonda's performance is far less exemplary. Although her social studies teacher calls her "extremely bright and very articulate," for the second year in a row she is well on her way to failing most of her classes. "I'm just praying that I do good enough to graduate onstage," she says, shaking her head. "That's all I'm thinkin' about now."

LaRhonda walks slowly, with a rolling, athletic gait, past a display of seventh-grade art projects, then past the library, which, since funds are scarce, is unstaffed this year. She is about to leave campus to buy a candy bar when Kimberly, a tall, rangy African American girl who is on the school honor roll, walks by on her way to the girls' bathroom.

Kimberly raises a hand in greeting. "Hi, LaRhonda!" she says.

LaRhonda turns to face her. "It's L!" she says. "You call me L. And it's 'Yo, whaddup!' Not 'Hi.'"

"Okay," says Kimberly, not wanting to offend.

"That's why they call you 'white girl,'" LaRhonda says, not unkindly.

"I'm not white," says Kimberly, who is, in fact, darker-skinned than LaRhonda. "It's just how I talk."

LaRhonda begins to walk away. "That's *still* why they call you 'white girl,'" she tosses back over her shoulder.

Later, sitting on the school's front steps, LaRhonda shakes her head over Kimberly's faux pas. "When you hang out, you want to blend in," she explains. "You got to have something that blends in: the way you talk, the way you dress, if you have something to talk about, something like that. If you talk white, you a schoolgirl, you a nerd. Last year, Kimberly, she'd come up to everyone and go, 'How are you doing?' We'd be like, '*What* you talkin' 'bout?' But I guess she's trying to change her ways."

I ask LaRhonda if she thinks she hurt Kimberly's feelings.

"Nah," she says. "We're friends. Anyway, I used to be like her in, like, fifth grade. I was good at school, I was focused. I used to hang out with a whole bunch of white girls, and wear my hair like them, my bangs and everything."

She laughs, and glances over to see how I'm taking this: it's not easy, after all, to offer up opinions on white girls to a white girl. I know, and knew throughout my reporting at Audubon, that I would learn a different story from some of these young women if we had race in common.

"The other girls used to say I acted like a white girl too," she continues, "but it was normal to me. Then, after fifth grade, we moved to the projects, and I started hanging around more with black girls and shaved my hair off in the back. I never grew it since."

LaRhonda puts a hand to her hair, which, without her artificial ponytail, is short and straightened, plastered against her head with gel, except for a few wayward tufts on top. "After that, you know, I didn't do so good in school," she continues. "I flunked most everything in seventh grade. I was too busy having fun, I guess, cutting class, hanging out and all, going to the store and buying candy. And then I had this incident at the end of sixth grade, too. There was these girls, a whole bunch of 'em, and they wanted to beat me up. But I beat *them* up, and after that people started to look up to me because I could fight. So now I get my respect."

The word "respect" comes up frequently, almost obsessively, in LaRhonda's conversation. "Getting respect," to her, is a matter of pride, an acknowledgment that in spite of the devaluation of both blackness and womanhood in our culture, she is no less human, no less worthy of esteem than anyone else. LaRhonda has already earned the respect of her peers, but her teachers are another matter. When they "disrespect" her, by insulting her intelligence or abusing their positions of authority, she can't prove her worth with her fists as she did with her friends; instead, she protests by opting out of class. "When the teachers disrespect me, that's it," she says. "I don't care who it is, I'm not going to let anyone disrespect me."

When we first chatted, in Ms. Raynes's science class, LaRhonda said that she planned to improve her school performance, both to avoid future wrangles with the legal system and to achieve her dream of graduating "onstage" to the strains of Audubon's school band mangling "Pomp and Circumstance." Now I ask if it's possible to do that without becoming like Kimberly, without becoming a "white girl" and losing her hard-won respect. Is there anyone else at the school she looks to as a role model?

"I don't know," she admits, mulling the question for a long moment. "Maybe." Then, suddenly, she brightens. "I know a drug dealer who sells drugs outside my house," she says. "Everybody hates him 'cause he go to high school and do his work, but he still sells drugs to make money, buy his clothes, all that. Everybody thinks it's dumb to go to school *and* sell drugs, that he should do one or the other. The other dealers call him schoolboy and they clown him, they won't let him hang with them. But he says, 'That's right, I'm a schoolboy,' like he proud of it."

She glances over at me, widening her eyes, to make sure the significance of such a statement is not lost on me. "I think he should be rewarded for that," she continues. "It's hard for him to sell drugs and go to school. I think he a good influence." She nods her head somberly. "He an influence for us all."

▪

Public and Private:
African American Girls and Self-Esteem

▪

One of the most newsworthy aspects of *Shortchanging Girls, Shortchanging America* was its findings about girls of color, especially black girls. Black girls, the report concluded, have higher overall self-esteem than white girls: they feel a greater sense of personal and familial importance, more entitlement to speak out, and are more satisfied with their appearance. And although black girls' self-esteem does decrease as they move through adolescence, the drop is only 7 percentage points, compared with a 33 percent plunge for white girls and 38 percent for Latinas.[1]

Certainly African American women and girls are subject to sexism and violence, both within their own communities and in the white world. Even so, they demonstrate a resilience beyond that of white girls, an ability to retain self-esteem—perhaps, in part, owing to a historically different conception of women's roles. In her analysis of autobiographical writings by African American women from slavery to the present day, educator Mary Williams Burgher found that, from the start, the model of European femininity—grounded as it is in delicacy, innocence, and an idealized helplessness—has largely been unavailable to black women. Instead, they have measured their worth through strength of character and a tenacious sense of self.[2] This is a true departure from white women's autobiographical legacy, in which, as Patricia Spacks has written, women who do express a clear and powerful sense of self "struggle constantly to lose it."[3]

There is, however, a consistent exception to black girls' self-esteem: in study after study, they report far lower academic self-confidence than their white counterparts, expressing more pessimism about both their teachers and their schoolwork.[4] So although black girls may feel a deep sense of personal satisfaction, that pride is not, for many, translating into academic excellence. To explain this discrepancy, some researchers have posited a vision of a dual self-esteem, with a "private" component that encompasses a child's image of herself in her community and a "public" component which involves her interaction with larger society.[5] For many African American children the "public" self is formed at school, where they are often stigmatized by teachers and undermined by low expectations and where, for underclass children in particular, the survival skills they've mastered are considered a liability.[6] As those inequities become apparent, some black students simply reject achievement as a source of self-esteem, insulating themselves from indignity by ceasing to care and by labeling academic success as "acting white." Others, like Kimberly, attempt to develop a kind of biracial identity, a way in which they can comply with the "white" demands of the educational system without being rejected by their black peers.[7]

To LaRhonda, "blackness" is essentially an oppositional stance, grounded in "gangsta" rap culture and mildly delinquent behavior. When I first met her, in Ms. Raynes's science class, she had just been released from Juvenile Detention after an arrest for petty shoplifting. She told me that during the apprehension the security guard at the Woolworth's store had forcibly restrained her. "I was yelling, 'Let me go!' and this guy was choking me and I couldn't breathe and my pants was falling down and everyone was looking at me," she said of the incident. "And this black lady, maybe twenty-five years old, yells, 'Don't cry! Don't cry! You let him choke you, but you don't cry!' "

When I looked confused, she explained further. "He was white, or maybe Mexican, and I'm black," she said. "And when you're black, you're supposed to be strong, so I tried to hold my tears in."

For LaRhonda, then, the compromise Kimberly has struck is untenable, erring too far on the side of "white" in both language and demeanor. Her drug dealer friend seems, for the moment, to have maneuvered more deftly between the two cultures. Of course, someday, he will have to choose between the street and the school, just as, someday, LaRhonda herself will have to choose.

▪

The "Junior Mother"

▪

Although all black children have to negotiate the dilemma of "white" achievement, girls like LaRhonda have another, unique obstacle to success: the pressure to place their family's well-being over personal advancement. Like many underclass African American girls, LaRhonda lives in a world of women:[8] her father is often in jail, as is her mother's boyfriend, who has lived with them intermittently for the last five years. Her uncle, as she says, "can't even take care of his own kids." That leaves her mother and her aunt, who are unemployed, as well as her grandmother to raise LaRhonda's entire extended family. Despite her own illegal activity, LaRhonda sees herself as part of that community of women and, as the oldest female child of her generation, she has begun to shoulder a large share of its burden.

On a Tuesday morning late in February, I meet LaRhonda shortly after the second-period bell has rung. She has just arrived at school: although she woke up at 7:20, giving her ample time to make it to class, she first had to supervise her four youngest siblings' morning ablutions, help them dress, make their breakfast, sign their homework, and walk them to elementary school. She arrives on campus still adjusting her earrings and dabbing at her lipstick, unsurprised that she has missed both English and gym. "I can't help it," she says. "I have to be responsible for my little brothers and sisters. My mom can't do it by herself. There's just too many of us."

LaRhonda's mother, Nicole, is only twenty-eight years old. Her own dreams of becoming a secretary died when she became pregnant with LaRhonda and left school after eighth grade. Two years later, she had another child by the same man, and subsequently has had four more with her current boyfriend. On the occasions when we've spoken, Nicole has talked about going back to school and getting her degree, maybe even learning a trade. But according to LaRhonda, her mother has said that before: lack of money and child care and her regular pregnancies always get in her way.

LaRhonda and I walk across the schoolyard, a desolate expanse of concrete and asphalt surrounded by a metal fence, and settle in on a bench from which we can see her gym class engaging in rigorous calisthenics. "I used to look up to my mother a lot," she says, gazing out at her classmates in their red-and-yellow uniforms. "But now I see she lives in the projects and she's on welfare and can't get no job because she didn't make it out of high school. It's no life, no life."

As LaRhonda talks, I find myself thinking about Becca at Weston. Like Becca, LaRhonda sees her mother as ensnared by the circumstances of womanhood; she, too, believes that, as the eldest daughter, she is obliged to alleviate her mother's suffering in a way that her brother, for instance, who is just a year behind her in school, is not.[9]

"*I* take care of my mother," she says scornfully, when I ask if he pitches in. "He's outside all the time being a boy. Or when he home he sit and watch TV and we have to treat him just like a little child. He's *very* helpless. When he try to do stuff around the house he just make a mess and I have to do it for him anyway."

LaRhonda's contempt for her brother's dependence is, equally, an affirmation of her own competence. And that is where her course and Becca's diverge. Whereas Becca feels powerless in the face of her mother's pain, LaRhonda can act. Whereas Becca becomes increasingly vulnerable, LaRhonda becomes increasingly competent; her assumption of what she calls the "junior mother" role is not only a source of dignity but also a mark of her maturity as a woman. "I like being the mom," she says, smiling shyly. "I like being responsible. Not all the time, but I like it, it makes me feel good."[10]

LaRhonda's commitment to her family, like her street smarts, encourages self-reliance, but it also gives her further cause to distrust and disconnect from school success. Several times during our conversation LaRhonda indicates that she feels threatened by teachers, who are insensitive to her priorities; she believes she is being forced to choose not only between school and her peers but between school and her family. And as far as she is concerned, there's no contest.

"Teachers get mad because I'm late," she says, placing a hand on her hip. "They say, 'I told you . . .' and I say, 'No, I told *you*. I have to help my mother and I ain't dropping my brothers and sisters for *no* schoolwork.' " She lets her hand fall and continues. "I have to help my mother and that's it. I have to make that choice."

LaRhonda knows few people who have completed high

school, and among those who have, she doesn't know many who have found good jobs. So for her, the benefits of education are both dubious and remote, while the rewards of caretaking and the self-esteem she derives from it are immediate. As much as LaRhonda does not want to repeat her mother's mistakes— "I'd give anything not to be like that," she's told me—she will not abandon her either; nor can she embrace a form of success that feels to her like betrayal. LaRhonda talks eagerly about getting a job when she's fourteen, and contributing half of each month's earnings toward household expenses (the other half, she says, "I'll keep for clothes and supplies and all that"). She contemplates transferring to a continuation school at sixteen— although she derides them "dumb-dumb schools where you don't learn nothin' "—because the move would cut her class time to three hours a day, thus making her more employable. Sometimes, as important as she knows school is, she considers dropping out entirely, a strategy which she regards as an assertion of self-sufficiency rather than what it is: a step toward self-destruction.

After talking to LaRhonda, I run into Ms. Leland in the hall. When I mention LaRhonda to the teacher, she sighs deeply, her usually gloomy expression becoming more dour. "I talked to her recently about high school," she tells me. "And she said, 'Maybe I'll drop out when I'm sixteen and get a job. I have to take care of my family.' I said, 'LaRhonda, you're *already* taking care of them!' LaRhonda is smart and very capable. She could be very good if she were motivated. But that's not what's important to her. Taking care of her family is important. Taking care of her mother is important. Survival is important. Being in school is not important."

■

Reaching Past the Mind

■

Danny Muriera, who teaches eighth-grade social studies and Spanish bilingual classes at Audubon, is a heart attack waiting to happen. He sits in the teachers' smoking lounge, his belly straining against his Hawaiian print shirt as he reaches for a cigarette. His face, leathery and deeply lined, is set in an angry frown, and when he talks, his voice is laced with bitterness. Mr. Muriera has been at Audubon for sixteen years, since just after the school opened, and, he says, by the end of last year he knew he couldn't watch another sharp-minded student cycle through the school and end up out on the street.

"You take a kid like LaRhonda," he says, waving his cigarette. "She's extremely bright, yet she's failing. The system is failing her. It's condemning her to becoming pregnant or landing in prison by age fifteen. Kids like her have real leadership potential. They aren't the best-behaved kids, but they are leaders, and their peers see them as leaders. There are no programs in this school to help those kids develop in a positive way."

So last year, with the permission of the departing principal, Mr. Muriera decided to try an experiment. Just before school adjourned in the spring, he asked each of the seventh-grade teachers to draw up a list of the most difficult children in his or her classes. Mr. Muriera calls these students "negative leaders" or, less formally, "the real pains in the butt." Any child who appeared on more than one list—and, as he recalls, LaRhonda appeared on several—was tagged in eighth grade for a new, two-period class he developed that would involve equal parts crisis intervention programming, group therapy, and community service projects along with their required dosage of American history. The balance between the cognitive development and the psychological support, Mr. Muriera believes, is the key to reengaging high-potential, low-achieving students like La-Rhonda.

"You just cannot take these kids and treat them like they're supposed to be intellectual sponges," he says, gesturing toward his head. "You can't just ignore the problems in their neighborhood and in their families. You can't learn if you see some of the things these kids see. You can't learn when you saw a drive-by shooting the night before, you just can't. You can't learn if you're being abused. You have to deal with the pain, the pain they bring into this building every day. Most teachers are only trying to reach the mind of these kids and as long as we just do that"—he slaps both hands hard against the tabletop—"we'll lose them."

I glance at the attendance roster which Mr. Muriera holds in his hand. There are a few familiar names among the fifteen students: LaRhonda, of course, along with her friend Sacha, a light-skinned African American girl who frequently explodes at her teachers. There is Michael, an African American boy whose inventiveness when insulting other students' mothers is peerless. And Ron, a Latino boy whose studied aloofness prompted one teacher to call him "the James Dean of Audubon." The class is a fairly even mix of boys and girls, although, Mr. Muriera says, that was not originally the case.

"You should have seen the original lists that the teachers submitted," Mr. Muriera says. "Every stereotype was there. There were no Asian girls; people think that the Asians are quiet and well behaved, but they don't see the problems or the potential there. And there were no Latina girls, not a single one. So I pulled four in from the bilingual social studies class I taught last year. They don't say much, but I'm working on it."

During the first semester, Mr. Muriera's class not only studied multicultural history but participated in gang prevention workshops; heard guest speakers on topics as wide-ranging as employment opportunities and child abuse; began a year-long discussion on how to effectively express anger; and spearheaded a successful campus-wide anti-litter campaign. Now, a month into the second semester, the students are transferring what they've learned to the world outside of Audubon: three days a week they leave campus for the last two hours of the day to tutor younger students at nearby elementary schools, or to volunteer in a soup kitchen, assist at a project for mentally disabled adults, or care for animals at the local Humane Society. The students are responsible for showing up on time, and in fact, for showing up at all: the class spent an entire forty-five-minute period practicing how to call in sick to a supervisor. Every two weeks, the students receive written evaluations from their "bosses" which will determine their grades. The idea, Mr. Muriera says, is to give these students a taste of adult responsibility, to instill self-discipline, and, perhaps most importantly, to help bolster a sense of personal efficacy. And although he's aware that working with small children may reinforce stereotypic gender roles for the girls in the class, Mr. Muriera points out that, for a girl like LaRhonda, the experience may act as a bridge between the skills that make her feel competent at home and the alienation that dogs her at school. "I believe kids learn better when they're involved," says Mr. Muriera, "and the best way to inspire kids is to let them teach what they know to someone else, to show them that they have something they can give . . . For these kids, that just might keep them in school."[11]

LaRhonda's volunteer assignment is to help a group of second graders at an elementary school that feeds into Audubon

—the same school, in fact, that three of her younger siblings attend. She arrives precisely at 12:40 every Monday, Wednesday, and Friday. The classroom she works in is dingy, crowded with thirty students, and poorly lit. The teacher, a grim-looking white man, and his aide, a large African American woman named Bernice, sit at their desks in the front of the room while the students toil over an English work sheet. LaRhonda makes her way to a child-size table in the back, and takes a seat next to two African American girls who are thrilled to see her. She pulls out a box of flash cards and they begin reviewing some basic sentences.

"It is a hat," one of the girls reads in a clear, strong voice, and looks to LaRhonda for approval.

"She has a cat," the second girl recites when LaRhonda flips the card.

When the girls get a word wrong, LaRhonda shakes her head and waits for them to try again. When a boy whose reading skills are weaker than the girls' joins them, she encourages him to sound out each letter before trying a whole word. Like any good teacher, she peppers him with encouragement, but will not provide him with answers. During her session with the children, LaRhonda's attention holds steady, and her patience never wavers.

When the bell rings for recess, LaRhonda offers to help Bernice correct a stack of spelling tests. The aide hands her the pile and a red pen.

"You know," LaRhonda tells her, "I think I might like to be a teacher. I like teaching these little kids."

Bernice puts an arm around LaRhonda and turns to me. "She is *such* a good role model for these girls," she says. "She is so helpful and considerate all the time; she's just doing *wonderfully*. You tell her teacher that for me, won't you?"

▪

No Respect

▪

Several weeks pass before I see LaRhonda again, and during that time her good intentions seem to crumble. Although she had not received a single detention or discipline referral all year, in early March she has two run-ins with her counselor, Mr. Morrissey. In the first, he catches her and several friends roaming the halls without a pass, and when she tells him, "I can't help it if people follow me around the halls—I'm a leader," a brief shouting match ensues. A few days later, Mr. Morrissey confronts her again in the cafeteria and, because hats of all kinds are prohibited on Audubon's campus, demands that she take off a flowered cap she is wearing which matches her outfit. LaRhonda refuses to comply, although she promises that she will after lunch, when she can go to the bathroom and comb her hair. From there, the dispute quickly becomes a showdown, played out in front of most of the school. Mr. Morrissey wants obedience; LaRhonda demands some slack. Mr. Morrissey's authority is threatened; LaRhonda's dignity is at stake. Mr. Morrissey raises his voice, and LaRhonda loses control. She calls him a motherfucker and the argument is over. She is hauled into the principal's office and suspended for the rest of the day.

The "hat rule" at Audubon is a curious thing. When I inquire about it, no one—not the teachers, not the counselors, not the principal—know exactly why students cannot wear hats on campus, especially in public spaces such as the cafeteria or the schoolyard. Yet, although it cannot be explained, the rule, a pure exercise in adult authority over children, is rigorously enforced (more strictly, it might be noted, than regulations such as the new sexual harassment law, which confers a measure of power on the students).

"I don't know why it's a rule," says Mr. Morrissey when we discuss his encounters with LaRhonda in his office on a wet March morning. "Maybe it's a bad rule and maybe it needs to be changed, but it's a rule. Maybe it's gang-related, but I don't really think so. What I know is that she wouldn't take that hat off. One of the teachers said that, because she's a black girl, she was sensitive about her hair, but other children don't have that problem. LaRhonda chooses to tangle with authority, to call me a motherfucker. Maybe the hat rule is dumb, maybe that's true. But it needs to be enforced because it *is* a rule."

He runs a hand through his thinning hair and glances out the door. Three students are waiting to see him, all holding the small pink slips that indicate they have been kicked out of class. "LaRhonda has been breaking other rules, too," he continues. "She comes in late for school whenever she wants to, sometimes after nine o'clock."

I ask if he has any idea why she might be doing that. "I don't know why she's late," says the counselor. "She probably doesn't want to get out of bed in the morning. I don't know why she's behaving this way, I don't know what her family situation is, but I think she might get weird."

"Weird?"

"She might get . . . delinquent."

I ask how, in a case like this, he goes about counseling a student. He glances out the door again. "I don't really have the time to do that kind of counseling," he says. "I have to deal with a lot of behavior stuff, kids being kicked out of classrooms for being kids, for wanting to play. A lot of times, I'm just over-whelmed with students who have been kicked out of class, so the kids who might drop out or have other problems get . . .

Well, I can't be as effective as I'd like to be. I end up doing this"
—he gestures toward the waiting students—"being a disciplinar-
ian."

A few minutes later, I find LaRhonda sitting on a bench
under an overhang outside the school watching the rain. She has
reattached her braided hair extensions and tied them into a
ponytail with a red and a blue bandanna, adornments which *are*
usually associated with gangs, yet, perversely, are not banned at
Audubon.

"Look," she says, gesturing toward the sky, which is heavy
with dark clouds. "It's raining right now and if I were out there
with a hat on my head they'd make me take it off.

"Lately my mom shakes her head and tells me, 'You ain't
gonna graduate on no stage,' because of all the trouble I'm getting in," LaRhonda continues. "I know I shouldn't have called
Mr. Morrissey a motherfucker. I should've just combed my hair
when he asked me. But he shouldn't have yelled at me like that
neither. He should've asked me in a polite way; he never did ask
me politely."

LaRhonda falls silent, staring glumly ahead. "You know, I
never used to trip when people yelled at me," she says. "I never
used to say nothing about it. But I'm sick and tired of people
yelling at me about things like hats. They always yelling about
things like hats. I just think it's time for people to give respect
back to me when I respect them."

In April, a month after her explosion at Mr. Morrissey,
LaRhonda and her mother receive written notification that she
is in danger of failing eighth grade. Believing that her fate is
already sealed, LaRhonda stops coming to school. She spends
her mornings babysitting while her mother, who says LaRhonda
is old enough to make her own choices, runs errands. In the

afternoon, LaRhonda goes out with her friends, who have be-
gun, sporadically, to sell crack on the street to earn extra money
for clothes and cosmetics. Neither LaRhonda's English teacher,
Mr. Krieger, nor her science teacher, Ms. Raynes, reports
LaRhonda missing. For them, there is just one less troublemaker
in the class. But when, after three days, neither Ms. Leland nor
Mr. Muriera has heard from her, they become concerned, and
Mr. Muriera phones LaRhonda at home.

"You're not flunking, LaRhonda," he tells her. "I've talked
to your teachers. I've talked to Ms. Leland. She says you're not
flunking yet, you can still pass and graduate, but you have to
come to school."

It takes three more phone calls over the course of another
week before LaRhonda agrees to return to school, but the re-
prieve is short-lived. Just three weeks before graduation, there is
a racially motivated stabbing on a city bus after school which
involves three Audubon boys; in its wake, LaRhonda spreads
rumors around the school that there is more violence to come.
Inciting violence on campus is a serious offense, far graver than
anything LaRhonda has done here to date. Although she claims
she was "just trying to be helpful, to warn people," her credibil-
ity among the school's administrators is too low for a compromise. Provisions are made for her to complete her course work
at a neighborhood youth center, and she is asked not to return
to Audubon for the rest of the year.

When he hears the news, Mr. Muriera tries to be philosophical. "I had hoped that the program would keep this kind of
thing from happening," he says, "and for most of them it has.
But I admit it, I've lost a few. Probably not as many as would've
left anyway, but a few. I'll tell you something, though. Every
single one of these kids, including LaRhonda, has gotten excellent evaluations from their supervisors." He pulls LaRhonda's
most recent evaluation from his grade book and reads it aloud.

" 'LaRhonda has been a great help,' " he reads. " 'She has a great attitude and has done her job in a serious manner, attaching an importance to her work that has helped her succeed in it, and conveying that importance to the children she has worked with.' " Mr. Muriera slaps the paper with the back of one hand. "What does that tell you?" he says. "On the job, they're treated like adults and they act like adults. Yet in school they're getting in trouble. These kids aren't dropping out—they're being *pushed* out. We have to stop pointing at them and start pointing at ourselves. You know, maybe the trouble LaRhonda has gotten into is more about the administration than about the students."

A week later, at eleven o'clock in the morning, LaRhonda has yet to check in at the youth center. She is home, babysitting her youngest sister, Quinisha. The Johnsons' apartment is just a few minutes' drive from the school. As I approach it, I see two eighth-grade boys, students at Audubon, sitting on the curb, watching for slow-cruising cars whose drivers might be interested in buying crack. They smile and wave as I pass by. Behind them, a young girl, a pale-skinned Latina who is, perhaps, fifteen, balances a baby on her hip and stares straight ahead, at nothing.

LaRhonda and Quinisha sit in the living room of the family's apartment, watching *Sesame Street* from the only piece of furniture in the room: a large, shabby gold couch. LaRhonda, who wears Walkman headphones on her ears, although she does not turn them on, says she will probably pick up her homework when her mother comes home, in an hour or so, but then again she may not. Since it is no longer possible for her to graduate onstage, she's not sure she wants to graduate at all.

"I wanted to graduate onstage," she explains. "And I still

don't want to move on until I do. And maybe if I repeat a grade, maybe I'd concentrate more and learn something this time. I could get good grades if I want to, I think."

I ask her what she believes hurt her most this year.

She stares into space. "I don't know," she says. "I don't know. I hurt myself, I guess. But I don't know. Sometimes I just don't understand things, sometimes people are talking to me, sometimes it's the teachers or whatever. I don't know . . . I guess if they make me move on, I'll just go to a continuation school next year, I think that's what I'll do. I don't think they're as bad as I said, for dumb-dumbs and all. Or maybe I'll go to some kind of night school or something like that. I don't know. I don't know what I'll do now. I guess I'll have to see."

9

"I Choose Not to Go down That Path": Unteachable Girls

■
■
■

This year has been an especially tough one for Mrs. Sandoval, who teaches seventh-grade math at Audubon and, on the side, coaches the school's cheerleading squad. Her class sizes have nearly doubled, and in mid-October there are still not enough math books for each student to take one home. Nonetheless, she persists, trying to review old material, introduce new ideas, and leave enough time for the students to complete "homework" in each class period.

Today, she stands before the class, a stout woman with chin-length black hair and a long nose, trying to review fractions. She has just asked for the proper way to say "two over five" when April Welch, an African American girl with reddish hair who sits smack in the center of the class, shoots up her hand.

"Mrs. Sandoval! Mrs. Sandoval!" April leans forward in her seat, waving her hand frantically. "Mrs. Sandoval!"

"Okay, April," Mrs. Sandoval says, smiling.

April drops her hand, relieved. "You can't change it," she announces, indicating that the fraction cannot be reduced—a fact the class has already established.

Mrs. Sandoval's smile tightens almost imperceptibly. "That wasn't my question," she says.

"Oh," April replies, turning away and rummaging in her backpack for a tube of ChapStick.

As the class proceeds, April volunteers continuously, each time with the same frenetic urgency. Occasionally, she simply wants to provide information, such as the whereabouts of another student who is cutting class. Other times she is trying to assist the teacher, offering to pass out math books or to take a note to the office. But most often April raises her hand in response to a question that Mrs. Sandoval has posed, and when she does that, the pattern of their interaction rarely deviates.

The class moves on to today's exercise, which is on number patterns. The teacher writes a series of numbers on the chalkboard: 1, 2, 4, 7, 11, 16, 23 . . .

"Okay, everyone," Mrs. Sandoval asks, "what kind of math is happening?"

Again, April's hand is the first in the air. *"Me! Me! Me!"* she shouts. But when Mrs. Sandoval calls on her, April's expression turns blank; in truth, she hasn't a clue as to the answer.

On the next problem she tries again. Mrs. Sandoval writes: 26, 24, 22.

"Are the numbers getting bigger or smaller?" she asks.

April thrusts her hand in the air. "Smaller."

"So it is . . ."

April's hand shoots up like a flag. "Subtraction!" she shouts.

"And so the pattern is . . ."

April stops and stares, slack-jawed.

"What's the difference between these two numbers?" Mrs. Sandoval asks her, gesturing toward the problem.

"They're both in the same range," April answers, looking discomfited, "but one of them is kind of . . ."

"Listen to my question, April. What is subtracted to get this number?"

April falls silent, more quiet than she has been all period, and darts her eyes desperately.

Someone stage-whispers, "Two."

She raises two fingers, hesitantly, still not speaking.

"So what would the next number be?"

Everyone, except for April, yells out, "Twenty."

April looks at the board, befuddled. "I don't get it," she mutters, but the class has moved on. As the lesson proceeds, April's confusion only deepens. Still she continues to raise her hand in response to every question.

There are only two students in April's class who come close to participating as much as she. One is Al, a Latino boy who, although he disrupts so frequently that he has been isolated among a sea of empty desks, nonetheless nails every answer. The second, Bonnie, is a demure white girl who is new to Audubon this year. Since her arrival, she has become her teachers' fallback student, the child who can be relied on to offer a correct response when no one else volunteers, or when other students answer incorrectly. Bonnie's compliance and Al's insolence are typical of the behavior patterns among boys and girls at Weston and in the honors classes at Audubon. But April is different. As she proceeds through the day, from math to science to English to social studies, she vies with Bonnie and Al for her teachers' attention and is called on nearly as often. Unlike them, however, her answers, except to the simplest of questions, are invariably wrong. Her teachers react with the same tense annoyance as did Mrs. Sandoval, and then, often without acknowledging her comments at all, impatiently move on.

"April is just a real talker," Mrs. Sandoval tells me after class. "But there's a time and a place for that stuff, and this isn't usually it, you know?"

■

Trying to Be Heard

■

When I first met April, in the spring of 1992, I was told by a student adviser that she would be an eighth grader the following fall. As it turned out, the adviser was wrong: April was at that time repeating sixth grade, so, unlike the other girls in this book, she was a seventh grader during the year I spent with her. For girls more than boys, grade retention is directly linked to dropping out. Just as high-achieving girls personalize small mistakes, low-achieving girls internalize their failures, viewing retention as a ruling on their own ineptitude; although both girls and boys who are held back drop out at twice the rate of their peers, the girls drop out earlier, and more frequently relate their decision to their retention.[1] At Audubon, since retained students are often assigned to the same classes with the same teachers and the same curriculum that failed to inspire them the first time around, the extra year proves useless in terms of skill building: although repeating students who attain a C average by the end of the first grading period are put up with their peers, that goal is seldom realized. At any rate, the students know that at age fifteen, no matter how many times they have been left back at Audubon—and regardless of whether they can read, write, or add—district policy is to promote them to high school.

April and I discuss her educational history on an early fall afternoon when the school year is still new and flush with the promise of a fresh start. We settle into a windowless, seldom used PTA office which doubles as a storage closet. As we talk April's eyes skip around the room to see what might be on (or under) a desk, what's tacked on the bulletin board, what's piled on a shelf. She is a broadly built, kinetic girl with dark, burnished skin and straightened hair pulled into a stubby top knot. Sometimes she wears oval wire-rim glasses which make her look oddly professorial for a girl who has a GPA of D minus.

"The first time I was in sixth grade, I hardly came to school at all," she says in her soft, raspy voice. "I was enrolled, but I'd just cut. I'd walk into school and walk right back out. I was scared, I guess. I'd just graduated from fifth grade and I thought middle school was a big old step. So I didn't want to go." She shakes her head, as if in disgust at her former self. "My mother didn't say nothin' 'bout it. She just said it was my life and I'd learn in my own time and I did. I learned that lesson. I tried to run from it: I wanted to start over at some other school, but I didn't. I knew I had to face what I did. I came back and started sixth grade again. It was kind of embarrassing, but that's how it had to be. I still haven't caught up neither. I mean, I have a little, but not how I want to. Not like I was in elementary school. Back then, I did good. I used to understand better back then."

I tell April that, watching her in class these days, I feel a bit mystified. Other students raise their hands when they know an answer. She seems to raise her hand simply because a question has been asked.

April shifts in her seat to look at the clock in the main

office and, in doing so, spies a paper clip on the floor. She picks it up and begins twisting it open. "I guess," she says, staring at her handiwork, "I guess I raise my hand because I want to be part of the class. I just . . . I just want to talk and feel part of that, you know?"

In her desire to be heard, April is a far cry from the young women at Weston, who refuse to raise their hands unless they are irrefutably sure of an answer (and, as Becca once said, "sometimes not even then"). In fact, April's attitude more closely mirrors that of Weston boys such as Nate, the clamorous young man in Amy's math class who once told me, "You yell out no matter what the teacher says because you want to be heard, because you have an opinion or an answer . . . it doesn't matter if you're right or wrong, you just want them to listen to you." Like Nate—and decidedly unlike the Weston girls —April is unhindered by failure. "I don't mind if I don't know the answer," she says, "because then they tell you what you did wrong and you learn. And no one's perfect anyway, so it's okay."

April's willingness to speak up in class, and to see the potential for self-improvement in failure, is far more common among the African American girls I speak with than it is among whites or Latinas. At Audubon, African American girls are more likely than other girls at either school to participate in class discussions, challenge their teachers, and otherwise seek attention. And like the boys in both schools, they participate freely whether or not their comments are germane to class proceedings.

Yet, although they assert themselves similarly to boys, there is a crucial difference: while some studies show that black girls in desegregated schools attempt to initiate more contact with their teachers than white girls (or boys of either race), they are also most frequently rebuffed, so they actually receive far less attention.[2] Further, in a fascinating transfer of the familiar pattern of gender inequity to race—which has profound implications for single-sex classrooms—sociologist Linda Grant found that first-grade teachers who do attend to their black female students are most likely to praise their social maturity, whereas they reinforce white girls' academic progress.[3] Even at that early age, Grant found, teachers directed the largest share of comments relating to course work at white boys, while black girls were most frequently consulted on nonacademic matters and were relied upon as assistant disciplinarians or "rule enforcers." When black girls did achieve on a par with white boys, their success was attributed to hard work, while the boys were dressed down for not fulfilling their potential.[4]

By middle school, the antics of white boys like Nate are still considered inevitable and rewarded with extra attention and instruction, but the assertiveness of African American girls has become menacing, something that, for the sake of order in the classroom, must be squelched. April's outbursts in class, for example, are rarely recognized for what they are—an ardent refusal to be ignored, a rebuke to the system that has already failed her. Instead, she is considered a nuisance, a girl who, since she has not been taught academic skills, must be pressed into disengaged silence.

Shortly after talking to April, I pass Mr. Hirsch, her second sixth-grade teacher, who is leaning in the doorway of his classroom. He asks me how April is faring this year and seems unsurprised when I respond that she is failing most of her courses. "She's a smart girl operating on a fourth-grade level," he says. "I don't know what the deal is."

As we chat, the bell signaling the end of a period rings, classroom doors fly open, and a horde of middle school children comes hurtling into the hallway, yelling and jostling toward their next class. April, who was in an English classroom down the hall, swings by at a more restrained pace, nodding cordially as she passes.

Mr. Hirsch points to her with a triumphant smile. "See what happens when you hold them back?" he says. "Last year she was bouncing off the walls, you could always hear April coming. But that extra year calms them right down."

When April is out of sight, we fall into a conversation about what he's observed about his students' self-esteem. I ask if he has noticed that, although their remarks are sometimes inappropriate, a number of African American girls at Audubon seem to bring a strong sense of self into the classroom.

He nods his head eagerly. "It's their role models," he says. "They . . ." He pauses, groping for words, and I think that, as an English and history teacher, he's about to explain that black women have traditionally been a source of strength and pride for the girls in their communities. "They . . . well, it's this sort of crack addict's idea of what maternal is," he continues. "Their mothers tell them to go out and just kick anyone's ass who gives them trouble. That's why those girls are more aggressive."

Such stigmatization of female assertiveness affects black girls whether they are middle-class or poor, whether they are in largely white schools or in urban schools like Audubon. In more affluent areas, African American girls—more than their male counterparts—endure social isolation for voicing a sense of self that is so out of sync with the subterranean conflicts of their white peers.[5] Meanwhile, underclass girls like April are considered deviant and, if they cannot be contained, are subtly pushed out of the system. Some of them, especially after years of encountering attitudes such as Mr. Hirsch's, do, indeed, subvert their own success by becoming their reputation. For those girls, disrupting in class, defying authority, and participating inappropriately become acts of resistance, assertions of self in the face of a school system that insults and rejects them—assertions of self in the face of the constant assumption that their mothers are all crack addicts. These girls may speak, but since no one listens to them, they are still silenced.[6] That may be why, in *Shortchanging Girls, Shortchanging America,* black girls report that, although they speak up readily, they nonetheless feel a strong sense of hiddenness, that people "don't know the real me."[7]

In their work on black girls and the development of self, educational psychologists Tracy Robinson and Janie Victoria Ward explored black girls' resilience, and suggested that they employ one of two strategies when confronted by psychic devaluation.[8] The first, "resistance for survival," encompasses the stopgap measures which appear to help girls preserve self-esteem temporarily, but prove harmful in the long run: disconnecting from achievement when confronted by educational discrimination, for instance, or attaining a sense of purpose and assuaging loneliness through too early motherhood.[9] The second, more comprehensive, approach requires broad-based support: in "resistance for liberation," black girls learn that their struggle is not individual, but collective, and are encouraged by their communities and school systems to work toward societal change.[10] Without access to that second, healthier path, however, too many African American girls are forced onto the first. And for April, whose mother really *is* a crack addict, "resistance for survival" becomes her only hope.

▪

"I Learned to Be a Positive Person"

▪

If, among some of her teachers, there is a tacit understanding that April is doomed by her family's circumstances, it is not an understanding that April shares. Ever since she was a toddler living with her grandmother (who died when April was seven), April has been battling fiercely—and largely unassisted—to keep her mother's addiction from defining her. Sitting in the school's litter-strewn back stairwell on a bleak winter day, she discusses that struggle. As she talks, April squirms uncomfortably, fiddling with the ornately braided ponytail she has woven into her hair. Throughout her story, however, her voice remains steady, and she speaks with a level of insight that goes untapped in the classroom.

April explains that after her grandmother died she became a vagabond, moving back and forth between her mother, who lives in a public housing project with April's ten-year-old brother, and one of her nearby aunts, who seemed more interested in the monthly foster care check she received from the state than in caring for her niece. Month to month—sometimes night to night—she was unsure of where she'd lay her head. But it wasn't until the summer after her first sixth-grade year, when her aunt moved in with a boyfriend and her mother succumbed to drug addiction, that April decided she had to find a better life.

"I was livin' with my mom back then," April says. "She was into the fast life, into drugs and all that. She wasn't at first, but then she took up with her boyfriend and he was, so she started doing it, too. She lost her job, and she was just doing crack with her boyfriend all day long. I used to call him 'Dope Fiend.'" She breaks into a small, wry smile. "We didn't get along too good. He'd yell at me and hit me sometimes. Once I got so mad at him, I took his drugs and crushed 'em up. He tried to slap me and I kicked him and he said he was going to throw me out of the house. That's when I told my mom, 'You gotta choose between us,' but then I didn't make her choose. I just left. I called the child protection services and they took me, and they took my brother, and they put us in a group home for about four weeks. I didn't want to go back with my mom after that, but my brother did. I wouldn't go back to that drug-infested hellhole. I told her that, too, and she cried. So I lived with another one of my aunties for a while until my mom broke up with her boyfriend after he stole some drugs and almost got her killed. My whole family told her to go into rehab then, but ain't nothin' gonna help if you don't want to help yourself. But then, she did.

"I moved back with her last summer," April continues, "and now I stick with her like everything. I watch every move she makes. When she first came back from rehab, she had money and she was going to the store. I followed her where she couldn't see, because I thought she'd buy drugs for sure. But she didn't. So the next time I trusted her, and she came back with food and no drugs, so I think it might be okay now. I pray to God it is."

April has been staring intently at an empty candy wrapper as she talks. Now she abruptly turns to face me.

"I would never do drugs," she says passionately. "I saw what it did to my family, and I'd never look at it even. But to this day I tell my mom, 'I don't hate you, I love you, but I hate what you took me through.' I would never, never take my children through what she took me through. Never. There was people in that house walking around like zombies; there was people with guns threatening to kill people. Once, my mom's boyfriend owed my cousin a thousand dollars for drugs, and when he didn't pay, my cousin put a gun to his head. I used to go in my room and lock the door and cry and I'd think I should just kill myself, it was so bad."

She turns away and stares straight ahead, at the gray light that trickles through the stairwell's frosted windows. "But I learned something, too," she says. "I think I learned to be a positive person. And I learned I would not put myself through that and I would not put my children through that. Not never. I learned all that, so that's okay."

■

She's Just a Distraction

■

Like the educators in Linda Grant's study, April's teachers are delighted to recognize her emotional maturity. One afternoon just before Thanksgiving, her English teacher, a nervous, fast-talking man named Mr. Lawrence, rushes up to tell me that an irate parent had come in after school the previous afternoon to threaten him with violence, and April, who was serving detention at the time, had slipped out and reported the incident to the office. "She defended me," he says. "It was very nice of her, very ethical. She didn't have to do that."

Yet when it comes to grappling with April's flagging academic skills, the same teachers who applaud her thoughtfulness shake their heads and pass the buck. "I don't know what to do about April," Mr. Lawrence says on another occasion. "I know how to teach kids who understand the words on the page. She's reading at a second-grade level."

By the end of the first semester, April's teachers had given up on her. "She's failing," Mrs. Sandoval tells me flatly when I run into her in the school office. "She doesn't come to class anymore. Maybe she comes three times a week, but math is built on structure, on one thing and then the next, so unless you're really bright at it . . . Sometimes she tries really hard and seems to get it, but she's just falling behind. I offered her after-school help, extra tutoring, but if she doesn't come, I can't make her do it."

I ask her how she thinks she could help April.

She answers quickly, smiling although her eyes narrow slightly and her tone becomes curt. "Hey, I got kids of my own," she says. Then her shoulders droop and she sighs. "Look, I know she's on the at-risk list, that they *know* about her. But there are so many kids in the class with so many needs . . . Someone like April, when she's not there much, it gets to be out of sight, out of mind."

Later that day, when I ask her science teacher if I can speak to April in the hall for a few minutes, he seems equally frustrated. "Go ahead, keep her the whole period if you want to," he says. "At this point, she's just a distraction."

April is a distraction, as would be any student who cannot catch up but will not drop out. Students like April are best, as her math teacher said, when they are "out of sight, out of mind": toward the beginning of the second semester, when April jokes too loudly and too often in her art class, the teacher sends her to the office with a discipline referral slip. On it, he writes in capital letters, underlined several times for emphasis: "IT IS MY OPINION THAT APRIL SHOULD HAVE BEEN *STAFFED OUT* LAST YEAR"; that is, labeled unmanageable and shipped to another school, where she would become someone else's problem—or someone else's student to ignore.

"I know I'm not doing good," April says when I find her wandering in the hall one afternoon. "But I'm not tripping or anything, 'cause I'm still gonna graduate after next year and go to high school."

No one at Audubon can explain how a child can reach seventh grade without being able to add or subtract, particularly a vocal child such as April, who makes her difficulties quite clear. When, toward the end of March, I question April's counselor, Ms. Peck, about this, she purses her lips and lets out a long, slow breath. Like Mr. Morrissey, Ms. Peck is responsible for "counseling" over three hundred students a year. She is a peevish woman with gray skin and sharp features. The first day of school, in an assembly for the entire eighth grade, she announced that the students' fate was already sealed, since their high school applications are based on their *seventh*-grade GPA. "It's already done and you can't change it," she told them, effectively extinguishing any motivation for improvement they might have been harboring. Today, sitting in her cramped box of an office, Ms. Peck leans across her cluttered desk to pull April's file up on her computer screen. She informs me that April has already racked up between twenty-five and thirty unexcused absences in every class.

Ms. Peck leans back in her chair. "She's missing an average of two days a week of school," she says defensively. "There's very little we can do if a child is not here. We contact home, but if she doesn't do the work required and she's not here . . . Well, there's very little we can do."

Audubon students who are most in danger of leaving school are placed on a special counseling list. Once a month, the counselors, the social worker, and other appropriate support staff convene an "at-risk roundtable" to discuss what can be done for these children. They request daily progress reports from the teachers (which are rarely provided), meet with parents when possible, and evaluate whether students require testing for learning disabilities. April was placed on this list in December, and, according to Ms. Peck, her case was discussed shortly thereafter. "I know we talked about her," Ms. Peck says, "but I don't remember what we said, and I don't remember what we were going to do."

I ask Ms. Peck how the school will ensure that April receives an adequate education. The question provokes a fresh burst of annoyance. "I don't know if there's anything that we can do to make a difference for April," she says. "I always say that success in school is a three-legged stool: the parent, the school, the child. If you're missing the parent or the child in that stool, you won't have much chance at success. From what I understand, April goes back and forth between her mother and her aunt; I don't have any idea of what goes on there, but she doesn't seem to have any parent backing."

Although there are no programs at Audubon designed for girls like April, no counseling to help her cope with her mother's drug addiction, no classes to help her build her skills and regain her academic self-confidence, no one who even remembers what was said about her at a meeting specifically dedicated to at-risk children, Ms. Peck insinuates that April's home life is solely responsible for her failure. Like the teachers who turn from April when she speaks inappropriately in class, Ms. Peck finds it easier to condemn the child rather than question herself. Yet when, during the spring semester, one of April's aunts calls and informs Ms. Peck that she would like to keep abreast of her niece's progress, the counselor does not offer to meet with her, nor does she invite her to participate in the at-risk roundtable. Instead, she writes the aunt's phone number on a small yellow Post-it, which quickly disappears on her desk. She cannot, Ms. Peck explains, be expected to keep track of every relative who calls when her caseload is so overwhelming.

"I don't have the time," she says. "I don't have the time to do much more than discipline."

A few minutes later, as I am about to leave her office, Ms. Peck makes a final remark, which sounds very much like April herself. "It doesn't matter how well or poorly she does, though," she says grimly. "She'll go on to ninth grade in another year anyway."

■

Taking Control: The Resilient Self

■

For months after April tells me about her mother, I try to meet Denise. We talk on the phone nearly a dozen times, and she seems eager to discuss April's school progress as well as her own attempt to reconstruct her life. But whenever we choose a time and place to meet, she stands me up. Three times we agree to meet at the school, but she never shows; later we agree to meet at a café near her apartment and I wait for two hours; twice we agree to meet at the corner of the housing project where she lives, but even when our talk is scheduled for just a few hours after a phone conversation, Denise forgets.

In early spring, I ask April if she'll bring me home with her one day for a kind of guerrilla interview, but she lowers her eyelids and shakes her head. "I can't do that," she says, playing with her fingers, her voice thick with pain. "I think . . . I think my mom might be on drugs again."

By May, I can no longer reach Denise: the family's phone has been disconnected because she has lost her job and cannot pay the bills. As her mother becomes increasingly incapacitated, however, April steps in to fill the void. Like LaRhonda, she begins caring for her younger brother, cobbling together enough money from relatives and neighbors to buy chicken wings and potatoes for dinner, giving him her own small portion when his is inadequate, and insisting that he attend school even when she does not. In early June, Denise begins stealing from the small stash of money that April has hidden in her room for emergencies, but April says nothing; she just buys a lock for the door of her room. When, a few days later, Denise breaks the lock and rifles through her daughter's possessions again, stealing April's VCR, the remainder of her money, and some of her clothing, April sits down on her bed and sobs.

"I know my mom," April tells me sadly one afternoon. "I can see what she's doing. She's doing drugs for sure and now there's starting to be prostitution, men coming into the house. I don't know what they're *doing* in there exactly, but I don't want those men coming after me next." April jiggles her foot and tugs on the neck of her T-shirt. "I don't know what I'm gonna do."

When the year's final grades are reported, April fails every subject except gym. She is still unable to add or construct a simple sentence, but, as predicted, she is promoted to eighth grade anyway. Yet although the school system has essentially dismissed her, and her mother has all but abandoned her, April perseveres. On a late June night she lies awake in bed, listening as the sound of her mother trading sex for crack drifts through the wall. She grabs two socks and jams one against each ear to block out the noise. When that doesn't work, she wraps a pillow around her head, the socks still in place. Lying there crying, she realizes once again that the only way she can save herself is to leave home.

"I was thinking I have to do something if I want to do something different in my life or I'll end up doin' like my mom's doing," she tells me later. "I'll end up doing prostitution for drugs and sleeping with all kinds of different guys and having all kinds of kids maybe. So I prayed to God that night. I decided I'd leave and go with my Auntie Lydia. And if she wouldn't have me, I'd go get a job and pay my own rent somewhere. But I couldn't stay there. I knew that."

The next morning, April called child protective services and was again placed in a group home. After several days, however, she phoned her great-aunt and uncle, Lydia and George Roberts, who agreed to take her in, at least on a temporary basis. To

April, her aunt and uncle are the stuff of fantasy: they both hold stable jobs—Lydia works in the accounting department of a large corporation and George has a job with the city—they go to church every Sunday, and the house where they live with their seventeen-year-old son is clean, calm, and safe.

"At first, my husband said this was too much for us, to take April on," Lydia told me when we spoke on the phone shortly after April moved in with her. "We have a child of our own, and we're not so young anymore. But somehow, April touched our hearts. The night after she called, my husband woke me up at two in the morning and said, 'I don't know why I'm saying this, but if you want to take April in, I'm with you all the way.' I asked him what happened and he said, 'I don't know, I just know you love her.' Well, I don't know about that, but I know she deserves a break. I know that much. April has potential, I believe that. She just needs someone to be there for her when she falls, to pick her up, push her back out there, and tell her she can do it. Someone to be there when she's in need. Someone had to get involved, so I did. I did it because I see a future for April, I have hope for her. She's very strong . . . I still have hope for her mother, too. Denise has come up from the gutter before, gotten a job even. But she's not what concerns me right now. What concerns me is whether April will hold out for the dream, whether she will hold out for all that she hopes for, for all that potential."

The last time I see April is during a visit to the Roberts' home, a whitewashed row house several miles away from the project where Denise lives. When I ring, April answers the door and immediately apologizes for her appearance. She is wearing purple sweatpants and a ratty T-shirt—what she calls her "kicking around" clothes—and her hair is pulled into a haphazard ponytail. She leads me to the living room, which is dominated by a large-screen TV, and I sink into an oversized gray sofa. April sits on the floor beside me and leans against a window, so she can monitor the progress of two boys across the street who are trying to coax an ancient car back to life.

April is noticeably less fidgety than in our previous conversations, and although she says, "I'm hurting. I'm hurting every night about my mom," she is filled with pride in her new life. "With my mother, she let us do what we wanted," she says. "You didn't have to go to school, you could just stay home. You could be out on the street selling drugs—my brother does that. He likes it like that. But I choose not to go down that path. I choose to do good for myself. So I made a change. And it was all me: if I hadn't decided to make that change, there would've never been no change."

If April's initial flight from home was a matter of survival, her new long-term goals, developed since she's moved in with her aunt, mark a shift toward a personal version of Robinson and Ward's "resistance for liberation." Whereas earlier this year April told me that she aspired to a career in cosmetology, she now says she wants to grow up "to help kids in the situation I was in. I want them to see me and say, 'Dang! April got through high school and college and all, and look at all she went through!'

"You know what I want?" she continues, looking down at my notepad. "I want to write my own book someday. I want to write my *own* book about my experiences so all the kids like me will know they can do better."

As April walks me to the door, I think back to what her counselor said, that there was nothing the school could do for a child who did not want to help herself. If success is, indeed, a three-legged stool, April has, despite profound adult indifference, secured two of those legs on her own. The question is whether she will be provided with the means to shore up the third—whether, during her final year at Audubon, she will receive the help she needs to convert her strength of will into educational success.

10

Slipping Away:
Lost Girls

■

■

■

For the past twenty minutes, Ms. Raynes has been trying
to explain a lesson on newspaper weather maps to her science
class. Every few sentences she interrupts herself in mid-thought
to call for order, whack her yardstick against the chalkboard, or
berate the class for its ignorance, and even the most attentive
students are growing surly with impatience.

"What are we supposed to be doing?" one girl asks, exasperated.

"What do we do now?" mumbles another, who sits a few
seats away.

"I don't understand this, Ms. Raynes," a third girl shouts,
several decibels louder than anyone else. "What are we supposed to do on number six?"

"I'm not going to do it for you," snaps Ms. Raynes.

"Fuck this," mutters one of the boys who, at the beginning
of the class period, had been participating avidly. "I don't understand none of this." He crumples up his paper and lobs it at a
friend who sits several tables away. The second boy promptly

responds with a return volley and, within minutes, the entire class has dissolved into gleeful warfare.

A wad of paper arcs toward the back of the room, bouncing off the head of a girl who is quietly picking the remains of some flaking pink polish off her fingernails. The girl, Marta Herrera, doesn't even look up. In keeping with the caprice of Audubon fashion, she is dressed in an oversized nylon warm-up suit in cobalt blue. Her dark hair, half grown out from a home permanent, falls across the expanse of her broad face, obscuring its expression. But I know, from the days I have spent in her company, that Marta's eyes are most probably impassive, her brightly painted lips turned downward in a frown.

Crystal, who sits next to Marta and saw the paper hit her, gives her a shove.

"Marta, what's doing with you?" Crystal says, astonished by Marta's passivity.

Marta merely smiles again, and Crystal, who is a cheerleader, turns away and begins to chant, "Be aggressive. Be, be aggressive," making pompon motions with her hands. She has been practicing the cheer periodically throughout the day, and seems oblivious to the relevance of her words. Marta, meanwhile, glances at the clock over the door, softly humming a salsa tune.

There was a time when Marta loved school. In third grade, she had a passion for computers, and even last year, in seventh grade, her interest was briefly piqued in an English class. "I liked the stories we read," she says now as we survey the melee around us. "We read this book called *The Outsiders* about these boys in a gang somewhere. I was the only one in the class who got an A plus on that and I was so happy. Everyone was surprised, because I usually do bad in all my classes and in this one —A plus! A plus!" Marta sits back and grins proudly. When she smiles, Marta looks warm and vulnerable, but her expressions of pleasure are all too rare. "It was so interesting to read the language," she rhapsodizes. "You know, all the different words they used. I liked how they dressed, too, and how they wore their hair. I wished I could be with them back then. Life seemed simpler."

At this last thought, Marta's smile collapses and she returns to her fingernails. "I started this year really ready for something special," she says, "because we're in eighth grade and it's our last year here. But it's the same thing. Go in the class, read the book, do the work sheet. Mr. Krieger forgets what he's saying in the middle of a sentence half the time." She gestures at Ms. Raynes. "And she doesn't teach us nothing. I hate school now. I'd rather work. At least then I would be doing something. And I'd make some money to spend on clothes and things, instead of coming here and being bored. This is stupid."

I ask Marta if she is thinking about dropping out. "Yeah," she says dully, nodding her head. "I mean no . . . I don't know. My parents wouldn't let me, but I would like to."

When the bell rings, Marta ambles out to lunch, but Ms. Raynes asks me to stay behind to discuss Tracey, whom she believes instigated the paper fight. Instead, I ask her about Marta's class work.

"Marta?" she says, squinting.

Marta Herrera, I say.

"Oh yes," she answers, nodding her head. "I think she's doing pretty well."

I'm skeptical, and ask her to check. Ms. Raynes flips through her grade book.

"Oh," she says. "Marta hasn't turned in anything all semester. She's failing." She closes the book. "I guess I had her confused with someone else."

Mr. Krieger has a similar response when I ask about Marta, who studied English with him in seventh grade and takes both

English and social studies from him this year. "I think there's a problem with her mother, from what I understand," he says vaguely. "She's not doing too well." When I ask what sort of problem, since, as far as I know, Marta's mother—who works in an industrial laundry and has only a fifth-grade education—is eager for Marta to succeed, he merely shrugs. "I don't know," he says. "She doesn't say much."

In schools such as Audubon, embattled institutions where every day seems to bring a fresh crisis, Marta's placidity renders her invisible. Every year since fourth grade, which she repeated, her teachers have written nearly identical comments in her student file: in order to perform at grade level, she needs extra help with her English and math skills. Each year, the recommendations have gone unheeded, and since neither of her parents speaks English she is unable to obtain help at home.

As she has proceeded through Audubon, Marta's grades have slipped from a mix of A's, B's, and C's in sixth grade to solid D's and F's at the end of the first quarter of eighth. Yet, unlike April and LaRhonda, Marta is not one of the children discussed at the school's at-risk roundtable; she's not one of the children sent to the school social worker or channeled into special programs, and her parents have never been called in for a special conference. Marta doesn't cause enough of a stir to warrant that kind of notice. In class, she doesn't disrupt and she doesn't argue. She just sits, silently. And since she is not an impediment to her teachers, the fact that she is hurting herself escapes attention.

■

Falling Through the Cracks

■

Girls who become pregnant, girls who join gangs, girls who marry young and leave school are often said to have "fallen through the cracks." At Audubon, "falling through the cracks" is almost a mantra, repeated so often that one begins to wonder if the school is comprised of anything besides great, yawning cracks into which students must inevitably tumble. But the girls who are statistically most likely to "fall through the cracks" at Audubon, or at any school, are the ones who are most frequently overlooked: Latina girls such as Marta.

Shortchanging Girls, Shortchanging America found that Latina girls report the greatest plunge in self-esteem of any girls surveyed.[1] Without the personal self-esteem of black girls or the academic opportunities enjoyed by many white girls, the consequences of silence and marginalization for Latinas are especially dire. In their teenage years, they have a more negative body image, are at greater risk of attempting suicide, and report higher levels of emotional stress—anxiety, depression, nervousness, insecurity, or exhaustion—than any other group of children, male or female, of any race or ethnicity.[2] Latina girls are particularly vulnerable to gang membership and are twice as likely as white girls to become teenage mothers.[3]

In school, Latinas' flagging self-image is not only ignored, it is reinforced. Latinas are less likely than other girls to be called on or to speak out in class, the least likely to be recognized as gifted, and the least likely to believe they can achieve their dreams. Meanwhile they are the group of girls most often held back from fifth grade onward (which they often internalize as a

199

message about their own self-worth), and most likely to report that, at age thirteen, they have never taken a single science course.[4] Given such profound disregard for their academic and social needs, it is unsurprising that, in 1990, Latinas in highly urban areas had the highest dropout rate of *any group* of students in the United States: in some communities they left school at a rate of 60 percent, and nationally nearly one out of two Latina girls leaves school without a diploma.[5]

Audubon's student body is over one-third Latino, and unlike at many schools, a number of the teachers as well as one of the counselors speak Spanish. Even so, when I arrived on campus, there were no services designed specifically for Latina girls and no programs geared toward helping them remain engaged in their education. The community workers who regularly visit the school as part of a gang prevention program are all male, and mainly African American, attuned to the kind of explosive violence usually associated with young men. Among the teachers, there is a resistance to seeing Latinas' leadership potential: when Mr. Muriera put out the call last spring for recommendations for his community service class, teachers submitted the names of a number of Latino boys, as well as African Americans of both sexes, but did not suggest a single Latina girl.

"As a teacher, you're combating so much with Latina girls," said Ann Armstrong, a young woman with a depleted expression who teaches bilingual classes at Audubon. "You're combating some really entrenched sex roles: from the time they're little, they have to take care of their siblings and the boys don't have to do that. Then you're combating the bias of people in the school. Like, if a girl mainly speaks Spanish, if her English isn't good, forget it. She'll *never* be recognized as a leader in this school no matter how bright and interesting and dynamic she is. She won't be asked to be a peer tutor, she won't be asked to do anything. The Spanish-speaking girls are just pushed to the side, and they end up leaving school, joining gangs, getting pregnant."

When I first met Marta, in the spring of her seventh-grade year, she was cautiously optimistic about her future. She told me shyly that she dreamed of becoming a lawyer. "It would be hecka fresh," she said at the time, "because you get to defend people who are really innocent and help them." Unlike Lindsay and Suzy at Weston, Marta did not see herself as being too "sweet" for her chosen field. Nonetheless, without encouragement (or even acknowledgment) from her teachers, without any clear career or educational guidance, Marta's hopes are quickly fading. I don't know whether, if she were a boy, Marta would be able to hang on to her goal more tightly, if she could more easily navigate the terrain of indifference and indignity before her. Perhaps not. But as she slides anonymously through her eighth-grade classes, progressively engulfed by disillusionment, the strategies Marta pursues to maintain self-esteem and seek alternative sources of self-worth are singularly, tragically female.

▪

Stay Home, Stay Safe

▪

The Herreras' apartment is just a block from the housing project where April Welch's mother lives, but in that block there is an abrupt shift from a neighborhood that is predominantly African American to one that is almost exclusively Latino. The doorbell to their ground-floor flat is broken, but when I shout out a greeting, Marta's mother, Delores, peeks out of the kitchen window. She is roundly built, like Marta, with the same flaking pink polish on her fingernails, but Delores' face radiates merriness and she laughs often, a light, sweet sound. Her bleached hair is pulled back from her face, revealing dark brown roots, and she wears jeans with a red T-shirt that says "Palm Springs" across the chest.

Delores and I chat over orange juice in her cramped kitchen. Her nine-year-old daughter, Veronica, scampers in and out of the room as we talk, sometimes stopping just behind my elbow to stare as I take notes. Marta has told me that her mother is the only person who supports her career aspirations, although Delores is unsure about the steps required for their realization.[6] But Marta's dreams are not on Delores' mind to-day, and she quickly brushes them aside to discuss something else: the fears that have beset her over the last year, since Marta has become a teenager.

"My niece, who lives with us, got pregnant when she was sixteen," she says in Spanish, lifting Veronica onto her lap and stroking the young girl's head. "I thought, 'Well, I guess that's it for her—she'll never do anything with *her* life.' I would die if that happened to Marta. I would die. And I'm not going to let it happen either. I'm going to protect her from that. I watch her carefully: I watch where she goes and I know what time she is supposed to be everywhere. And, so far, she tells me every-thing." Delores pauses, considering this. "At least I think she does. I don't know for sure. But she tells me because I accept it, I don't make her afraid of me and I rarely get mad."

As if to prove her mother's point, Veronica squirms out of Delores' grasp, knocking a sugar bowl off the table in the pro-cess. Without a word of reprimand, Delores stoops to clean up the mess. As she gathers the broken pieces of crockery, she says that Marta's father (who refused to talk to me) tends to be far less understanding. "Marta and her father have been having a lot of problems lately," Delores says gravely. "She wants to go out and her father doesn't want her to. I feel sorry for her, because I wanted to go out, too, when I was a girl and my father wouldn't let me either. But Ignacio worries that if she goes out she'll get involved with boys and he's right. It bothers me that they fight so much, but there's nothing I can do. He wants her to stay home and study, and stay safe."

The girls at Weston may have been taught to repress their blossoming sexuality, but Marta's parents unwittingly reduce her to it, using "safety" as their justification. Marta's neighborhood is, indeed, violent, and dangerous for girls, but it is treacherous for boys as well. During one two-day period shortly after school began, five people were murdered within blocks of the Herreras' apartment: three of the victims were adolescent boys. Yet Marta's teenage cousins and half brothers (from both parents' previous relationships) who live with her family are never ordered to stay inside, even when their lives are in jeopardy. Instead, for better or worse, they are taught that they have a right to self-determination. For Marta, it's different. For her "protection," her maturing body is cast as a source of anxiety, and she is denied even a small measure of independence. As she realizes her passage into womanhood is circumscribed by peril and repression, her despair only deepens.

When Delores and I finish talking, she allows Marta to walk me to my car. Her father, a burly fellow who works in a hotel laundry, lounges on the front stoop among a knot of men. He nods as we pass, and she smiles back, saying, "Hi, Poppy!"

A few steps later, when her father is out of sight, Marta launches into a bitter diatribe against him. She complains that he wants her to model herself on her cousin Teresa, a young woman whose purity recalls Lyn Mikel Brown's and Carol Gilligan's "perfect girl."

"My father says, 'Why can't you be like Teresa?' " Marta says. " 'She goes to school, she doesn't wear lipstick or nothing.' He wants me to be like a little saint who only has girlfriends, and who likes all those girl things. My father wants me to say to my friends"—she switches to a sugary falsetto—" 'Oh, come over to my house, I can't go outside! Let's go smell roses!' "

Marta shakes her head in disgust. "He says Teresa is such a good student. He says, 'You don't see *Teresa* going out on the street. You don't see *Teresa* hanging out with boys.' But it's not even true. She sneaks behind her parents' backs. They just don't know. So I tell my dad what Teresa really does. I like to get him confused, to change things around on him. He gets really mad, but he doesn't say anything, he just shuts up completely."

I ask Marta, since she does not want to be a "little saint," what she would like to become instead. "I don't know," she says. "I want to be how I am. I don't know how I am, but that's how I want to be. I want to be able to go outside to the corner— just to the corner. And I want to be a lawyer."

Quite suddenly, Marta dissolves into tears, her face crumbling into such severe distress that I think, at first, that she's teasing me. "My dad is just so different than he used to be," she sobs. "He used to hardly even pay attention to me. Now he thinks I'll get pregnant, so he's after me all the time to stay away from boys."

During the course of our conversations, Marta cries often, her bouts of tears always beginning with the same startling force. It is at these moments that this girl, whose anger and despair are so undiscernible in the daily chaos of her middle school, admits to thoughts of suicide "because of all the pressures" to submerge her ego. She tells me she hates herself and confides that her father calls her worthless and a whore.

"My dad says to me, 'You're not going to be nothing in the world, you're going to be a *puta*,' " Marta says now, crying harder. "I say, 'No, you'll see me be something, I'll be sure of that. All this time you're giving me a hard time, you'll see me do something.' My mother says, 'Yeah, you'll see her be something.' But my father just says, 'You'll be a *puta*.' "

▪
Guys Protect You from Other Guys
▪

In her home, in her neighborhood, even at school, Marta sees that young men command more respect than she does, and that they're entitled to more freedom. During one of her crying jags, she tells me that she doesn't want to be a girl at all. She wishes she were a boy, she says, "so my parents would let me do anything I want." Since becoming male herself is impractical, Marta chooses the next-best option, swiftly turning for affirmation to the very source her father fears most. She has begun to sneak out of the apartment at night to flirt with a group of young men in her neighborhood, most of whom are more than five years older than she and delinquent.

One morning in Ms. Raynes's class, Marta opens her purse and pulls out a wallet-sized pink photo album embossed with cartoon kittens. It contains snapshots of her new male friends. They grin out at us defiantly, dressed in dark T-shirts and black jeans, each holding a different combination of shotguns and pistols. Marta points to a picture of an acne-scarred man toting two rifles who looks about twenty years old. His name is Berto, she tells me, and over the past several weeks she has twice sneaked out to meet him.

"I don't know why I hang around Berto," Marta says, her eyes shining. "I know he's bad for me. He's older and . . . I don't know, he's bad. He sells drugs and everything. But it's very exciting. We go in his car and he drives really fast, all over the city. It's fun!"

If Marta is oppressed by the constraints of femininity, the brash masculinity of men like Berto—who, like the fictional

205

"outsiders" that so captivated her imagination, have their own argot, dress, and hairstyles—offers her a release. Berto and the string of other men she would tell me about through the year provide an exhilarating foil to the "perfect girl" her father wants her to be, and their attention infuses her with the sense of power she so lacks. Without a healthy sense of self, however, Marta is unable to distinguish between liberation and domination. She cannot see that the men she views as redeemers will just make the snare around her tighter, that they will just take away more of her self.

A month after she shows me her photographs, Marta and her friend Alanna ask me to drive them home from school. As we walk toward my car, three young men cruise up in a blue Datsun. One is Berto, who has emphasized his scarred face by slicking back his hair. The men try to convince Marta to join them, negotiating with her in Spanish. Berto motions to Alanna and me—perhaps we'd like to come with them instead? Marta tells them she won't go with them and they drive off.

"He pisses me off!" she says, smiling broadly. "He wants me to go in the car with him, I tell him having a car don't make him bad—he thinks it does. I hate him! I hate him so much!"

Yet she doesn't move. The next time the car rolls by, the principal, Mr. Pirelli, rushes over. "Hey, you girls!" he shouts. "I want to talk to you. That blue car is circling the school and they've got their eyes on you. That doesn't look good. We don't want that here. We don't know who those men are—they may be high school boys or older, and they're driving around here trying to get girls to get in their car. We can't allow that. And you know what happens if you get in? They tell you that you're pretty, and you get in and they take you up to the hills somewhere. Sometimes you never hear from those girls again."

Marta avoids the principal's gaze, but when the car comes around again, she yells in Spanish for Berto to leave quickly, saying that the principal is on to him. As the men depart in a screech of rubber against pavement, Marta reveals that her infatuation with Berto ended two weeks ago when he moved to another neighborhood with a fifteen-year-old girl. Apparently, though, that hasn't stopped him from pursuing Marta.

"Yesterday," she says, "that girl was in the car with him, and he *still* drove by me and said, 'You're looking good!' He makes me so mad!"

I ask, in that case, why she's still smiling so broadly. Her response recalls a remark by Amy at Weston, who, along with her friends, wanted to remain desirable to a boy whom they knew had manipulated them.

"Even guys we hate," she says, gesturing toward Alanna, "if they show us attention, I like it."

A week later at lunch in the school cafeteria, Marta tells me that, the day after I saw her, she and Alanna did accept a ride with Berto, his friend César, and the third man, whom she doesn't know. She instructs Alanna to tell me what happened. Alanna is a smaller, thinner girl than Marta, with deep red lipstick, heavily lined eyes, and a glossy ponytail that tumbles to the middle of her back. She proceeds gingerly, trying to tell her story in sanitized language, to avoid using the words "whore," "*puta,*" or "bitch."

Alanna says that when the men reappeared the next day, Marta's initial reaction to them was the same. " 'No way,' she told them. 'I wouldn't go with you.' But she's smiling all the time. They keep saying, 'Come on, we'll show you fun, why are you mad at us? You know you want to go.' Then Berto talks to her real nicely, like a gentleman: 'Please, girls, won't you let us give you a ride home? We'll be very nice.' And she says yes."

In truth, Alanna says, Marta wanted to go all along. Alanna did, too, but she didn't know the men, except by name, so she was a little nervous. They crowded into the back seat of the car, with the man they didn't know, whose name they never remembered. He wasn't good-looking anyway, Alanna says. Then César, sitting in front, locked the door with an electric button.

Alanna looked at Marta and whispered, "They locked the door."

"Don't trip, Alanna, we can unlock it," Marta said.

But when Alanna tried, she couldn't. César kept his hand on the automatic lock, and she couldn't get the latch up. That's when the girls became scared.

"So," Berto said, "you took a ride with us. You thought we'd be nice. Well, we won't. We're going to take you in the hills and fuck you. We're going to rape you . . ."

"Let us out!" Marta yelled, hitting César on the back and shoulders. "Let us out of the car!"

But Alanna just sat there, not saying anything, not doing anything.

"I wasn't letting myself think about it," she says now. "I was too scared."

After a while, the stranger in the back wanted to let the girls go, but César said no. "They haven't given us anything yet," he said. The men argued back and forth, and finally Berto and the other man made César unlock the door.

They pulled over about a mile from the girls' homes.

"Get out," Berto said.

Alanna scrambled from the car, but when it was Marta's turn, the man in the back grabbed her ankle and Berto lurched the car forward. She tripped and fell into the gutter. The men sped off laughing.

Marta and Alanna walked toward the bus. "Those bastards," Marta said, brushing at her pants. A block later, the car cut them off, and César rolled the window down. He was holding a gun.

He aimed it at Marta. "You fucking *puta,*" he said, and clicked the trigger.

The gun wasn't loaded, and the men roared off again.

"I don't think they really would've raped me," Marta says, when Alanna finishes talking. "Maybe. I don't know. I didn't let myself think about it."

Neither Alanna nor Marta "let themselves think about" rape, but, as Marta talks further, it appears to be the only kind of sexual encounter she can imagine. Marta is a virgin, but she is resigned to the notion that, if the men she knows want to, they can force themselves on her at any time. This expectation may be derived partly from her own father's repeated warnings, but the idea of rape's inevitability is not challenged by the school curriculum, either. As at Weston, Audubon's consequence-driven "family life" course, taught by Ms. Raynes as part of eighth-grade science, shrouds young women's bodies in silence, providing neither information about contraception nor opportunity for a discussion of their right to sexual autonomy. Without a model for how a healthy relationship might be conducted, girls such as Marta are left to find whatever pleasure they can amid the victimization they expect, to recast mistreatment as excitement, and exploitation as romance. For them, female desire becomes not merely taboo but unfathomable.

"Guys get in the mood and they want to have sex," she explains. "For girls, it's more if the guy wants it and she wants to let him. And you don't know, you can think you love a guy, but then he forces you to do it. Men stink."

I ask her why, if the men she knows are so disreputable, she wants to be with them at all.

"Because guys protect you from other guys," she says simply.

Guys may protect you from other guys, I respond, but who protects you from the protector?

She gives a disinterested shrug. "I don't know," she says, with a small crescent of a smile.

◼

Jumping In, Dropping Out

◼

Sexual abuse and violence affect girls of all races and classes. However, for low-income urban girls like Marta, it has an accepted, codified venue, in gangs. Media reports on gang violence have centered on what boys do to one another, the ways in which they try to exert and maintain control through bloodshed. But, increasingly, gangs are made up of girls as well as boys.[7] Like boys, girls turn to gangs for protection in dangerous neighborhoods, for camaraderie, and to attain the feelings of self-worth denied them at school or at home. But although their reasons for joining are similar, the hazing required for entree is different for young women than for young men. Boys are "jumped in"—that is, beat up by other gang members—or asked to commit a crime. But girls, although they also may be jumped in, more often have to prove their loyalty by having sex with a succession of gang members, and sometimes with every male in the gang. In one notable 1993 case, five Latina girls showed up at a Planned Parenthood office in San Antonio, Texas, asking for HIV tests—during a gang initiation rite they had each engaged in unprotected intercourse with an HIV-infected man.[8]

"Bad" boys exert power, "bad" girls succumb. "Bad" boys strike out, "bad" girls get struck. There could not be a more effective message transmitted about how some of the boys in these girls' neighborhoods perceive them, or a clearer signal sent to us about how the girls view themselves. Inside the gangs, the

210

hierarchy of male power remains intact. As one girl who is peripherally involved with a gang in Marta's neighborhood told me: "The girls shoot sometimes, but they don't control nothing. The boys decide everything—when to do the drive-bys, when to do the shoot-outs—everything. The girls, they don't say nothing, they just do what the guys tell them."

It is difficult to gauge exactly how many Audubon students are involved in gangs. Although Mr. Pirelli claims that gang presence on campus is minimal, students and teachers say the opposite. According to one of the community workers who tries to dissuade Audubon students from joining gangs, up to a quarter of the school's student body are gang members, another 30 to 50 percent are what he calls "wannabes," "and the rest," he said, "they're just trying to go to school, and it's a shame for them."

When I first met Marta, she was derisive about gangs. "Kids in gangs think they're so bad," she told me during lunch in the school cafeteria. "The kids in my neighborhood, they're all like, 'Oh, a gang's so cool! If you're in it, you can have all the protection you need!' So they all want to get in them. But me and Alanna know that if you get in a gang it's more dangerous, because if you're from one gang, the other gangs are always trying to get you."

Marta gestured with her chin to a heavily made-up Latina girl leaning against the cafeteria wall. "That's Arianna," she said. "She's in a gang. I don't like her way of being. She thinks it's all about being in a gang. She slept with a lot of those guys in the gang to get in. I know, because I know some of the guys that she slept with and they told me. That's gross to me, because they just want her for a toy or something. They don't really care about her. They just want to sleep with her. And she still falls for it."

By the spring of eighth grade, however, Marta's attitude

has reversed. One May morning, she falls into step beside me in the first-floor hallway. Her curly permanent has now grown out completely, and she has gelled her hair into a tight topknot. Along with her dark lipstick, she has also begun wearing thick black eyeliner that extends past the outer corners of her lids.

When I ask how she's doing, she shrugs.

"Okay," she says. "My friends want to jump me into the First Avenue gang, and I don't know if I want to. The gang doesn't like this guy that I like now, so I couldn't see him anymore. If I could see him, I'd do it. But I don't want him to have problems."

Marta dismisses the idea that her parents would protest her gang membership. She doesn't think they'd find out. "When I come home, I tell my mother I've been with a friend, and it's true," Marta says. "It's just that my friends are in the gang."

As for the sexual submission required for initiation, Marta, characteristically, says, "I don't think about that. Anyway, sometimes they just beat you up, so I don't know."

We arrive at the door to her math classroom, and Marta leans against a locker, her eyebrows knit with concentration. "I don't know what I'm going to do," she says. "If it wasn't for this guy I would do it for sure. But I don't know. The guys in the gang, they're all in jail, or just out of jail. They're proud of it, they brag about it. I don't think that's good. But they're funny, too, and they're good friends. And I feel sorry for some of them. Yesterday these two boys in the gang asked me and my friend for food, and we were laughing at them. But they meant it. Their parents kicked them out of their houses, and they were really hungry, so we got it for them. I think that's why they jump people sometimes. They need money for food or for drugs."

When I see Marta the following week, just over a month before graduation, she is still vacillating, not about whether she should jump into a gang, but about which one to choose. When she discusses her prospects, her tone is excited, like a college student being rushed by rival sororities, and, like any potential new pledge, she's taking her time, weighing her options before deciding. "I want to join one gang," she says. "But I don't know, because I live in the territory of its enemy, so that could be bad, I could get hassled. They'd understand if I don't want to join because of that, but I think I might join anyway. Or maybe First Avenue, I don't know."

I ask Marta, since it is so close to the end of the semester, how she thinks her year at Audubon has turned out. Her expression immediately shifts from delight to indifference. "I'm getting pure F's," she says flatly. "I don't know if I'll even graduate, but there's nothing I can do about it now, even if I tried. I don't like school. And anyway, hardly anyone in the gang finishes school, so it doesn't really matter."

▪

Talking Revolution

▪

In early spring, the director of a local YWCA chapter approaches Audubon's counselors to invite them to participate in a new program the organization is starting: a series of in-school support groups for Latina girls. And not just for the supposed highest-risk girls either, but for girls who are simply quiet, girls who slide by unnoticed in school, girls without discipline records, even for girls who are maintaining a C average, which, by Audubon's standards, is considered respectable. The school officials eagerly accept. There will be two groups, they decide, both for eighth-grade girls, which will meet during the students' gym classes on the last seven Fridays of the school year. The groups will be led by Jessica Diaz, herself a student of health sciences at a nearby branch of the state university, who has directed a similar program at the YWCA for two years. Marta is one of the girls chosen by Mr. Morrissey to participate in the program. Helen and Carolina, her friends from Mr. Krieger's class, as well as Alanna, are placed in the group with her.

Jessica, who asks the students to call her by her first name, is round-faced with wide eyes and waist-length hair. She grew up in the same neighborhood as the students, dresses like them in jeans and combat boots, and speaks in the same vernacular. She runs the groups out of a cramped conference room next to the school's main office, which is so small that the nine girls who join her today for their group's second meeting are forced to sit knee to knee around the table. Nearly all of the girls wear deep red lipstick and most have pulled their hair into topknots. They wear T-shirts and jeans, and some wear oversized jackets, which they don't remove. Marta is absent today. It has been only three days since our last conversation, but I wonder if it is too late, if she has already been jumped into a gang.

Jessica likes to begin each session with what she calls a "check-in," asking the girls, one by one, to tell her anything they'd like about the last week. "Tell me if you're happy, mad, angry at a teacher, if you cut all week, whatever you did," she says.

There is silence. The group is still too new; the girls are shy and, perhaps, a bit suspicious. After a minute, one of the girls asks Jessica to start, so she breaks the ice by saying she's "stressed and worried" over the three final papers she has to write before the end of her college term. She then turns to the girl sitting next to her, whose T-shirt depicts the Virgin of Guadalupe surrounded by a halo on one side and a crucifix wrapped with roses on the other.

"Do you want to go next?" Jessica says.

The girl shakes her head.

"Come on," Jessica urges, "I just want to hear your voice." But the girl only stares.

"Just tell me about your T-shirt," Jessica tries.

The girl shrugs.

"Does it mean anything to you?"

The girl shakes her head again. During the course of this one-sided conversation she has, unconsciously, placed her hand over her mouth. Her friend, who sits beside her, bats it away, but the girl still won't talk.

Jessica turns to Helen, who also loathes speaking in front of others. When she's called on in class, Helen writhes in her seat. Once I saw her eye the clock, trying to determine whether she could stall the forty-five seconds until the bell rang.

Now she looks around shyly.

"Well," she begins, "a teacher called my house because she saw me holding hands with a boy and told my mother I was going with him, but I wasn't. I was just giving him something. And when my mother found out, she said I couldn't go back to school ever again. It took me a while to make her believe it wasn't true. She said it was okay, but if it ever happened again, she would take me out of school."

"I'm mad at a friend," Carolina pipes up. "She got stabbed, and she won't say why and she won't go to the doctor. I'm worried about her."

"Is she kind of into gangs and colors and that mess, is that why she got stabbed?" Jessica asks.

Carolina nods.

"Have you seen the cut?"

"She won't show it."

Jessica and Carolina discuss her possible options for a few minutes, then the group falls silent again.

"It's a trip," Jessica says, using one of her favorite expressions. "In some schools everybody talks and talks, and in some schools people are so quiet."

Jessica has told me that, to her mind, the purpose of the group is to pierce through the girls' silence, to uncover the ways they have been taught to suppress the self. Over the long run, she hopes to help them develop such a clear sense of pride and self-worth that they won't be tempted into gangs or duped into sexual victimization. To do that, she believes, her students need to understand two things: the beauty of their culture and their entitlement to their own desire.

Jessica takes a breath and looks around the table.

"Today we're going to talk about sexuality," she says. "Does anyone know what that is?"

"Yes," Helen says. Then, after pausing for a second, she whispers, "No."

"No one knows?" Jessica says, looking from girl to girl. "Sexuality has to do with being a man and with being a woman. It has to do with good feelings and with bad feelings about yourself. And it has to do with what your church and your family tell you about sex. Not that we always listen. But maybe they say you shouldn't have sex before marriage because that's bad. But then you have it anyway, and you feel guilty about it because they taught you to feel it was bad. So you feel bad about your sexuality."

Jessica uses the word "sexuality," but what she's really telling the girls is that they have—and they have a right to—sexual desire. As she talks, the girls watch her a little dubiously, as if they're waiting for the catch.

"It's kind of weird," Jessica continues, "but everyone is sexual, from real young little kids to real old people. Like, you don't like to think about your mom and dad doing it, right? Like, you think they did it once to have you and that's it."

The girls smile and nod. Carolina covers her face with her hands.

"Or your grandparents"—the girls giggle—"but everyone is sexual. It's part of *everyone*.

"I'm mentioning all this not because I think you guys are having sex—maybe you are and maybe you aren't. I'm mentioning it because, if it hasn't come up yet, it's going to come up extremely soon, when you have boyfriends. And it's important to talk about it before that happens, so you can think about what's right for you. Like how would you like a relationship to be, how do you think about it?"

The girls smile, but they don't answer.

"Do you think that a relationship is about being pressured?"

A few girls shake their heads no.

"No? That's not how you think about it? Because a lot of girls do. How many of you think about it like romance"—Jessica changes her voice to a singsong—"like candles and flowers."

There's giggling assent.

"Yeah, sometimes you think it'll be that way, you get a lot of that from movies and TV. But it's a trip, they never show you how it really is on TV. They never show you some guy stopping to pop a condom on to show he cares. And that's important—it's important to prevent getting pregnant and diseases. There's lots of diseases you can get. You can get HIV, and you die from that. Or you can get herpes, with sores, and that disease never, never goes away. And you can get one called chlamydia. With that, you can become sterile. You know what sterile means?"

The girls shake their heads and she explains. "And another thing is, you have to have a pelvic exam once a year if you're sexually active. Has anyone told you that?"

The girls shake their heads again. Their "family life" class included no such information. Jessica walks them through a typical doctor's visit, swinging her feet on the edge of the table to illustrate gynecological stirrups. The girls wrinkle their noses and blush, but they never take their eyes off Jessica, and they listen carefully.

By the time the class period ends, Jessica has informed them of the existence of both the clitoris and the female orgasm (neither of which the girls had heard of) and has explained that women often derive more pleasure from oral sex (which she defines) than from intercourse. At no point does she encourage the girls to have sex. In fact, she actively stresses alternatives to intercourse, especially during the early teenage years. But she does want her students to have enough information about their own bodies and their own desires to be able to make their sexual decisions from a position of strength—to be able to responsibly determine whether, if they have sex, they are doing it as agents of their own pleasure or as victims of someone else's.

"A lot of girls tell me that when they have sex it hurts," Jessica says at the end of the session. "A lot of times, when you're too young, your body's not ready yet. But they do it anyway, and you have to ask, why would you want to do something that hurts you?"

After the girls leave, Jessica shakes her head. "This group is really quiet," she says. "But I think that will change. I can tell you from experience that when you start teaching them about their culture they lift up." Jessica turns both palms upward, and sits straighter, extending her spine. "But where are they supposed to learn about that? In school, in society, Latinas are invisible. These girls don't see themselves reflected anywhere at all. Maybe there are lots of negative models for black girls, but they can find positive ones, too. Latina girls can't. But at schools where there is a La Raza club or girls are involved in one of the

Latino community groups, then it's different: they've learned to speak their minds. Those girls are the same age, from the same neighborhoods, but they just can't wait to talk. But not these girls. They're ashamed. They've learned there's nothing good about being Latina."

She rifles through a file lying on the table next to her and pulls out a handful of multiple-choice surveys that the girls completed at the beginning of their first meeting, to help Jessica assess their family environment, risk-taking behaviors, and overall self-esteem.

"Look," she says, handing the pile to me. "Look at the first one, 'I am a beautiful person.' "

I flip through the papers. Nearly all of the girls have chosen "rarely or never" as their response to that statement.

"These girls are taught by the mainstream culture that they aren't beautiful. I mean, look at what they play with as kids—blond Barbies. I'm not trying to clown white people or nothing, but they always blame the way the girls are on our culture. Well, we're living in a white, patriarchal society that's run by white men, so don't talk to me about *our* culture."

Because of conflicts with graduation festivities and the eighth-grade class outing, Jessica's group meets just twice more. She spends another session on sexuality, debunking six common sexual myths, such as "Having sex shows a couple is really in love," which she's typed up as a handout for the girls.

"Okay," she says as they read down the list. "How about this one? 'If a girl has sex once, then there's no reason not to have it again.' "

"That's true, 'cause she's a ho'," Helen says, then adds, "Just kidding. But sometimes some girls do it just because they think some guy is cute, and that's a ho'."

"You gotta think about that, Helen," Jessica cautions. "If a girl does it with a guy just because she thinks he's cute, she's a ho', but if men do it with young women 'cause they think the girl is cute, then they're cool. So before you go calling your friends and sisters ho's, you have to think, 'Where did that come from?' It's men who put that out. They go and fuck you and then afterward they call you a ho'. That shit's messed up. So when they call our friends and our sisters ho's, it's up to us to say, 'Hey, that's not even cool,' to those guys."

If that myth challenged the politics of male conquest, the next one reveals how deeply the girls have disconnected from their own desires, how, amid the tangle of that submersion, they do not imagine consent as saying "yes," but as saying "no" in a particular way.

" 'Boys need sex more than girls,' " Jessica reads.

"Yes," says a girl named Paula, who is holding a compact mirror and applying lipstick. "I mean, maybe. No. I don't know."

"I say yes," says Helen decisively. "Boys get horny."

All the girls laugh at this.

"Yeah," Paula says, "but girls get horny, too. Maybe she wants to have sex but she can't ask."

Marta, who, it turns out, has not decided about entering a gang, has attended the group today and now speaks for the first time. "Maybe if she wants to do it, she won't say so," she says. "But she'll kind of lead him on to do it instead. Girls do that sometimes. They say 'no,' but they don't really mean it."

"Yeah," says Alanna, "we're evil."

"No, we're not evil," Jessica says quickly. "But there isn't any evidence that guys need sex more than girls."

"They don't need it more," says another girl, "but they want it more."

"In our society men are pushed into sex young," Jessica says. "For guys, you're supposed to have sex as young as you can. You're supposed to want it all the time or you're not a real man. You're supposed to be like these macho men you see. But with girls, if you want it, it's back to being a ho' again, and that ain't even right."

At the group's final meeting, Jessica passes a stack of books about Latino culture among the girls. "You need to know what your roots are," she says at the beginning of the session. "You need to know that in order to feel pride about yourself. You need to know your culture to have self-esteem."

Unfortunately, her discussion of culture ends up being far shorter than she had planned. With each subsequent week, the number of girls attending the group has swelled. Today, there are fifteen girls in the room, nearly twice as many as the first week and too many to wedge, even uncomfortably, around the small table. Because of the unwieldy number, the weekly check-in becomes the central focus of the meeting, taking up a full forty minutes of the forty-eight-minute class period. Although this inhibits Jessica's curricular goals, the bits and pieces of the girls' lives that emerge during check-in give her the chance to suggest participation in other community groups appropriate to their individual interests and needs, groups which can engage them beyond June 18, when the school year ends.

Jessica proves right about one thing: over the few weeks they have met, the girls have become more talkative. This week, Carolina confesses that Mr. Krieger called her a bitch, and Helen adds bitterly, "He's always judging the girls, how pretty you are." Jessica writes the information on a small notepad. Another girl says that her family may be forced to return to El

Salvador, and a third airs the details of a recent heartbreak. Throughout check-in, though, there is one consistently recurring theme: the effects of living amid gang violence.

When it is her turn, Nathalie, an unusually chatty girl who is in Mr. Muriera's community service class, looks anxiously around the table. Earlier this week, she announces, she was jumped by four girls. "They said I was from another gang," she says. "They hit me with a rag on my face and stole my chain and my ring."

One of the girls asks if she knew her attackers. Nathalie looks nervous again.

"They used to go here," she says. "Now they're in First Avenue." Several of the girls steal glances at Marta, to see how she'll react to this. Nathalie does, too.

Marta looks down, but a small smile plays across her face.

"This gang stuff is really affecting people," says Jessica, who has noticed not only what has been said but what has not. "I hear it in every group I go to, all around the city, people are talking about gangs."

"I'd like to kill the person who started gangs," Helen says vehemently. "Kill them forever."

"What do you get from gangs?" Jessica asks the group. "It's your posse, your support system, right? And that feels good. And if you're in trouble, your posse backs you up and that's good, too."

Marta looks away.

"They tell you, 'You wanna get in? You wanna get in?'" says Nathalie, who, with Mr. Muriera's help, resisted joining a gang earlier this year. "But it'll mess you up in school and everything."

"Anyone else have anything to say?" Jessica says, looking directly at Marta.

"I have nothing to say," Marta says.

222

"No, you gotta talk, Marta," Jessica insists.

Marta shakes her head. "I pass."

"No passing," Jessica says. "We're stopping right here until Marta talks."

"Come on, Marta," Paula says.

"*No se,*" Marta says, switching briefly into Spanish. "Nothing happened to me this week. I go to school, I go home."

"Marta," Jessica chides. "You don't go to school and go home."

"Yeah, I go home. I go out. I pass by First Avenue, I talk to them. I go to my friend's house, I go back home."

Jessica tries another approach. "Do you know how you get into a gang?" she asks Marta.

"They jump you in," Marta answers, then adds, "Or you do something with a guy."

"You have to be 'trained,'" Jessica says, using the slang word for sequential sex with a group of men.

"I heard that," Marta admits, "but they told me it was just one guy."

"But if you just do it with your boyfriend, someone has to see," says Nathalie. "They have to watch you."

"Have you ever asked the girls who say they slept with guys to get in, how many they slept with?" Jessica asks.

"No," Marta admits. "They just say that their boyfriend got them in."

"Well, maybe you should ask," Jessica says. "You should check that out. 'Cause that's not what I heard. I heard you had to be done by all the guys to get in."

"But they want to jump me in anyway," Marta says.

"Hmmm," Jessica replies. "Have you decided what you're going to do?"

"I don't want to be in First Avenue," Marta says, sidestepping the question.

By the time the bell rings, I've decided to break my promise of confidentiality to the girls once again. I stay behind to tell Jessica what I know about Marta, and ask her if there's anything she can do to help.

"There's another community group with a good program that tries to keep the kids out of gangs, that gives them alternatives," she says. "They go out in the street to talk with the kids and reach them that way. I'll tell them about her." She makes another note in her pad.

"This is exactly why we wanted to do this group in the schools," she continues. "If we can catch a girl like Marta before she joins, maybe we can do something about it. But we can't catch them if we don't know about them. I don't know, though. It's hard to do much at the end of the year. I'll try, but the group isn't meeting again, so it's hard. But next year I'll be able to do more—maybe the group should go all year. Then I'll really be able to get somewhere with girls like her."

11

Rising Above:
I Like Myself

.
.

.

Dashelle Abbott is about to confront LaRhonda Johnson. This is big news at Audubon, potentially a major event.
Aside from LaRhonda, Dashelle is the toughest girl in the eighth
grade, and a fight between the two of them might be the only
fair match either one ever faces. LaRhonda has speed and agility
on her side, but Dash has sheer physical force: she's a generously
built young woman, who looks closer to eighteen than thirteen,
with wide shoulders and hips, an ample chest, and a rounded
stomach. The stand-off takes place just outside of Mr. Muriera's
community service classroom between fifth and sixth period on
a late January afternoon. At issue is whether, during a fight last
Saturday with Dashelle's best friend, Tracey, LaRhonda boasted
that she not only would flatten Tracey but next time she saw her
would pound Dashelle as well.

Now the girls eye one another, their mood tense, but controlled.

"Tracey said that you said, 'Fuck Dashelle. You go get her
and I'll whip her ass, too,' " Dashelle says, her head cocked to
one side, her hands planted on her hips.

"I didn't say nothin' like that," LaRhonda responds, indignant. "I said, 'You run and get Dash, I can tell that's what you want to do, and I'll beat her up, too.' "

Dashelle weighs this new information for a moment; LaRhonda's version of events shifts the onus from Dashelle back onto Tracey, implying, quite rightly, that she is too cowardly to fight her own battles.

Dash drops her hands. "Yeah," she says, shrugging. "I figured it was something like that."

LaRhonda relaxes her body, too, but Tracey, a smaller, slighter girl, who has been standing a few feet behind Dashelle, isn't so easily appeased. After all, LaRhonda is proving her to be not only gutless but a liar. She peers around Dashelle's broad shoulder.

"Fuck you," she says to LaRhonda.

LaRhonda's eyes flash, and Dash glances back and forth between them.

"It's over," she says. "You two just don't talk to each other."

LaRhonda seems about to heed this advice. She takes a deep breath and turns to walk away, but, in the end, cannot resist. "Fuck *you!*" she spits at Tracey.

"Just stay away from each other," says Dash, still trying to placate.

But LaRhonda is livid. "Fuck you, you punk-ass bitch. *Fuck* you. I'll whip your ass again."

Dash grabs Tracey's arm and drags her away. "Fuck you!" Tracey screams back over her shoulder. "You see that, Dash? You see what that bitch called me?"

"Fuck you, you punk-ass bitch," LaRhonda repeats.

"It's over," Dash says as she pulls Tracey toward her next class. "Let it be over."

"No, it's not over," LaRhonda retorts. "And it ain't

gonna be over. I'm not gonna let her disrespect me like that."

"It's over," Dash repeats, and since Mr. Muriera pokes his head out of the classroom to call LaRhonda back inside, for the moment it is. Tracey and LaRhonda may mix it up later, goaded by the girls in their neighborhood, but at school, where Dashelle stands between them, the two will reluctantly get along.

Dashelle Abbott is an unlikely peacemaker. There was a time when, if a scuffle broke out on the schoolyard, Dashelle would be in the center, egging the adversaries on, if not jumping in herself to exchange a few blows. Other students used to describe Dash as the girl at Audubon you "don't want to mess with." Principal Pirelli once confided, "Even some of the boys are afraid of her." When I first approached her, during the spring of her seventh-grade year, Dashelle wouldn't even talk to me; she wanted nothing to do with a white woman writing a book.

Back then, teachers considered Dash one of the most nettlesome girls at Audubon. They complained to Mr. Pirelli that she was out of control, uneducable, and dangerous to them as well as other students. According to Ms. Leland, Dashelle was the only student to ever draw blood in her class, when, as a seventh grader, she rose from her seat after a perceived insult, dove at another girl, and punched her in the nose. Mr. Krieger, who has also taught Dashelle, in both seventh and eighth grade, was blunt. "I hated her," he told me. "I didn't see any potential in her at all; she was a pain in the butt." Unsurprisingly, Dash barely passed seventh grade.

"I was real bad," she told me toward the middle of this year. "I thought, 'F school,' you know? I was like other kids: I thought it was nerdy or acting white or something to do good at school. I'd come to class and get kicked out and just sit in the office all day listening to everyone else's business. My friends would be sent in, and I'd see them come in and go, 'Girl, let me see your [discipline] referral!' and we'd laugh."

But that was the old Dashelle Abbott.

■

The Change

■

Several days after her averted fight with LaRhonda, Dashelle meets me in an empty cubicle in the school's front office. This year, she's happy to talk, but she can't conceal her irritation that I've scheduled our chat during her English class. Her reproof stuns me: no girl—whether at Audubon or Weston—has shown any reluctance to skip an occasional class for an interview. "I don't want to miss anything," she explains. "I don't like to miss none of my classes."

We sit down in two chairs facing each other. Dashelle crosses her legs, folds her hands in her lap, and looks up at me expectantly. She wears a light blue work shirt, meticulously pressed pants, and, looped around her neck, a handful of gold chains; a spray of acne erupts along the cheekbones of her broad face, and her processed hair is styled in a neat pageboy. Dashelle has the exceptional poise I often see among the older daughters of large families. Her father, a city bus driver, married her stepmother when Dashelle was an infant. In addition to the four children the couple brought into their new relationship, they now have seven more. According to Dashelle, it was the youngest of her brothers, Demetrius, who jolted her into the decision that has changed her life.

The revelation came, she says, the night before school began in September. Dashelle had already gathered her supplies together and she'd ironed and laid out the new outfit she had bought in which to make her debut as an eighth grader. Although it was getting late, she wandered into Demetrius' bedroom and told him that, if her parents were looking for her, she'd be outside with her friends.

Demetrius eyed her coolly. "You know," he drawled, "I used to look up to you, but you ain't gonna be nothin'. You get in trouble at school, you go out every night . . . You still gonna do all that this year?"

Dashelle draws in her breath at the memory and clasps a hand to her chest. "It, like, shocked me," she says, her eyes wide, "because no one ever sat down and told me nothin' like that before. I said 'Demetrius!' And he just said it again: 'You ain't gonna be nothin'.' "

Dashelle shakes her head. "It was like, 'Wake *up*, girl,' " she continues. "I know I'm not stupid. And all my little brothers and sisters, they probably look up to me like Demetrius. I thought, 'If I go down the bad path, then they might, too.' That would hurt me so much, to see them doing the wrong thing. And I know me and my older brother and sisters can stop them. We can set an example for them. If I do good, they'll see they can do it, too. It always works like that." Dash nods her head decisively. "It *always* works like that."

When school began the next day, Dashelle marched into Ms. Peck's office and announced that she was a changed girl.

"You're going to see a big difference this year," Dashelle says she told the counselor. Ms. Peck looked up at her dubiously, but Dashelle just smiled. "You'll see," she remembers saying. "You'll all see a new Dashelle Abbott."

Dashelle had vowed to apply herself before, but this time her determination seemed boundless. She went to class every day, and did all of her homework assignments. When, in Mr.

Krieger's English class, other students ran through the aisles, Dashelle worked studiously on a crossword puzzle. When, during a test in Ms. Raynes's class, other students shot rubber bands and yelled to one another across the classroom, Dashelle moved to a table by herself to complete the exam. (Although when Ms. Raynes subsequently ordered her back to her seat and, in spite of Dashelle's explanations, threatened to call her mother if she did not obey, Dashelle raised her fist and shouted, "Fight the power," before complying.)

"I went through my file the other day and pulled out a stack of discipline referrals an inch thick that I'd given her in sixth grade," Ms. Leland told me when we discussed Dash one afternoon. "She used to do terrible things. She'd have outbursts, she'd call me names I don't even want to say. But this year she's focused, she's directed, she's just shining."

When the first-quarter report cards came out, Dashelle made the honor roll with a 3.33 average. The principal hung her report card on the door under a heavily inked declaration: "Most Improved Student." Her goal now, she tells me, is to pull her grade point average up to a straight A before she graduates from middle school.

"I tried to change before," Dash explains, "but it used to be, I'd say, 'I'm going to class,' and my friends would say I was a nerd or acting white or something, and I'd give in. I'd say, 'All right, I'm gonna come with you then, because for sure I ain't no nerd.'

"Maybe I'm just getting mature now, becoming a young lady," she continues, "but now they call me a nerd and I say, 'I'll be all that. But I'm doing the right thing now, I'm taking care of business.' "

Dashelle's self-esteem is palpable: it's in her speech and in her eyes, but it's the grace of Dashelle's carriage that I find particularly striking. I remembered the lunch periods I'd spent with some of the girls at Weston, discussing their anxieties about food and fat. Dashelle, by their standards, is significantly overweight, but when I ask whether she's concerned about her size, she looks baffled. "It don't affect me none to be healthy," she says. "My mother and my sisters—we're all healthy. It's not my body that's going to get me somewhere, it's my brain. I could be the biggest person, bigger than this, and it's still my brain, not my body. So I'm not trippin' if I'm big or small or nothing. That don't matter."

If Dashelle were one of the girls at Weston, her "healthy" proportions alone might overwhelm her academic accomplishments and wreak havoc on her self-worth. Those girls are so often defined by the invisibility of the self, both in the classroom and, most poignantly, in relationship to their bodies. If they are thin, they aren't thin enough. If they are heavy, nothing can compensate for that blow to their self-esteem. Yet for Dash, it's quite the opposite. Although the key to her future, as she so aptly points out, is her brain and not her body, her size has served her well: it is, in fact, the genesis of her power.

Some of the difference in body image between Dashelle and the girls at Weston is, no doubt, cultural, attributable to the divergent conception of the female self among black and white women. While middle-class white girls are steeped in the contradictory messages of assertiveness and compliance, of achievement and containment, writer Toni Morrison has said, "Aggression is not as new to black women as it is to white women. Black women seem able to combine the nest and the adventure. They don't see conflicts in certain areas as do white women. They are both safe harbor and ship; they are both inn and trail. We, black women, do both."[1]

Certainly a brief foray into the world of rap videos makes it clear that black girls have their own tyrannical standards of beauty to contend with—the glamorizing of light skin and straightened hair, the fetishizing of large breasts and rears—yet Morrison's definition of African American femininity also offers an alternative vision, an affirmation of an expansive self, with, perhaps, an expansive body allowed to go along with it. This may, in part, explain why, in *Shortchanging Girls, Shortchanging America* as well as other studies, black teenage girls not only report healthier body images than their white peers but also hold consistently higher aspirations (even though inadequate educational standards and poor career guidance more often thwart their dreams).[2]

At times Dashelle has misused her strength. But her physical competence has given her a sense of efficacy and personal entitlement, the kind of confidence usually associated with girls' sports or self-defense classes. Unlike the girls at Weston, she is not afraid, literally or figuratively, to throw her weight around —to assert herself in class or to hazard appropriate risk. And although she believes she is now becoming a "young lady," Dash does not associate that phrase with emotionalism, weakness, or hypersensitivity. Instead, she views the transition to womanhood as a time to channel her prodigious strength toward a more productive end: a time to use her power to catapult herself to the top of her class.

Because she has found a constructive way to channel her energy, the teachers and administrators at Audubon have embraced the newly transformed Dashelle. Instead of demanding her removal from the school, they now regard her as Audubon's star role model. In many ways, she's a sanitized version of LaRhonda's drug dealer: a student who is loud, tough—who can act "black"—but can use her grit to work toward academic excellence.

"I think God gave me a gift to be so wise, because I sit back and watch and learn," Dashelle says. "I listen to the things I hear and put them together. Like I see that these days people are getting laid off from their jobs and stuff, and you need more than a high school degree—you need a *college* degree. In order for me to get a good job and get paid enough to live off, me and my family, when I have one, you have to get a college degree. My parents won't be here to help me and pay my rent all my life. I have to do what I'm going to do, and I have to do what's best for me, for Dashelle Abbott." Dash emphasizes her point with another curt nod of her head, the gesture she uses to indicate that her assertions are indisputable.

▪

Dreams and Doubts

▪

Beginning in February, Dashelle is selected to participate in Audubon's peer tutoring program, which is run by Marisa Hamilton, an energetic young African American woman who tests Audubon students for learning disabilities. During the first two months of the program, the thirteen trainees meet daily to practice communication skills and conflict management techniques and to study teaching methods. Those tasks mastered, they spend the remainder of the semester tutoring both their classmates and younger students in math, science, English, and social studies. Like Mr. Muriera's community service course, the tutoring program aims to boost students' academic confidence by showing them how much they have to offer their peers; but this program is designed to encourage students at the other end of the Audubon spectrum, students who are already motivated.

Today, Ms. Hamilton has split the class into pairs to work on "active listening skills": learning to hear and immediately paraphrase another person's ideas. Dashelle and her partner, a Latino boy named Dominic, relocate to the back of the class.

Since both students find their assigned discussion topic—the relative merits of a year-round versus a nine-month school year—profoundly unappealing, their attention wanders, and the conversation drifts toward their own educational plans. Dominic says he would like to join the army, providing the government upholds its ban against "fags" in the military. At the mention of homosexuals, the two boys next to us begin a noisy round of gay bashing and Dominic abandons our conversation to join them. Dash, meanwhile, turns to me.

"When I finish high school, I want to go to community college and learn all that little mess," she says. "Then I want to go to the university and study medicine. I want to make, like, penicillin and that kind of thing and maybe I'll help some kids, you know, maybe kids with cancer or something will take my medicine and they'll get better."

Dashelle has a powerful personal voice, a strong will, as well as healthy self-esteem, but that may not be enough to surmount the obstacles that stand between her and her dreams. As she continues to talk, the specter of what she has called "the other path"—the one she hopes she and her younger siblings can avoid—slowly begins to emerge. Higher education is a luxury in Dash's large family, so, she says, after high school she plans to work at "a little minimum-wage job" until she can save enough for college tuition, a process she reckons will take about two years. Yet if, as she insists, younger siblings are destined to follow their older brothers' and sisters' examples, there is scant hope that Dashelle will ever raise those funds. Her older sister disappointed Dash by becoming pregnant and leaving school last year at the age of seventeen. At nineteen, her older brother supports his fiancée and baby daughter as a delivery van driver; Dashelle considers him to be a creditable example, but, she admits, "that's not really where he should be, though."

"Studying medicine is my goal and I have my mind set on

it," she says. "And I hope that's what I'll do. But I don't know what will happen between now and then. Something may happen to me. I don't know, something could, you know . . ." She trails off. "I don't want to . . . I don't want to drop out of school. I'm planning not to because I don't want to. But you don't know what will happen to you. You could die. That happens to people. You can get pregnant, or you can . . ." She stops again, looking pensive; when she continues, she seems to be talking more to herself than to me. "You say you want to do this, but then you get up to high school and it's a big step. You can say, and then you can't say, that you'll go to school and you'll go to college, because you don't really know. I might just switch my mind again, too. I might . . . but I know—well, I *hope* I don't."

Usually, when I ask Dash a question she launches promptly into a response, which emerges in a single stream-of-consciousness sentence. I have to fight to find a caesura in which to probe an idea or pose a new question. When I ask her what she thinks might make her "switch her mind" about her ambitions, though, she answers slowly, her speech sprinkled with half-finished thoughts and extended pauses.

"You know, it's . . . my friends. I . . . I don't want to go to a high school with my friends, I want to expand into different things and I don't want my friends to . . ." She catches herself before using a phrase like "hold me back" or "pull me down," and starts again, cautiously. "I don't want to go to a high school where I know too many people. I'd be distracted. If I do that I'd . . . I'd get off the track and I want to stay on the same track that I'm on."

Dash's fantasy, she confesses, would be to go to a high school where she knows no one and to keep it that way; such cultural isolation seems both impossible and improbable for a teenager, especially for Dash, who, when I ask what she likes

235

most about herself, says, "I like that everyone likes me, that I can crack jokes and make all my friends laugh." Yet a thread of apprehension about friendship runs through my conversations with a number of Audubon's more achievement-oriented girls. Instead of viewing their peers as a source of support, they seem to consider disengagement as the necessary price of success. Shortly after her encounter with LaRhonda, for instance, Dashelle begins eating lunch alone, to avoid what she calls "the trifling mess" of petty skirmishes and trumped-up challenges that punctuate lunch in the schoolyard. Dashelle claims to be reconciled to her solitude, yet she also expresses an undercurrent of regret, a concern that her choice may be seen as a betrayal of both her peers and her community, thus jeopardizing the sense of self she's fostered there.

"My friends wonder about me," Dashelle says. "They say, 'Dang, you're getting these high grades, that's cold.' They're just playing with me, but, you know, Tracey and me, we aren't as close as we was. She met new friends now, who'll hang out with her. I hope we'll still see each other and go out and things like that when I'm in high school, but at the high school I want to go to, people want to go to college and I want to be in with that. But I don't want to stop hanging around the friends I grew up with neither. I don't want to be snotty, like I'm too good for them now."

There is only one diversion more worrisome to high-achieving girls at Audubon than distraction by their female friends: the lure of involvement with boys. At Weston, the girls speak of boys' power to ruin their reputations, to undercut their self-esteem by branding them sluts. Yet, in spite of those hazards, they are still keen to lose themselves in love and are as syrupy as a Harlequin novel in their infatuations. At Audubon, academic-minded girls shy from liaisons of any sort. Instead of a source of pleasure, they view relationships with apprehension, fearing that boys could do something far worse than bruise their reputations: they could permanently derail their dreams.[3] Helen Ortiz, for instance, the girl who believes that Mr. Krieger's negligence will harm her in high school, once told me that she dreams of going to college, then added, "I think that boyfriends could get in my way, though. You fall in love with a boy and then you don't want to do anything. You just do what he wants to do and then you do nothing. So I don't want to fall in love. I know a girl who went with her boyfriend when she was fifteen, and she got pregnant and that was it. You have to keep your eyes open, and you can't fall in love, that's important."

Dash and I discuss romance one day on the school's front steps, during one of her solitary lunches. Like Helen, she's suspicious of male attention. She says that she saw its consequences when her sister became pregnant, and views that experience as a cautionary tale. "I was mad at her for a while," Dash admits, "because she didn't finish her last year in school. But now she's going back to a special school to graduate and I'm glad about that. I respect that. And, you know, I can't be mad at her forever. But that got in her way, getting pregnant, it held her back and it'll keep on holding you back.

"Girls want boyfriends and all that little mess," she continues, "but to me, I think boys distract you from school and everything. They can knock things out of your mind. So I don't want a boyfriend . . ." She lets her thought drop, and, as is so often the case with Dashelle, when she picks it up again her initial conviction seems to have faded. "But I don't know. I wish I could talk to you in two years when I'm in high school. Maybe I'll have a different attitude then; maybe more things come at you in high school and maybe you do want a boyfriend, I don't know. I don't know . . ." She pauses again. "But on the other hand, I know it's up to me if I let boys get in my way, though. Other girls let boys get in their way. They think about them all the time, they think about sex, they get all depressed. But I could never get to that point. No, I don't think so."

Between disengaging from her friends and shunning romance, the portrait Dash and Helen paint of their high school years seems hopelessly austere. Because they have so clearly linked accomplishment to denial of pleasure, it seems a dangerous vision as well: it's a fair bet that they will "fall in love" before their educational goals are attained, and if, like many academically inclined Audubon girls, they see that as a reason to relinquish both their goals and their egos, it is hard to imagine that they can ever realize their dreams.

According to Ms. Leland, who has been coaching Dashelle in the math skills she missed during sixth and seventh grade, the girls' extremism is warranted. "I've talked to teachers who've kept track of their students," she tells me when I stop by her classroom after school. "They say the ones that succeed have to completely deny themselves a social life." She puts her hands up to the side of her face like blinders. "They have to focus on their work and just not have anything else. Can they do that? Will they give in? Will they get pregnant? Will they have caring adults there to help them? I don't know. Dash is atypical in that her achievement is recognized by the staff here, and that has kept her going, and she's pleased with herself. Dash never questions her pride, and that's a big plus. But I don't know. Will that be enough?"

▪

Just Look at Those A's

▪

At the end of the third quarter, Dashelle strides up to me in the hallway, holding three blue ribbons in her hand, one for each quarter she's made the honor roll. I accompany her to the counselor's office, to show Ms. Peck—who had been so skeptical about Dash's potential—both the ribbons and her latest report card: Dashelle has earned a 3.67 grade point average, an all-time high. Although the grades were awarded this year, too late for high school applications, Dash's exceptional progress has helped her gain special entree into a high school for college-bound students.

"Just look at those A's," Ms. Peck says appreciatively. "And not a single 'unsatisfactory' in citizenship."

"I'm really proud of that," Dash says, smiling. "All 'satisfactories' and 'excellents'!"

Dashelle tells us that the PE teacher, who oversaw the assembly in which the honor roll ribbons were conferred, announced that the school was especially proud of Dash's achievement, of how much she had improved during the last year.

"It took something out of my heart when he said that," she says, her voice heavy with emotion. "I felt so good because they noticed. That means something. I can show my children these ribbons when I get older, and tell them, 'Look, I made the honor roll in school.' I can show it to anybody and they'll know I *was* somebody in my life. Everyone is so proud of me, but I'm proud of myself, too. Because I couldn't have done it without my brain, I couldn't have done it without me. None of this could've been possible without me, Dashelle Abbott."

Dash turns to me, her expression intent, and says something that I haven't heard from any other girl at either school. "You know," she says, "I love my life. I *love* my life. I'm so proud of myself. When I walk down the street, I can have a pocketful of change and I see some homeless person and I'll just give it to them, because I know they probably messed up their lives, and my life is so good, I want them to have a chance, too."

Like LaRhonda, Dashelle dreams of finishing her eighth-grade year by "graduating onstage"—that is, participating in commencement exercises in Audubon's auditorium, which requires a 2.0 GPA. And with the support of the school's staff, the moment promises to be a memorable one for Dashelle: she is scheduled to receive three special awards during the course of the ceremony, more than any other student.

Two weeks before school ends, however, one of Dashelle's cousins, a boy not much older than she, is murdered. The loss isn't something she can talk about. "It makes me too emotional," she tells me when I ask her about it. Because of the death, Dashelle misses the final week of school, as well as the eighth-grade mathematics awards ceremony, where she was to receive a special trophy for her improvement in Ms. Leland's class. Under the circumstances, walking across the stage suddenly seems unimportant, too, and Dashelle decides to skip commencement.

Dashelle's story might have ended there, but Ms. Leland believed that it was vital, especially after such a harsh personal blow, for Dash to be reminded of the redeeming potential of her scholastic achievement. In the days before graduation, the teacher called Dashelle at home several times and begged her to come to the ceremony. "You're getting all kinds of awards," she told Dash. "It was going to be a surprise, but I'm telling you because you just have to show up."

But Dashelle would make no promises.

On graduation day, Audubon's auditorium is blazing hot and most of the parents attending have folded their programs into ineffectual paper fans. The stage is ringed by bouquets of pastel flowers, and a yellow banner with white letters reading CONGRATULATIONS, CLASS OF '93 is draped grandly across the proscenium. The eighth graders who have earned their place in today's event are strutting around the auditorium grinning broadly. The boys are dressed to the nines in natty suits (some in Day-Glo colors), and the girls are turned out in elaborate frocks that would seem more appropriate at a prom than a commencement. Many of the students, especially those with foreign-born parents, are the first members of their families to attain this level of education. Others were not so lucky: roughly a quarter of the class—including LaRhonda Johnson and Marta Herrera—were ineligible to attend today's proceedings because of their poor grades.

Just before the processional begins, Dash shows up, without her family, and takes a seat in the audience toward the back of the auditorium. When Ms. Leland spies her, she bustles up the aisle. "You have to come up onstage with everyone else, Dashelle," she insists. "You *have* to."

Dash folds her arms across her chest and shakes her head, but when the teacher continues to plead, she finally relents. With a heavy sigh, Dashelle stands up and follows Ms. Leland to the back of the auditorium, where the other graduates are assembling. The school band strikes up a tortured, vaguely disco version of "Pomp and Circumstance," and Dashelle, looking embarrassed, lumbers down the aisle with her classmates. Onstage, she slides into the back row, although her turquoise sweater

241

makes her easily visible. When she is presented with her first award, conferred each year by an African American sorority upon an outstanding female student, Dash trots across the stage, looking humbly pleased when the audience claps. With her second award, however, her enthusiasm increases. By the time Dashelle accepts her final prize—a special plaque commending her for outstanding leadership—she returns to her seat slowly, with her fist held aloft in triumph. The entire 1993 graduating class bursts into raucous applause.

When the ceremony ends, and it is time to leave the middle school for the last time, Dashelle can't stop crying. "I'm so happy," she says over and over through her tears. "I'm so proud of myself and I'm just so happy."

She looks around the foyer of the school, where the graduates are introducing one another to proud parents, snapping photographs, and making promises of everlasting friendship.

"I'm just so happy," Dashelle repeats, wiping her cheek with the back of her hand. "This is the happiest day of my life."

Part III

Through the Looking Glass

.

12

Anita Hill Is a Boy:
Tales from a
Gender-Fair Classroom

.
.
.

There is no single magic formula that will help girls retain their self-esteem. Scores of educators around the country are working to develop gender-fair curricula in all subjects and reexamining traditional assumptions about how children best learn. Some educators are developing strategies to break down gender and race hierarchies in cooperative learning groups.[1] Others are experimenting with the ways that computers, if used to their best advantage, can enhance equity in math and science courses.[2] Individually, teachers find that calling on students equitably, or simply waiting for a moment rather than recognizing the first child who raises his hand, encourages girls to participate more readily in class. On a national level, the Gender Equity in Education Act, which should be implemented in 1995, includes provisions for improved data gathering, for the development of teacher training programs, for programs to encourage girls in math and science, and for programs to better meet the needs of girls of color.

In trying to address the thornier issues of the hidden curriculum, some school districts have offered self-defense classes for girls, introduced aspects of sexuality education as early as kindergarten, or developed curricula that explicitly take on sexual harassment.[3] A few principals in embattled urban neighborhoods have recast their schools as round-the-clock community centers, offering recreational activities, adult education, medical care, and a flotilla of social services.[4] Others have begun mentoring programs or sponsored mother-daughter activities to help raise educational attainment rates and career aspirations among girls of color.[5]

Meanwhile, heated debate has arisen over whether mere reform—such as adding a few prominent women to existing texts or what has been called the "add women and stir" approach to gender equity[6]—is, indeed, adequate. In science, for instance, educators question the merits of a repackaged, "girl-friendly" curriculum versus a more radical examination of the very nature of objectivity and evidence collection.[7] Is it enough to simply call on girls more often or to introduce cooperative learning without changing the core of the male-dominated curriculum? Is it enough to change the substance of the curriculum but retain traditional classroom structures?

My own gender journey ends where it began, in the classroom of one teacher who is trying not only to practice equity but to teach it, to change both boys' and girls' perspectives on the female self. Judy Logan has been teaching for twenty-six years, twenty-two of them at San Francisco's Everett Middle School, where she currently coordinates the Gifted and Talented Education Program (GATE). Her students are an ethnically diverse lot, and although her classes have the highest proportion of white children in the school, about 40 percent of the pupils are Latino, Filipino, Asian American, or African American. As sixth graders, they spend three hours each morning with Ms.

Logan learning language arts and social studies. Over the next two years, the students take quarter-long required and elective courses from all four GATE teachers which combine English and history. But whether she is teaching classes on Greek mythology or world cultures, American history or English literature, Ms. Logan has an agenda beyond the standard lesson plan: she aims to blast the hidden curriculum wide open.

Stepping into Ms. Logan's classroom from the drab hallways of Everett is somewhat of a shock. There are images of women everywhere: the faces of Abigail Adams, Rachel Carson, Faye Wattleton, and even a fanciful "Future Woman" smile out from three student-made quilts that are draped on the walls. Reading racks overflow with biographies of Lucretia Mott, Ida B. Wells, Emma Goldman, Sally Ride, and Rigoberta Menchú. There is a book on Jewish holidays and one on Muslim women. There is a section on Pele, the Hawaiian goddess of volcanoes, and a coffee table book on artist Judy Chicago's famed "Dinner Party." On the back wall, there is a display of student submissions to this year's city-wide National Organization for Women (NOW) essay contest on "Women We Admire." For the eighth year in a row, Ms. Logan's students—an equal number of girls and boys—won first or second prizes in all three grades. A giant computer-paper banner spans the width of another wall proclaiming, "Women are one-half of the world's people; they do two-thirds of the world's work; they earn one-tenth of the world's income; they own one one-hundredth of the world's property."

It almost seems wrong. Looking around Ms. Logan's classroom, I find myself wondering, 'Where are the men?' Then it dawns. This is a classroom that's gone through the gender looking glass. It is the mirror opposite of most classrooms that girls will enter, which are adorned with masculine role models, with male heroes, with books by and about men—classrooms in which the female self is, at best, an afterthought. This is what a classroom would look like if women were the dominant sex. Educator Emily Style has written that the curriculum should be both a window and a mirror for students, that they should be able to look into others' worlds, but also see the experiences of their own race, gender, and class reflected in what they learn.[8] In Ms. Logan's class, girls may be dazzled by the reflection of the women that surround them. And, perhaps for the first time, the boys are the ones looking in through the window.

■

When Boys Are Girls

■

Forty-one sixth graders crowd into Ms. Logan's classroom each morning, and when I visit on a mid-February day, there isn't an extra chair in the house. Normally, the students sit at long, low tables arranged in vertical rows, but today those have been pushed aside, and the sixth graders have turned their child-sized chairs toward the front of the classroom. Ms. Logan sits among them, a fiftyish woman, with a round, pleasant face made owlish by her red plastic-framed glasses. She is dressed casually in an oversized African print shirt, leggings, and knee-high boots.

Today is the culmination of their African American history class. As a final project, each student has researched the lives of two prominent African Americans (past or present) and must now perform brief dramatic monologues as those people. The students have gone to great lengths to fulfill their assignment: the room is awash with costumes, props, audiotapes, books, and athletic gear. Although they had the option to recite their piece alone for Ms. Logan, most have chosen the limelight, and the posterity of the video camera, which is positioned at the back of the room.

Before class began, Ms. Logan told me that the first year she introduced this project she assigned only one monologue, but she noticed that while girls opted to take on either male or female personae, the boys chose only men. "It disturbed me that although girls were willing to see men as heroes, none of the boys would see women that way," she said. This was no surprise: I recall observing the same phenomenon among the student-written myths from Weston's English classes. At the time I wondered how the boys, who could only see male experience as relevant, would ever learn to see girls as equals.

Faced with the same concern, Ms. Logan decided to add her own hidden curriculum to the assignment. She began requiring two reports, one from the perspective of a man and one presented as a woman. To ask a group of boys, most of whom are white, to take on the personae—to actually *become*—black women forces an unprecedented shift in their mind-set. Yet Ms. Logan found they accepted the assignment without question.

"As long as it's required, they accept it," she explained. "But it wouldn't occur to them to choose it."

When the students have settled into their chairs or onto pillows on the floor, Ms. Logan asks for volunteers to begin. Jeremy is among the first to perform his female monologue. He saunters up to the stool that Ms. Logan has placed at the front of the room, a gangly white boy whose loose gait and rubbery features remind me of a Muppet. Like many of the boys, he has minimized the indignity of being required to "become" a woman by performing without a costume: he wears an orange baseball jacket, jeans, and untied sneakers.

He looks around uncomfortably. "To understand the blues," he begins, "you have to understand black history. When we were slaves, the only way we could express our pain was to

249

sing, so we started singing about racism and about love. And that was the blues. To sing the blues, you have to live them, and I'm an example of that. My name is Etta James."

There is muffled tittering from the class.

James goes on to detail her life, starting with her discovery at age fifteen by R&B front man Johnny Otis, and including an incident in which she was threatened at gunpoint in a Texas restaurant for using a whites-only rest room. She touches on her heroin addiction and descent into petty crime, then finishes up with her recent triumphant comeback.

"It wasn't that we wanted to sing the blues," James concludes. "We women had to. And even though men owned the record companies, even though men were the deejays and they controlled the world, we had to sing and be heard. And we were so strong, we women singers—it was scary."

James walks to one side of the classroom, where she has stashed a small tape recorder. She presses a button, returns to center stage, and begins to lip-sync to a bluesy ballad. This is too much for the class to handle, and the disbelief they've so valiantly suspended for the past five minutes comes crashing down. A boy begins to laugh and more join in, as do some of the girls. James tries to keep a straight face, but even she knows that the image of an eleven-year-old white boy syncing the blues is ridiculous, and a struggle for control ensues: Etta briefly gives way to Jeremy, who starts to giggle. Then she regains the upper hand for a moment before losing out to the boy once more. The whole performance ends up more comedic than respectful, and although Jeremy receives a vigorous hand when it is over, he has opened the door for the boys to make a mockery out of the feminine part of their assignment.

"Ms. James," Ms. Logan says when the applause dies down, "did you apologize when the restaurant owner threatened to kill you?"

"Yes," James answers, hopping back onto the stool.

"And how did that feel?"

"I felt really bad about it," James says. "I guess I wasn't used to racism."

Ms. Logan nods her head. "I'd like to ask Ms. James to step aside now and let me ask Jeremy a question."

Jeremy jumps off the stool, takes a few steps and turns around, now himself.

"Was it hard for you when you got up here to sing because some of the people were laughing?" Ms. Logan asks.

Jeremy shrugs. "Sort of," he says.

"Was it different when you practiced it at home?"

"It was more serious at home," Jeremy answers, ducking his head. "I did it seriously."

"Class, I'd like you to understand the interaction between the audience and the performer," Ms. Logan says. "If you laugh, it's very hard for Jeremy to stay in character, but if you support him, he can take risks. How you respond has tremendous impact on what a performer can and can't do. Jeremy, you took some real risks up there and I thought that was great."

As Jeremy returns to his seat, one of the boys turns to another, who had instigated the laughter. "I didn't think it was funny until you had to go and laugh like that," he says. "I would give him an A if I was grading."

A third boy says, "Me, too," and slaps Jeremy five as he walks by.

As the reports proceed, it becomes clear that the subtexts of Ms. Logan's lessons are not just about gender, nor, in fact, are they about race. Muhammad Ali's monologue sparks a discussion about the price one pays for success. West Indian writer Jamaica Kincaid inspires comment about noninvasive tourism. And when Charles, a shy African American boy costumed in gym shorts and a sleeveless jersey, finishes his report as Michael

251

Jordan after a near-disastrous stumble partway through, Ms. Logan steps to the fore and puts a hand on his shoulder.

"I'd like to ask you as Charles," she says, "how did it feel for you to stand up here like this?"

"I didn't like it," he says, his voice trembling slightly. "It was hard for me. I didn't like it at all."

"And how could we, as your audience, have helped you out?"

"You were fine," he says. "You listened and didn't laugh when I messed up. It was me. I'm sorry."

Ms. Logan addresses the students. "How many of you have one thing in this class that's really, really hard for you?" she asks.

Most of the sixth graders raise their hands.

She turns to a small, alert-looking boy. "What's your hard thing?" she asks.

"I don't know," the boy replies, "but I'm sure there is one."

"Well, okay," Ms. Logan says, turning to a girl who has raised her hand. "What's yours?"

"Stage fright," the girl says, giving a mock shudder.

"How many of you have stage fright, a little bit or a lot?"

About a third of the students raise their hands.

"And what can we, as an audience, do to help?"

"Don't laugh," says Charles.

"Listen," says a girl.

"Smile and look encouraging," says another girl.

"Yes," says Ms. Logan, "show expressions of support. Charles, it was really brave of you to get up here and do this when you had the option not to. You have nothing to apologize for. I know how hard it was, and it took a lot of courage."

Charles leaves the stage smiling. Although this mini-lesson on the value of supportiveness and appropriate risk taking was conducted surrounding a boy's experience, it seemed especially relevant for girls. I thought about the exaggerated fear of humiliation among the young women I have met, a fear so acute that they often silenced themselves in class. Like Weston's history teacher, Ms. Nellas, who stressed that " 'dumb' questions lead to learning," Ms. Logan has confronted her students' anxieties and taken the shame out of imperfection. Later, when a minute Asian American girl begins lip-syncing "What a Difference a Day Makes" as Dinah Washington, the class begins to giggle again and she falters.

"Remember what we learned about the audience and performers, class," Ms. Logan warns, and the students simmer down. By the end of the piece, the girl's performance is so precise that the class is mesmerized, and they finish out the last chorus along with her: "What a difference a day makes, and the difference is you!" (I'm surprised that they know the words, until I remember that the song is also the advertising jingle for the California state lottery.)

Over the course of the next few mornings the students are visited by nearly eighty-four prominent African Americans. Ida B. Wells talks at breakneck speed, reeling off an account of her life as a journalist, an activist, and co-founder of the National Association for the Advancement of Colored People (NAACP). Jackie Robinson discusses the difficulty and rewards of breaking the color barrier in baseball. The class is introduced to a fiery Angela Davis and a very nervous Frederick Douglass. Sculptor Richmond Barthé informs them, "You probably don't know me because certain people who write certain history books didn't put me in them because of my certain color," and poet Paul Laurence Dunbar recites his "Ode to Ethiopia." There are flashes of humor, as when Miles Davis' tape recorder goes on the fritz and Ms. Logan suggests that someone else step in until the trumpeter is ready.

"You know how temperamental these artists can be," she confides to the class.

There are also moments of true poignancy. Maya Angelou, for instance, in the guise of a freckle-faced white boy, discusses the trauma of being raped by a supposed family friend. When the man was subsequently murdered, she explains, looking sorrowfully at the class, "I didn't know whether to laugh or cry, whether to feel sorrow or joy." (Later, when recalling her first pregnancy, Ms. Angelou also asserts that "the pain of childbirth is overrated.")

After two hours of reports, the sixth graders take a fifteen-minute break, during which they have a snack and read to themselves. I join three girls in a corner who are chatting quietly over apples and boxes of juice. Holly wears glasses, has a precocious expression, and speaks in a clipped voice. I ask how she has enjoyed her year in Ms. Logan's class. "I like that Ms. Logan does things on women and women's rights," she answers. "She never, never discriminates against girls, and I'm glad that someone finally got that idea." She takes a bite of apple and chews thoughtfully. "But sometimes I think the boys don't like it."

Jill, a chubby-cheeked girl with dark eyebrows, who seems meek in Holly's presence, pipes up. "My older brother had Ms. Logan," she says. "And he said all she ever talked about was women, women, women. He didn't like her."

"I guess it's because all the other teachers ignore women," Holly says. "But sometimes I worry about the boys, that they get kind of ignored."

"Look at this room," complains Dana, who is Chinese American. The girls turn and scrutinize the walls. "There's all this stuff on women everywhere."

"That's true," says Holly. "But I'm still glad someone finally got the idea that we're all the same. I mean except for a few things, of course. That's good, I guess."

As the girls talk, I recall what a teacher at Weston once told me, that "boys perceive equality as a loss." Apparently, girls are uneasy with it, too. Even these girls, whose parents have placed them in this class in part because of Ms. Logan's sensitivity to gender issues, have already become used to taking up less space, to feeling less worthy of attention than boys.

I wander to the back of the room, where Mindy, who is an eighth grader, lolls near the video camera. Mindy is a model of grunge chic, dressed in a faded plaid shirt, battered jeans, and purple Converse sneakers. She has lank brown hair which hangs to her jaw, and a pair of oval granny glasses balanced on her snub nose. Mindy has been in Ms. Logan's class for three years, and is taping today's proceedings as a favor to her teacher. I ask her opinion, as a veteran of the class, about Ms. Logan's attempts at gender-fair teaching.

"The boys definitely resent it," she says matter-of-factly. "They think Ms. Logan is sexist. But you know what I think? I think that it's the resentment of losing their place. In our other classes, the teachers just focus on men, but the boys don't complain that *that's* sexist. They say, 'It's different in those classes because we're focusing on the important people in history, who just happen to be men.' "

Mindy rolls her eyes and adopts a long-suffering expression. "The girls like having all the women's history stuff, though," she continues, "unless they like some guy and worry about what *he* thinks about it. But I don't think that's so true by eighth grade. In sixth grade the girls are nervous about what the boys think because they're not used to it yet. But now I enjoy it, and a lot of the other girls do, too."

Of all the African American history monologues Nick's, which is performed just after the break, makes the strongest

255

impression. Nick is a thin boy with carrot-colored hair, milky skin, and freckles. He performs as Anita Hill and, like many of the boys, has chosen to proceed without the aid of a costume. Unlike some of the other female monologues delivered by males, there is complete silence as Professor Hill relates her personal history and her now notorious encounters with her onetime boss, Clarence Thomas. The sixth graders are old enough to remember seeing Hill on television when she testified before the Senate Judiciary Committee, and they watch intently, recognizing the importance of her words. Hill declines to go into detail about what, precisely, Judge Thomas said to her, because, she explains, "in the end, no one will really know what happened between us, except us."

Hill ends her report by looking straight into the video camera. "I had to have the courage to speak out against sexual harassment for other women in this country," she says solemnly. "So they could speak out, too, and become strong."

When she is finished, Professor Hill blushes to the roots of her red hair.

"Dr. Hill, I'm a great admirer of yours," Ms. Logan says, "and I'd like to know whether, even though Judge Thomas was confirmed, you feel some good came out of the hearings?"

Hill nods her head. "I showed other women that they can come forward," she responds. "They don't have to take that kind of behavior from *anyone*."

"Give her a hand, everyone," Ms. Logan says, and even though she is gesturing to a boy—who in most cases would undoubtedly be ashamed to be called "her" in front of forty peers—no one even flinches. Instead, the students burst into applause. And Nick, who has, if only for a few minutes, lived the experience of a sexually harassed woman, takes his seat.

▪

Education That Includes Us All

▪

After the bell rings, and the students leave for lunch, Ms. Logan and I sit across from each other at one of the low tables. "This is learning from the inside out," she explains enthusiastically. "They do the research, they connect into that other life, and they really *become* the person. People always ask me how you can get boys to stop being so totally male-oriented. I say, 'You just do it, and they'll pick it up as you go.' If you do a project like this, they really have to take on a female persona in a serious way, in a way that's respectful to the woman and her role in history. "It's a thrill for me to hear the way boys stand up for women's rights in their monologues. And I think it's meaningful for them, too."

I tell Ms. Logan about my conversation with the sixth-grade girls, about how, in spite of their gratitude toward her for treating them fairly, they worry that equity excludes boys. Before I can even finish my thought, she begins to smile. This is a comment she's heard before.

"It's true," she says. "Sometimes the kids resist the idea of gender equity, and it isn't always the boys either. One year, during a quilt project, a sixth-grade girl said, 'Why do we always study women, Ms. Logan? I feel like I'm not learning anything about men and I don't think that's right.' But she waited to say that until we were in the library and the librarian *and* the principal were listening. Later, I took her aside and said, 'We've done the NOW essay contest and this quilt, and I don't think that's so much considering that women are half of humanity. This is your history we're talking about!' It turned out that she was concerned that the boys would feel left out by those lessons."

Ms. Logan explains that, in fact, only two of her sixth-grade projects focus exclusively on women. Others, such as the African American history reports, simply ensure that women are given equal time. "But because I do that," she explains, "because I *include* women, I'm seen as extreme. If I took those lessons out and concentrated only on men's experience for a whole year, *that* would be 'normal.' "

Ms. Logan can't pinpoint exactly when she began teaching what she calls an "inclusive curriculum." "I never had a moment of 'Aha!' " she says thoughtfully. "I wish I could say I did, that I knew exactly when I started to think this way or teach this way. I do know that if you grow as a person, you grow as a teacher. So, in the 1970s, when I took some classes and started learning more about women myself, women came into the classroom."

For years, Ms. Logan taught her unconventional curriculum gingerly, keeping, as she says, "my mouth and my classroom door shut," to avoid undue notice. Then, at a 1986 women's history conference, she met Peggy McIntosh, a former middle school teacher. Now associate director of the Wellesley College Center for Research on Women, McIntosh had developed a five-phase curricular model based on the changes she'd seen educators go through when trying to teach inclusively.[9] Using history as an example, McIntosh describes Phase One as "Womanless and All-White History," which most of us learned as children. In Phase Two, teachers notice that there are no white women or people of color in the curriculum, and they cast about for a few exceptional achievers to sprinkle in. During Phase Three, the politics of the curriculum are unmasked and the focus is on issues: sexism, racism, classism, and victimization. Phase Four heralds a new era, in which the daily lives of women and minority men are themselves considered worthwhile subjects of intellectual inquiry. Only when those four phases are combined does Phase Five become possible: "History Redefined and Reconstructed to Include Us All." In McIntosh's ideas, Ms. Logan found confirmation of her unorthodox approach to education. In Ms. Logan's teaching, McIntosh found her theories brought to life. The two quickly became friends and colleagues.

Inclusive education, as defined by both Ms. Logan and McIntosh, turns the conventional student-teacher relationship on its head. Students may become the "experts," producing their own curriculum, as in the African American history class, and teachers become learners. Like many educational philosophers, McIntosh and Ms. Logan also question the grounding of classroom interactions in competition rather than cooperation, in individual "right" and "wrong" answers rather than a collective search for meaning. In her own book, *Teaching Stories*, Ms. Logan writes that, during lessons that explore gender roles, which can easily turn into opportunities to cast blame for inequities, emphasizing tolerance is especially important. "If my class seems anxious at the beginning of a 'woman's unit,' I reassure them that women's studies is not about 'ruling over,' it is about 'existing with,' " she writes. "It is important to be explicit with these reassurances right away. Feminist teaching is not about allowing a win/lose situation to develop between boys and girls."[10]

On the other hand, sitting in her classroom today, Ms. Logan admits that delicacy has its limits. "I present women's lives without apology," she says. When I question her again about occasional student resistance, she shrugs. "I usually find that boys only resist studying women when they're presented as 'lesser,' " she says. "And if they're presented as 'lesser,' girls don't want to study women either. And I can't blame them."

■

If You Start with Sexual Harassment, You'll Get to Susan B. Anthony

■

In late April, several weeks after the African American history monologues, I visit Ms. Logan's afternoon elective for seventh and eighth graders entitled American Women Making History. This is the second week of the course, which meets every other day. There are thirty-five students in the class, and nearly half of them are boys. Some are even boys whom I've heard deride Ms. Logan's classes as too women-oriented. They are here, nonetheless, either because their friends have chosen the class or simply because they think Ms. Logan is a good teacher. "I was absent the day they passed out the descriptions of the class," explains one boy whom I've heard make sexist jokes. "So I didn't even know what it was called when I signed up, but I figured whatever Ms. Logan was teaching would probably be okay."

Ms. Logan kicked off the first week of the course by explaining Peggy McIntosh's phase theory, the remnants of which is still on the board. She explained that she wanted the class to be a combination of Phases Two, Three, and Four: they would look at women who had achieved great things, they would study the struggles of women to attain equal rights, and they would culminate with individual or group reports that could cover famous, nonfamous, or infamous women.

At their second meeting, the class read a short story by Jamaica Kincaid entitled "Girl." Written in the voice of a short-tempered mother, the piece is a fast-paced, single-sentence list of the messages about gender that an unnamed protagonist received as a child, such as ". . . on Sundays try to walk like a lady and not like the slut you are so bent on becoming . . ."[11] As a homework assignment, Ms. Logan asked the students to write their own "girl" or "boy" pieces. Today, they are reading them aloud to one another. In many ways, this exercise echoes the "gender journey" that I saw some of the same students undertake last spring as sixth graders. That earlier assignment allowed them to explore the ways that gender shaped their perceptions of one another. This assignment asks that they look at how stereotypes affect themselves.

After winning the toss of a coin, the boys begin, but their pieces are a mere litany of parental nagging, a series of "don'ts" that would apply to any child. It is almost as if they did not understand the assignment, or, perhaps, as boys, cannot imagine that their experience is mediated by gender. On the other hand, their very neutrality may reveal that, at times, silence can affect boys as profoundly as girls. I peek over the shoulder of Andrew, a frail, bespectacled boy, who opted to pass when his turn came. He has written "Boys don't cry" in his essay. Ms. Logan has told me that Andrew is often mocked by other boys because of his small size and gentle nature. He may be, then, in the best position among his peers to understand the limitations of conventional masculinity, yet he also has too much to lose by articulating them.

The assignment proves much easier for the girls. Although a number of their essays are tributes to their parents, who urge them to "be myself no matter what" and have helped them navigate the messages of sexism that they are bombarded with at school and in the media, they still amass an impressive catalogue of the ways they feel diminished as girls. By now, the list is all too familiar: the despised frilly dresses, the expectation that they will be tidy, the curtailed freedom in comparison to their brothers, the assumptions that they are emotionally fragile or bad at sports, the fear of being branded a slut. But unlike other, similar conversations about femininity which I have both over-heard and instigated, this discussion is taking place in the presence of boys, as part of the overt school curriculum.

After the first burst of energy subsides, the girls turned to a topic that has come up at every school I have visited this year: sexual harassment on campus.

"Sexual harassment in school is the worst," says Mindy, who is in this class, too. "It's like if you wear a tight shirt, you're asking for it."

"I feel safer if I wear big clothes," says Alissa, a curvy girl with wild blond hair that she pushes from her face every few minutes. "I buy my clothes three sizes too big. It's the fashion, but it makes me feel better. My mom says I look like a freak, and I say, 'Mom, dude, it's because I don't want people commenting on my body. I *have* to dress like this.' As a girl, you can't be accepted unless you wear big clothes. Then it's like, 'Oh, a girl,' not like, 'Oh, a body.' "

"I managed the boys' basketball team this year," says Shannon, who tries to make her freckled face look more mature by wearing lipstick, mascara, and eyeliner. "And this boy, Fred, walked up during practice and he just reached out"—she extends both arms—"and he grabbed both of my tits. And this other boy standing there said, 'Did he just touch you?' I said, 'Yeah,' and he said, 'Fred, you shouldn't do that.' Fred said, 'I didn't do anything!' and walked away. Then this guy turns to me and says, 'Next time you should really watch yourself.' Like it was my fault!"

"How long would a girl last in this school if she went up and grabbed guys you know where?" Mindy asks rhetorically. "Not long. She'd be out of here."

"But it's not just boys," says another girl. "When I'm shopping, I think, 'Would people think I'm a ho' if I wear this?' Girls, too. Would Shannon think I was a ho'? Would Alissa? I think about that."

Alissa glances away, brushing her hair from her face yet again. Shannon looks down.

When the girls have talked for over ten minutes, Ms. Logan interrupts. "I want to stop and check with the boys," she says. "They've been very patient and I'd like to hear what this experience of listening to this has been like. But I want to tell the girls, I'm not leaving it at this. There are places we can go from here. This is a very important, scary, and profound conversation you're having."

"It's true that some guys are assholes in school," says a small, pale boy in a paisley shirt. "But there are nice people, too. And there are things that are harder for boys. When it comes to gay and lesbian issues, it's much harder for boys. You can't, like, hold hands with another boy."

"Has it been easy or hard for you boys to hear this?" Ms. Logan asks. "Can you separate yourself from it, or do you hear the girls and feel persecuted or defensive?"

"I can separate myself," the same boy continues, "but I feel angry at the boys who do that."

"Boys who do that to girls learn it from their families," says another boy, who is tall and athletic with a rattail haircut.

"I think it's also a lot of peer pressure from other guys," says Alissa.

"Of course it is," says Luis, a Latino boy who has pulled his 49ers jacket up over his mouth and nose.

"It's like how boys learn to see girls," says one of the girls. "I mean, you turn on *MTV Spring Break* and there's these stupid girls with huge breasts and the tiniest bathing suits dancing around like pieces of meat, and all these boys going crazy in the audience. It makes me feel, like, totally degraded."

"But if you're a guy," says Luis, "you see all those great

bodies, and you think you want a girl like that. You think you *should* have a girl like that."

"I didn't really know it was this bad," says another boy. "This has kind of changed the way I think. You hear all these girls talk at once and you realize it's kind of a big deal. I'll try to treat girls better. And I think other boys need to learn how to talk to girls, too."

"I'd like to point out that today you girls heard many voices that had experienced what you had," says Ms. Logan, "but you also had allies among the boys. We have to be careful not to assume that all boys engage in this behavior. And we have to be careful that boys feel that they can take an active part in changing this kind of behavior, in changing the behavior of others. Because it's not just a female job to change it, but a male job as well. Many men have been involved in the feminist movement since suffrage, and that's very important in making change. Part of talking about history is talking about the things that are handed down to us over the years in terms of gender. Maybe one idea for a class project for some of you might be to collect the stories and the experiences with gender in this school and make them into a book."

"Boy, I'd like to do that!" says one of the boys.

"Maybe people need more education and we can provide some of that," Ms. Logan says.

When the bell rings, signaling the end of the day, the students stand up as usual and place their chairs on top of the tables, but they don't leave the room. Instead, they cluster together to continue their conversation about today's lesson.

"Some of the boys," Alissa says to me, "the ones that talked? I thought, how *totally* cool that they're saying something about this!"

Fifteen minutes later, there are still a handful of students loitering near the chalkboard. They are reluctant to leave, even when Ms. Logan shoos them out the door.

"Okay, you guys," the teacher says, laughing. "Get out of here! Go home!"

When the last student has finally gone, Ms. Logan moves about the room, picking up books and straightening tables. I ask her whether pursuing a project on sexual harassment will really allow her students to learn about women's history, about such things as suffrage, abolitionism, and temperance. "Peggy McIntosh always says that if you start your Civil War class with *Diary of a Slave Girl* you'll get to Abraham Lincoln," Ms. Logan says. "But if you start with Lincoln, you'll never get to *Slave Girl*. Well, if you start a course on women's history with sexual harassment, with something that connects to the students' experience, you'll get to Susan B. Anthony eventually. And it will mean more to them, because they can relate it to their own experience. But if you start with Susan B. Anthony, you may never get to sexual harassment, and you lose that important connection to their lives."

When the American Women Making History class convenes again two days later, the students continue their discussion on sexual harassment. But one of the boys asks Ms. Logan if, instead of calling out their comments, they can proceed more formally, by raising hands. That way, he says, the boys won't be trampled by the girls, who continually interrupted them during the last class. Ms. Logan shoots me a look. But this turn of the tables comes with a difference: the girls openly concede that they have been unfair, and they apologize.

"It was good to get our feelings out the other day," says Mindy, "but they were so forceful that we excluded the boys, so they didn't get to talk. I hope they can talk more today."

Although they try to comply with the boys' request, the girls simply have too much to say to be patient, and, once again, they begin blurting out their thoughts. The boys, meanwhile, continue to raise their hands whenever they'd like to speak. Eventually, the students begin to wrestle over what, exactly, constitutes sexual harassment, an issue that the United States judicial system has not yet fully resolved.

"If you say a girl is beautiful, it's not sexual harassment," advises one girl. "If you say she's got big boobs and she's a slut, it is."

"Is it sexual harassment if you write a note to someone, but the girl doesn't see it?" asks an intensely serious African American boy.

"It could be sexism if you write a note," Shannon says, "but not harassment. I mean, don't you have to *harass* them, like say it out loud and bother them?"

"It's not sexual harassment to write notes," says another boy, whose blond bangs fall nearly to his nose, "but it can start sexual harassment because it gets around and everyone starts believing it and saying it to the girl. The note can *lead* to sexual harassment."

"I think we have a double standard," a Latina girl says. "Sexual harassment happens to girls more, but we go up and feel on guys, too. Maybe some of them like it, but maybe some don't and they don't want to say anything."

"That's a good point," Ms. Logan says. "It's how the person feels about it, not if the person is a boy or a girl."

But it's Alissa who brings up the most complex issue for young women who, although steeped in the ethos of desirability, are struggling to come to terms with harassment: the conflicting feelings of shame and pleasure that boys' remarks can evoke. "Sometimes," she says slowly, "it's like you're almost flattered that the guy is paying attention to you. So you say it bothers you, but deep inside, you kind of think it's flirting. But it's not really flirting, it's something else. And when you realize it's something else, you feel really bad, like you can't believe you thought there was anything good about this. It's totally confusing."

The girls nod their heads and the boys look thoughtful. I consider the myriad articles I have read discussing sexual harassment, all of the television reports devoted to the topic. These children have helped each other puzzle through the most salient controversies in less than a quarter of an hour.

"I want to stop the discussion here," Ms. Logan says after a few more minutes. "We've gotten a lot done on this and it's very important, but the class isn't about sexual harassment. It's American Women Making History. Next time we'll see a video called "How Women Got the Vote" that ties in with what you're talking about today, in terms of how women and men can change history when they feel discriminated against. The women and men of the suffrage movement worked long and hard and some of them didn't see change in their lifetimes. They developed many strategies about how to change their environment and change history. Those lessons should not have to be reinvented today. You have many, many lessons to learn from the men and women who came before you and changed history."

The class takes a break, and I go over to talk to Luis, who during today's discussion pulled his chair into a corner apart from the rest of the class.

"I'm one of the guys that talks that crap about girls," he says, by way of explanation. "I always tell them I don't mean it. But if I said that here, I'd get blamed for all the things I've said and I couldn't really defend myself, because it's true."

He looks away from me, as if he's embarrassed. "Men are pigs, you know?" he says.

"Do you think so?" I ask.

"Well, I guess we don't have to be," he admits, "but I'm just trying to have fun before I get old. I don't know, maybe I'll do it less now, though."

Luis tells me that he chose to take this class because he was interested in the topic. "But I don't tell my friends," he says. "If I told them I was interested in women's history, they'd call me a fag. So I just take it and don't talk about it."

By early June, the seventh and eighth graders have learned about Susan B. Anthony as well as Rosie the Riveter. They've heard speakers from the city's Latina community and studied the internment of Japanese Americans from the female perspective. They've analyzed images of women in the media and visited a feminist bookstore. They have learned as individuals as well as cooperatively, utilized the creative as well as the cognitive, thought in the concrete and in the abstract. The students have also researched their individual or group reports, which they are scheduled to present today.

About a third of the class has participated in some aspect of the sexual harassment project. When their turn comes, the first team, comprised of two boys and two girls, steps to the front of the class. They have chronicled the instances of harassment that they have witnessed over the past several weeks in classes, on the schoolyard, and in the hallways. The slurs are, essentially, identical to the ones leveled at Weston and at Audubon, but some—especially "suck my burrito"—inspire bursts of laughter, which the teacher does not ignore.

"I want to point out," says Ms. Logan, "that laughing releases tension, but it's disparaging to laugh at things that are serious. Sexual words are uncomfortable, and sometimes that makes us laugh, but I see laughter as partly participating in it."

The second group of students, who call themselves "the policy committee," offers up the legal definition of sexual harassment as well as the school's official punishment for it, which is outlined in the district's student handbook. One of the girls, who interviewed the school counselor, proclaims, "She says she has and will enforce the rules."

"But," a boy in the committee adds, "she had no approximate number of how many times sexual harassment has been reported or how many times she's actually done anything. Only one person has ever been suspended for sexual harassment, for one day, for actually holding a person against a wall and touching her."

The team that undertook a teacher survey reports discouraging results: only six out of seventy-two teachers cared enough to fill out the several-page questionnaire. One girl on the committee says that she saw a teacher use the back of his survey to write out a hall pass. Meanwhile, the group that surveyed students about their attitudes was also disappointed. Of seventy-five surveys handed out to boys, only twelve were returned. Among those, the responses were often facetious, such as "I harassed her because she deserved it," or "because her butt's too big," or "because she has big tits."

"So what they're saying," Ms. Logan points out, "is that the responsibility for the harassment rests with the female."

The students on the committee nod, considering this.

The female students were the only segment of the school's population that promptly completed and returned their surveys. Like the girls in Ms. Logan's class, they reported that they were harassed frequently—sometimes daily—and felt that harsher penalties should be enforced against their tormentors. Most of the girls said that they tell no one when they are harassed, and they often blamed themselves or their choice of clothing for provoking unwanted attention.

269

"Most girls thought there was no point in telling the counselors because they wouldn't do anything," concludes Alissa, who helped administer the survey.

"Well," says Ms. Logan, "there seems to be little awareness by the girls that they have the right not to be treated that way. Girls can only ask the counselor to do something if they know they have that right."

Ms. Logan pauses and looks around the class. Then she does something unique among the teachers I've observed: she defines the hidden curriculum. "Class," she says, "there's something you need to know about, called the hidden curriculum. The hidden curriculum is all the things teachers don't say, but that you learn in class anyway. Sometimes, the hidden curriculum is what you learn the most. Sexual harassment is part of the hidden curriculum for girls, and for boys, too, because they learn whether it has anything to do with them or not. The girls in these surveys are trying to be inconspicuous so they won't be harassed. They're trying not to be in the wrong place at the wrong time, trying not to dress a certain way. They learn to become silent, careful, not active or assertive in life. That's what the hidden curriculum teaches girls."

The students listen with solemn expressions.

"So what should we do about it?" Ms. Logan asks. "Reporting to each other is good, but what else can we do?"

"Let's make a booklet," says one girl. "Maybe we could hand it out with the student handbook to all the students and teachers."

"And there should be guidelines," a second girl offers.

"There should be an assembly," says a third.

"We have to work on getting girls not to be ashamed," Mindy says fiercely.

Ms. Logan nods her head in agreement. "This year is over," she says, "but this topic is not. I'll be home this summer, so if anyone wants to work on a booklet for next year, we can do it." Several students eagerly raise their hands.

After class, I ask Luis what he thought about the reports. Over the last few weeks, he has had it pretty rough. Shortly after their first discussion of sexual harassment, he made an obscene comment to one of the girls in the class. All of the girls immediately banded together and stopped speaking to him, even though he subsequently apologized. "He talks like that all the time," one girl told me angrily. "He always apologizes, but then he does it again. We don't have to take that anymore."

"I know they look at me when they talk about guys who do this," Luis tells me now. "It's embarrassing, but I guess they want me to learn. And I guess I've got to learn sometime."

Luis still averts his gaze and smiles nervously when he talks to me, so it's hard to tell if he means what he says. But at least he's been in the room this quarter, at least he hears it. And if the girls do, indeed, decide that they will not socialize with boys who mistreat them, he may yet have to learn his lesson.

▪

Stitching It All Together

▪

For the last four years, as a final, unifying project, Ms. Logan's sixth-grade class makes a quilt with a women's history theme. Like the essays for the NOW competition, most of the quilts feature "Women We Admire." The students each pick a woman—who may be fictional or actual, past or present, famous or anonymous—and create a muslin quilt square in her honor. Some of the students draw faces, others draw symbols of their honorees' achievements: a gorilla for Dian Fossey, a double helix for Rosalind Franklin, a family tree commemorating a beloved great-grandmother. An adult volunteer (usually someone's mother) then sews the squares together and the children help by ironing the seams and knotting the back of the quilt to the front through the cotton-batting center. They also compose essays about the women they have honored. Last year, Ms. Logan, who is adding science to her sixth-grade curriculum, asked her students to make a quilt entitled "Some Women in Science." In the center of the piece there is a large muslin square, painted blue and decorated with the phases of the moon. It bears a quote by nineteenth-century astronomer Maria Mitchell which encapsulates Ms. Logan's educational philosophy: "In my younger days," it reads, "when I was pained by the half-educated, loose and inaccurate ways that we [women] had, I used to say, 'How much women need exact science.' But since I have known some workers in science who were not always true to the teachings of nature, who have loved self more than science, I have now said, 'How much science needs women.' "

When I visit them during the last week of the school year, the sixth graders are busily finishing their quilt squares. Ms. Logan is engaged in a discussion with one of the boys, Jimmy, who has represented tennis star Monica Seles by drawing a bloody knife lying across a tennis racket.

"What do you admire about Monica Seles?" she asks.

Jimmy shrugs. "She was in the paper," he says. "She got stabbed."

"This quilt is about honoring women we admire," Ms. Logan responds. "It's okay to choose her because you admire her, but it's not okay to do a square on her because she was stabbed."

Jimmy begins to sulk. "But without being stabbed she's just another tennis player!" he complains.

"This quilt is not about violence toward women," Ms. Logan says firmly. "You can make a square with tennis rackets if you want to."

I've noticed that, during each of the projects I've observed —the African American history monologues, the American Women Making History class, and the quilt project—the boys who are most resistant to studying the female experience choose to focus on women in sports, especially tennis or track. When I mention this to Ms. Logan, she nods. "That's what they can best relate to," she says. "When boys feel like they're being forced to admire women they try to pick one that they think behaves sort of like a man. It's a step in the right direction. If they don't go beyond that at any point, I guess I'd see it as a failure, but sometimes you have to meet children where they're ready to learn."

I continue walking around the room, glancing at the students' work. Holly has chosen Kristi Yamaguchi, while her friend Dana has chosen Polly Bemis, the Chinese American heroine of the book *A Thousand Pieces of Gold*. Several students have decided to honor the subjects of their African American history monologues and still others have chosen to honor relatives. One Latino boy is drawing a picture of his aunt. "She's a single mom," he explains, "and her baby is in the hospital and she has two other kids at home. She has to work really hard, so I admire that."

A number of Ms. Logan's students are focusing on women in the arts. One of the boys tells me that Frida Kahlo is a big inspiration to him. One of the girls, a redhead named Kristi, has chosen the Japanese artist Mayumi Oda. Oda's paintings depict women as goddesses, as founts of power. They are described in one collection as "a feminine view of the positive self." Kristi tells me she just thinks they're "neat."

Jimmy stares despondently at his new square, which looks

rather stark with just a tennis racket. "I've decided to do Billie Jean King instead of Monica Seles," he says. "But I thought it was kind of important, a tennis player getting stabbed just so she wouldn't win. I don't know why that's not appropriate."

Jeremy is sitting on the floor near the door, putting the finishing touches on a square commemorating Rosa Parks, whom he first learned about in elementary school. His journey this year has taken him from Anita Hill, whom he wrote about in the NOW essay contest, to Etta James to Parks. He shrugs when I mention this, more intent on the fact that one of the girls is laughing at his rendition of Ms. Parks's face—the eyes seem, somehow, to have gotten slightly crossed. When I press him further, Jeremy turns to me in exasperation.

"I don't see what the big deal is about women," he says, and I prepare to hear him say that he's tired of Ms. Logan's unfair focus on the female sex. But I've judged Jeremy too quickly. "I mean, as long as they're interesting, what's the difference if they're women? Women are people, too, you know."

Jeremy completes his square and brings it to Ms. Logan. She places it with several others that will be sewn together later and smiles. "This is how you teach about gender," Ms. Logan says to me as Jeremy sifts through the finished squares. "You do it one stitch at a time."

Afterword

■

■

■

In the fall of 1990, the attention of the nation was focused on education reform. An "education President" was in
office, and America's governors were developing national education goals and strategies to achieve them.

But these attempts to rescue a "nation at risk" ignored the
needs of girls. Twenty years after the passage of Title IX (the
federal law banning sex discrimination in school programs), research indicated that girls still receive an unequal education in
our nation's schools. Whatever the measure—test scores, textbooks, or teaching methods—study after study showed that girls
are not living up to their potential as boys are.

Shortchanging Girls, Shortchanging America was commis-
sioned by the AAUW to bring attention to the need to include
girls in the nation's education goals. The poll provided factual
evidence of years of research documenting systemic gender bias
in American education. It also alerted the media to this crucial
issue, sparking interest from parents, teachers, policymakers,
and journalists like Peggy Orenstein, who sensed the people and
stories lying behind the "facts" of the poll and who understood
the impact they could have on the struggle for educational equity.

Four years later, in this book, she has given voice to America's schoolgirls. Neither scientific subjects nor victims, the girls she came to know at California's Weston and Audubon schools are the girls I see every day in the Illinois high school where I work. Their stories are all works in progress: *SchoolGirls* leaves them in eighth grade—the middle of the adolescent free-fall in self-esteem from which some will never recover. Others, however, will emerge from adolescence strengthened—empowered, perhaps, by a parent, a mentor, or an instructor like Judy Logan who puts equity at the center of her classroom and teaches about gender "one stitch at a time."

Providing girls with opportunities to have such teachers is part of the AAUW's equity agenda. Through a package of gender equity bills now before Congress, we are working to incorporate gender equity language into the Elementary and Secondary Education Act. Such language will ensure that schools can use federal funds to provide professional development in gender-fair teaching methods and strategies and to address the needs of students of color and students with disabilities, limited English proficiency, and low socioeconomic status.

Furthermore, the AAUW Educational Foundation is committed to a ten-year research agenda focused on educational equity. Two pieces of that project have been completed—*The AAUW Report: How Schools Shortchange Girls* and *Hostile Hallways: The AAUW Survey on Sexual Harassment in America's Schools*—and a third piece is now in progress on programs in schools that have proven to be effective for girls. In addition, the foundation's Eleanor Roosevelt Teacher Fellowship program provides classroom teachers with opportunities for additional study on how best to teach girls to reach their potential. And across the country, more than 1,700 local AAUW branches serve as community resources and coalition builders working with schools, PTAs, parents, and girls to promote educational equity.

We live our lives through stories, says feminist scholar and author Carolyn Heilbrun. To date, too many stories tell girls to become "Little Women." While I once wept over Louisa May Alcott's beloved story of Meg, Jo, Beth, and Amy, today I weep for a different reason. "We are only girls," says the high-spirited Jo, and to become a "little woman," she must conquer her independent nature and learn to be agreeable—all the while cursing her fate at being born female.

Girls today deserve better. Their gender journey must end in self-affirmation and full participation in the educational, economic, and social life of this nation. True educational reform will happen when girls, as well as boys, become all they can be.

—Jackie DeFazio
*President, the American Association
of University Women*

Notes

Introduction:
The Bad News about Good Girls

1. Kenneth Eaky, "Girls' Low Self-Esteem Slows Their Progress, Study Finds," San Francisco *Examiner,* January 9, 1991, p. A1. Suzanne Daley, "Girls' Self-Esteem Is Lost on Way to Adolescence, New Study Finds," New York *Times,* National Edition, January 9, 1991, p. B1. The students who participated in the survey were drawn from twelve locations. The sample was stratified by region, and the students included were proportionate to the number of school-aged children in each state.

2. By high school, nearly half of boys strongly agree with the statement "I am happy the way I am" compared with less than a third of girls. American Association of University Women, *Shortchanging Girls, Shortchanging America: Executive Summary,* Washington, DC: American Association of University Women, 1991, p. 4. Boys are also more likely, by a margin of 18 percent, to reject the assertion "I wish I were somebody else," and 10 percent less likely to say "Sometimes I don't like myself." American Association of University Women, *Short-*

changing Girls, Shortchanging America: Full Data Report, Washington, DC: American Association of University Women, 1990, p. 17.

3. Although girls attempt suicide far more often than boys, because boys use more lethal methods such as guns, they are more likely to complete the act. The American Association of University Women, Educational Foundation, *The AAUW Report: How Schools Shortchange Girls,* Washington, DC: The AAUW Educational Foundation and National Educational Association, 1992, p. 79.

4. AAUW, *Executive Summary,* pp. 6–7. Twenty-one percent of girls mention an aspect of physical appearance as "the thing I like most about myself," compared with 12 percent of boys. Confidence in "the way I look" is the most important element of the self-worth of white middle school girls. AAUW, *Full Data Report,* p. 47.

5. AAUW, *Executive Summary,* p. 8. Thirty-five percent of girls strongly agreed with this statement, compared with 28 percent of boys. AAUW, *Full Data Report,* p. 59.

6. Twenty-eight percent of boys strongly agreed with this statement, compared with 15 percent of girls. AAUW, *Executive Summary,* p. 6, Graph C.

7. The AAUW Educational Foundation, *The AAUW Report,* p. 28; Peter Kloosterman, "Attributions, Performance Following Failure, and Motivation in Mathematics," in *Mathematics and Gender,* Elizabeth Fennema and Gilah C. Leder, eds., New York: Teachers College Press, 1990, p. 119; Elizabeth Fennema and Julia Sherman, "Sex-Related Differences in Mathematics Achievement, Spatial Visualization and Affective Factors," *American Educational Research Journal,* 14, 1 (1977): pp. 51–71.

8. Patricia E. White, "Women and Minorities in Science and Engineering: An Update," Washington DC: National Science Foundation, 1992, pp. 3–4; National Science Board, *Science & Engineering Indicators,* Washington DC: National Science Board, 1991, p. 51; Marcia C. Linn, "Gender, Mathematics and Science: Trends and Recommenda-

tions," paper presented at the Summer Institute for the Council of Chief State School Officers, Mystic, CT, July–August 1990, pp. 12–13.

9. Forty-eight percent of white boys say this is always true, compared with 47 percent of black girls, 32 percent of white girls, and 27 percent of Latina girls. AAUW, *Full Data Report,* pp. 19, 28. Even so, black boys still report stronger self-esteem than black girls, leading them by 18 percent on measures of general happiness and confidence in their abilities, and 17 percentage points in satisfaction with their appearance, p. 21.

10. AAUW, *Executive Summary,* pp. 8–9. The percentage of Latinas who report that "I like the way I look" drops 36 points during adolescence, from 47 percent to 11 percent. The percentage who strongly agree that they are "pretty good at a lot of things" drops 33 points, from 51 percent to 18 percent. AAUW, *Full Data Report,* pp. 22–23.

11. U.S. Bureau of the Census, *Educational Attainment in the United States: March 1991 and 1990.* Washington, DC: U.S. Government Printing Office, 1992, pp. 29–35, 68–76.

12. Harter and Rosenberg's definition combines the theories of self put forward by William James, Charles Horton Cooley, and G. H. Mead. Susan Harter, "Self and Identity Development," in *At the Threshold: The Developing Adolescent,* Shirley Feldman and Glen Elliot, eds., Cambridge, MA: Harvard University Press, 1990, pp. 352–87.

13. Grace Baruch, Rosalind Barnett, and Caryl Rivers, *Lifeprints: New Patterns of Love and Work for Today's Women,* New York: Signet Books, 1983, p. 32.

14. AAUW, *Executive Summary,* p. 4. The number of girls who strongly agree that "I like most things about myself" drops 13 points between elementary school and middle school, but only one additional point between middle school and high school. AAUW, *Full Data Report,* p. 18. Carol Gilligan and her colleagues found that the young women in their studies of girls' psychological development began to submerge their strong sense of self at around age eleven. Carol Gilli-

gan, Nona P. Lyons, and Trudy J. Hanmer, eds., *Making Connections: The Relational Worlds of Adolescent Girls at Emma Willard School,* Cambridge, MA: Harvard University Press, 1990, p. 11.

15. "The Breakdown for Minorities," *USA Today,* February 16, 1994, p. 4D.

16. National Center for Education Statistics, personal interview, May 11, 1994.

17. Arlie Hochschild with Anne Machung, *The Second Shift: Working Parents and the Revolution at Home,* New York: Viking Penguin, 1989, p. 3.

18. Simone de Beauvoir, *The Second Sex,* New York: Alfred A. Knopf, 1952, as cited in Deborah Tolman and Elizabeth Debold, "Conflicts of Body and Image: Female Adolescents, Desire, and the No-Body Body," in *Feminist Perspectives on Eating Disorders,* Patricia Fallan, Melanie Katzman, and Susan Wooley, eds., New York: Guilford Press, 1994, p. 305.

1

Learning Silence

■

1. Myra Sadker and David Sadker, "Sexism in the Classroom: From Grade School to Graduate School," *Phi Delta Kappan,* 67, 7 (1986): pp. 512–15; Sadker and Sadker, "Sexism in the Schoolroom of the '80s," *Psychology Today,* March 1985, p. 54; Sadker and Sadker, "Is the OK Classroom OK?" *Phi Delta Kappan,* 66, 5 (1985): pp. 358–61. For a summary of the academic literature on gender bias in teacher-student interaction, see The American Association of University Women Educational Foundation, *The AAUW Report: How Schools Shortchange Girls,* Washington, DC: The AAUW Educational Foundation and National Educational Association, 1992, pp. 68–74.

2. Sadker and Sadker, "Sexism in the Schoolroom of the '80s," p. 56. See also Joannie M. Schrof, "The Gender Machine," *U.S. News & World Report,* August 2, 1993, p. 43.

3. Clifford Adelman, "Women at Thirtysomething: Paradoxes of Attainment," Washington, DC: Office of Educational Research and Improvement, 1991. Adelman tracked over 12,000 high school graduates from their high school graduation in 1972 until they were thirty-two. Although the women received higher grades, were awarded more scholarships, and completed their BAs faster, they subsequently received lower pay than their male counterparts, were awarded fewer promotions, and were more frequently unemployed. Women who had taken two or more math courses in college were the sole exception to this pattern.

4. Confidence is the variable most strongly correlated with achievement in math, particularly for girls. Yet even when they perform as well as boys, girls' confidence drops significantly during their middle school years, with girls who view the subject as "male" showing consistently poorer performance than girls who do not hold that view. The AAUW Educational Foundation, *The AAUW Report,* p. 28; Margaret R. Meyer and Mary Schatz Koehler, "Internal Influences on Gender Differences in Mathematics," in *Mathematics and Gender,* Elizabeth Fennema and Gilah C. Leder, eds., New York: Teachers College Press, 1990, pp. 91–92; Peter Kloosterman, "Attributions, Performance Following Failure, and Motivation in Mathematics," *Mathematics and Gender,* p. 119; Elizabeth Fennema and Julia Sherman, "Sex-Related Differences in Mathematics Achievement, Spatial Visualization and Affective Factors," *American Educational Research Journal,* 14, 1 (1977): pp. 51–71. American Association of University Women, *Shortchanging Girls, Shortchanging America: Executive Summary,* Washington, DC: American Association of University Women, 1991, p. 13, Graph G.

5. Heather Featherstone, "Girls' Math Achievement: What We Do and Don't Know," *The Harvard Education Letter,* January 1986, p. 3. Girls are also more likely than boys to lose heart after a failure in math and, subsequently, to achieve at a lower level. This may largely be due

to a difference in what psychologists call "effort attribution." When girls do well, they assume it is because they've worked hard or are lucky, while boys attribute success to ability. Meanwhile, girls blame failure on incompetence, while boys ascribe it to laziness or bad luck. Girls' relatively poorer performance on standardized tests may derive from this difference: since girls attribute success to hard work, they approach a test that purports to measure raw ability with less confidence than do boys. Unfortunately, standardized tests determine students' futures. In 1993, three out of five semifinalists for the National Merit Scholarship, which is based on Preliminary Scholastic Aptitude Test (PSAT) scores, were boys. That same year, a new federally funded college scholarship program intended to encourage students to enter math- and science-related fields used students' performance on the American College Testing Program Assessment (ACT) as its sole criterion, and conferred 75 percent of its awards on boys. Malcolm Gladwell, "Pythagorean Sexism," Washington *Post,* March 14, 1993, p. C3; "Boys Predominate in a Contest, Fueling Complaint of Test Bias," New York *Times,* May 26, 1993, p. B7; Michael Winerip, "Study Finds Boys Receive 75% of New Science Scholarships," New York *Times,* November 17, 1993, p. B7.

6. The "math gene" is a persistent, mythical explanation for girls' disinclination toward math. Yet Patricia B. Campbell points out that in studies conducted after 1974 (not, incidentally, coincident with the rise of the feminist movement in this country), gender differences in achievement have declined by 50 percent. Even the oft-cited gender difference in spatial ability declines dramatically when girls are exposed more frequently to spatial tasks. If math skills were biologically determined they would be impervious to changing political ideology. Nor can the "math gene" explain why girls' math achievement relative to boys' varies across ethnic lines: in a study of students in Hawaii, for instance, non-Caucasian girls both outperformed and outnumbered males in top math classes. Further, the studies that are most often used to support gender differences in math—conducted by Camilla Benbow and Julian Stanley of Johns Hopkins University—are flawed. Not only did they rely on the Scholastic Aptitude Test (SAT), which is considered by many to be biased against both girls and minority boys, but

they assumed that, because the students were in the same classes, they had identical learning experiences. Finally, according to biologist Robert Sapolsky, the studies turned up enormous overlap between boys' and girls' scores, making it impossible to predict who would perform better in any randomly selected pair. Given these factors, a biologically driven achievement gap does not explain girls' reluctance to pursue math: a confidence gap, however, does. Patricia B. Campbell, "Math, Science and Too Few Girls: Enough Is Known for Action," documentation developed under the auspices of the Women's Educational Equity Act by Campbell-Kibler Associates, Groton, MA, 1991; Marcia C. Linn and Janet S. Hyde, "Gender, Mathematics, and Science," *Educational Researcher*, 18, 8, pp. 17–27; P. R. Brandon, B. J. Newton, and O. Hamond, "Children's Mathematics Achievement in Hawaii: Sex Differences Favoring Girls," *American Educational Research Journal*, 24, 3 (1987), pp. 437–61; Robert Sapolsky, "The Case of the Falling Nightwatchmen," *Discover*, July 1987, p. 44.

7. National Assessment of Educational Progress, *The Science Report Card: Elements of Risk and Recovery: Trends and Achievement Based on the 1986 National Assessment*, Princeton, NJ, Educational Testing Service, 1988. During that same period, the gender gap in math scores declined. Although the gender gap in science is significant, and present across racial and ethnic lines, the gap between all white children and children of color remains even larger. Further, although American boys may be achieving better than girls, neither sex is doing well in science. American children ranked ninth of twelve international populations in a survey of the science skills of thirteen-year-olds. Meanwhile, the Department of Education reports that American eighth graders lag behind their peers in eleven other industrialized countries in mathematics. Archie E. Lapointe, Nancy A. Mead, and Gary W. Phillips, *A World of Differences: An International Assessment of Mathematics and Science*, Princeton, NJ: Educational Testing Service, 1989; Carole Feldman, "U.S. Students Trail Industrial World in Math," Associated Press, December 1, 1993.

8. NAEP, *The Science Report Card*; Marcia C. Linn, "Gender and Learning: School Science," in *The International Encyclopedia of Edu-*

cation, Torsten Husén and Neville T. Postlethwaite, eds., 2nd ed., volume 4, New York: Pergamon Press, 1994, pp. 2436–40.

9. Even science toys designed to explode fusty myths about science fall prey to gender stereotypes. For instance, *Explorabook,* a compendium of fun experiments by John Cassidy and San Francisco's Exploratorium, only depicts boys and men engaged in scientific activity. The two exceptions are a cartoon of a woman in a nurse's outfit and a photograph of two girls performing an experiment that involves a handheld hair dryer. In several toy stores I visited, *Explorabook* was displayed next to another title by the same publishing company: *Braids,* a book on hairstyling, whose cover pictures a smiling (and well-coiffed) girl. John Cassidy and the San Francisco Exploratorium, *Explorabook,* Palo Alto, CA: Klutz Press, 1991.

10. The AAUW Educational Foundation, *The AAUW Report,* p. 27. High school girls, even those with excellent academic preparation in math and science, also plan to pursue related careers in disproportionately low numbers.

11. Patricia E. White, *Women and Minorities in Science and Engineering: An Update,* Washington, DC: National Science Foundation, 1992, pp. 3–4; National Science Board, *Science & Engineering Indicators,* Washington, DC: National Science Board, 1991, p. 51; Marcia C. Linn, "Gender, Mathematics, and Science: Trends and Recommendations," paper presented at the Summer Institute for the Council of Chief State School Officers, Mystic, CT, July–August 1990, pp. 12–13. Meanwhile, after a twenty-year rise, business schools report a significant drop in the number of women seeking MBAs. David C. Walters, "Number of Women in MBA Schools Is Dropping," *Christian Science Monitor,* November 16, 1992.

12. Linn, "Gender, Mathematics, and Science," p. 13.

13. Jacqueline Madhok, "Group Size and Gender Composition Influences on Discussion," paper presented at the Berkeley Women and Language Conference: Locating Power, Berkeley, CA, April 1992. Madhok videotaped fifty-one eighth-grade science students in their laboratory groups. She found that in majority-female groups, girls de-

ferred to boys, and boys discouraged dissenting opinions. In majority-male groups, boys insulted and ignored girls until the girls gradually ceased participating at all. Interestingly enough, single-sex groups did not necessarily improve girls' performance. In all-female groups, Madhok found that girls had nearly equal interaction, but they showed a lack of confidence in understanding the material and difficulty with even basic procedures (perhaps in part because, in other science classes, these girls had been in groups with boys in which they'd been sidelined from the proceedings). The groups in which boys and girls interacted most equitably, in which boys were least hostile, and in which girls had the most "hands-on" time were equal male-female groups.

2
Toeing the Line
■

1. *Shortchanging Girls, Shortchanging America* confirmed that children believe teachers like girls more, but boys receive more overall attention. American Association of University Women, *Shortchanging Girls, Shortchanging America: Full Data Report,* Washington, DC: American Association of University Women, 1990, p. 65.

2. American Association of University Women, "Equitable Treatment of Girls and Boys in the Classroom," *AAUW Equity Brief,* June 1991, p. 3.

3. AAUW, "Equitable Treatment," p. 3.

4. Bruce Bower, "Gender Paths Wind Toward Self-Esteem," *Science News,* 143, 20, (1993): p. 308.

5. Richard L. Luftig and Marci L. Nichols, "Assessing the Social Status of Gifted Students by Their Age Peers," *Gifted Child Quarterly,* 34, 3 (1990): p. 111. Luftig and Nichols found that gifted girls were the least popular among their peers of all ability/gender groups.

6. Lyn Mikel Brown and Carol Gilligan, "The Psychology of Women and the Development of Girls," paper presented at the Laurel-Harvard Conference on the Psychology of Women and the Education of Girls, Cleveland, OH, April 1990, p. 16. See also Brown and Gilligan, *Meeting at the Crossroads: Women's Psychology and Girls' Development*, Cambridge, MA: Harvard University Press, 1992; and Carol Gilligan, Nona P. Lyons, and Trudy J. Hanmer, eds., *Making Connections: The Relational Worlds of Adolescent Girls at Emma Willard School*, Cambridge, MA: Harvard University Press, 1990. Brown, Gilligan, and their colleagues' work was conducted largely among white middle-class girls at all-girl schools and so is, perhaps, most appropriately applied to girls such as Lindsay and Suzy, who are demographically similar.

7. Carolyn G. Heilbrun, review of *Meeting at the Crossroads*, by Lyn Mikel Brown and Carol Gilligan, in *The New York Times Book Review*, October 4, 1992, pp. 12–13.

8. Sandra M. Gilbert and Susan Gubar, *The Madwoman in the Attic: The Woman Writer and the Nineteenth Century Literary Imagination*, New Haven, CT: Yale University Press, 1979, pp. 22, 336–71. See also Tillie Olsen, *Silences*, New York: Delacorte Press, 1965; reprint, New York: Delta/Seymour Lawrence, 1989, pp. 213–16. Olsen cites Virginia Woolf's "Professions for Women," in which Woolf wrote that the angel in the house "bothered me and wasted my time and so tormented me that at last I killed her," (p. 213).

9. Joan Jacobs Brumberg, *Fasting Girls: The Emergence of Anorexia Nervosa as a Modern Disease*, Cambridge, MA: Harvard University Press, 1988, pp. 61–62.

10. Charles L. Richman, M. L. Clark, and Kathryn P. Brown, "General and Specific Self-Esteem in Late Adolescent Students: Race x Gender x SES Effects," in *Adolescence*, 20, 79 (1985): pp. 555–66. There is a significant body of research showing that, among their peers, high-achieving boys compensate by clowning or through athletics; these options are ineffective for girls.

11. Louise Bogan, *What the Woman Lived: Selected Letters of Louise Bogan,* edited and with an introduction by Ruth Limmer, New York: Harcourt Brace Jovanovich, 1973. Quoted in Tillie Olsen, *Silences,* p. 145.

12. Lynn Jaffee and Rebecca Manzer, "Girls' Perspectives: Physical Activity and Self-Esteem," *Melpomene Journal,* 11, 3 (1992): pp. 14–23. Jaffee and Manzer also found that, although physically active girls had higher self-esteem than their nonactive counterparts, when sports activities were coed—such as in school gym class—girls' confidence in their abilities plummeted. Two other studies, both published by the Women's Sports Foundation, have also touted the positive effects of sports participation on girls' self-esteem, finding, among other things, that high school sports experience is especially beneficial in building Latina girls' feelings of efficacy. However, sports participation is not a panacea. Dedicated female athletes often regard menstruation as a sign of excess body fat and, through exercise and undereating, arrest their periods, causing irreversible bone loss. Additionally, girls in some sports—such as gymnastics and ballet—are especially vulnerable to eating disorders. Women's Sports Foundation, *The Women's Sports Foundation Report: Minorities in Sports,* New York: Women's Sports Foundation, 1989; Wilson Sporting Goods Company in cooperation with Women's Sports Foundation, *The Wilson Report: Moms, Dads, Daughters and Sports,* New York: Wilson Sporting Goods Company and Women's Sports Foundation, 1988. Jane Gottesman, "A Harmful 'Blessing' for Women Athletes: Amenorrhea Linked to Osteoporosis," San Francisco *Chronicle,* July 8, 1993, p. C1.

13. Between 1983 and 1988, cosmetic surgeons' caseload doubled to 750,000. Susan Faludi, *Backlash: The Undeclared War Against American Women,* New York: Crown Publishers, 1991, p. 218.

3

Fear of Falling

■

1. Psychologist Deborah Lynne Tolman notes that, in his early work, Freud identified an unhealthy silence surrounding female sexual desire, although he later veered off to proclaim that mature female sexuality involved being "the object, and passivity." *Voicing the Body: A Psychological Study of Adolescent Girls' Sexual Desire,* PhD Diss., Harvard University, 1992, p. 9. See also Deborah Lynne Tolman, "Daring to Desire: Culture and the Bodies of Adolescent Girls," in *Sexual Cultures and the Construction of Adolescent Identity,* Janice Irvine, ed., Philadelphia, PA: Temple University Press, forthcoming.

2. Germaine Greer is cited in Naomi Wolf, *The Beauty Myth,* New York: William Morrow and Company, 1991, p. 154.

3. Simone de Beauvoir, *The Second Sex,* translated and edited by H. M. Parshley with an introduction by Deirdre Bair, New York: Alfred A. Knopf, 1952; reprint, New York: Vintage Books, 1989, p. 337.

4. Audre Lorde, *Sister Outsider: Essays and Speeches,* Freedom, CA: The Crossing Press, 1984, p. 57.

5. In *Erotic Wars: What Happened to the Sexual Revolution?,* New York: Farrar, Straus & Giroux, 1990, Lillian Rubin writes that "male condemnation of girls who violate the norm of monogamy is ubiquitous. I never heard anyone speak about a boy with equal disparagement." What's more, Rubin notes that there are "no words in the lexicon of teenage life that would give evidence that any serious stigma attaches to a sexually promiscuous male" (p. 71).

6. Naomi Wolf, *The Beauty Myth,* p. 156.

7. Deborah Lynne Tolman, "Just Say No to What? A Preliminary Analysis of Sexual Subjectivity in a Multicultural Group of Adolescent Females," paper presented at the American Orthopsychiatric Association, Miami, FL, April 27, 1990, p. 5. Sex-negative attitudes do not

discourage sexual activity, but they do discourage contraception use. By contrast, they found that teens with sex-positive attitudes were more consistent and more enthusiastic about contraceptive use. The United States, which encourages a "just say no" sex-negative attitude in its education policies, has among the highest teenage pregnancy rates, abortion rates, and birth rates in the developed world (and California has among the highest rates in the United States). According to the Alan Guttmacher Institute, the countries with the lowest rates of teenage pregnancy and childbirth have the most liberal attitudes about sex. Further, children whose parents are involved in their contraceptive education practice birth control at a far greater rate than those whose parents tell them nothing: 91 percent versus 50 percent. William A. Fisher, Donna Byrne, and Leonard A. White, "Emotional Barriers to Contraception," in *Adolescents, Sex and Contraception*, Hillsdale, NJ: Lawrence Erlbaum, 1983, p. 234. Mark O. Bigler, "The Facts: Adolescent Sexual Behavior in the Eighties," *SIECUS Report*, 18, 1 (1989): p. 8.

8. French feminists Luce Irigaray and Helen Cixous argue that "expressions of female voice, body, and sexuality are essentially inaudible when the dominant language and ways of viewing are male." Quoted in Michelle Fine, "Sexuality, Schooling, and Adolescent Females: The Missing Discourse of Desire," *Harvard Educational Review*, 58, 1 (1988): p. 34.

9. Personal interview, March 1, 1993.

10. Fine, "Sexuality, Schooling, and Adolescent Females," pp. 34–37. See also Michelle Fine and Pat Macpherson, "Over Dinner: Feminism and Adolescent Female Bodies," in *Disruptive Voices: The Possibilities of Feminist Research*, Ann Arbor, MI: University of Michigan Press, 1992, pp. 175–203; and Michelle Fine, *Reframing Dropouts*, Albany, NY: SUNY Albany Press, 1991.

11. Fine, "Sexuality, Schooling, and Adolescent Females," p. 40.

12. Daniel P. Orr, Mary L. Wilbrandt, Catherine J. Brack, Steven P. Rauch, and Gary M. Ingersoll, "Reported Sexual Behaviors and Self-Esteem among Young Adolescents," *American Journal of Diseases of*

Children, 143 (1989): p. 86. Other studies estimate that at least twenty-eight percent of children engage in intercourse before they are fourteen; of those, the average age of sexual initiation is twelve. Among sexually active girls under fifteen, only 31 percent report using contraceptives. By age fifteen, the number increases to a still-low 58 percent. By age nineteen, however, 91 percent of girls say they use contraception. The American Association of University Women Educational Foundation, *The AAUW Report: How Schools Shortchange Girls,* Washington, DC: The AAUW Educational Foundation and National Educational Association, 1992, p. 76.

13. Each day in the United States 2,795 teenagers become pregnant and 1,295 give birth. Debra L. Schultz, *Risk, Resiliency, and Resistance: Current Research on Adolescent Girls,* New York: Ms. Foundation for Women National Girls Initiative, 1991, p. 2.

14. The California state framework encourages teachers to promote abstinence as the only sure way to avoid disease and pregnancy, but allows communities to devise their own sex education guidelines. Weston's approach is typical of towns across the state. Department of Education, personal interview, January 28, 1994.

15. On average, secondary schools offer only six and a half hours a year of sex education, and fewer than two of those hours focus on contraception and the prevention of sexually transmitted disease. "Sexual and Reproductive Behavior Among U.S. Teens," *Fact Sheet,* New York: Planned Parenthood Federation of America, Inc., 1991.

16. In *The Beauty Myth,* Naomi Wolf writes that instead of asking, "Whom do I desire? Why? What will I do about it?" young women learn to ask, "Would I desire myself? Why? . . . Why *not?* What can I do about it?" (p. 157). Sandra Lee Bartky places a Marxist spin on the politics of desire, noting that girls lose control of the production of their own self-image, ceding it to those who are "neither innocent nor benevolent . . . In sum, women experience a twofold alienation in the production of our own persons: The beings we are to be are mere bodily beings; nor can we control the shape and nature these bodies

are to take." *Femininity and Domination: Studies in the Phenomenology of Oppression,* New York: Routledge, 1990, p. 42.

17. Robert Coles and Geoffrey Stokes, *Sex and the American Teenager,* New York: Harper Colophon Books, 1985, p. 73.

18. Robert Selverstone, "Adolescent Sexuality: Developing Self-Esteem and Mastering Developmental Tasks," *SIECUS Report,* 18, 1 (1989), pp. 1–3. Selverstone writes that increased difficulty in feeling capable places a greater emphasis on the need to feel lovable for all teenagers.

19. Twenty-one percent of girls cited an aspect of their appearance as "the thing I like most about myself," compared with 12 percent of boys. In addition to feeling more confident in their talents, half of boys strongly agreed that they were "pretty good at a lot of things," compared with less than a third of girls. Boys' confidence in their abilities seems to cushion their uneasiness about any changes in their appearance at adolescence, but the centrality of appearance to girls' self-esteem—and in particular to white girls' self-esteem—magnifies their anxieties. American Association of University Women, *Shortchanging Girls, Shortchanging America: Executive Summary,* Washington, DC: American Association of University Women, 1991, pp. 6, 7; American Association of University Women, *Shortchanging Girls, Shortchanging America: Full Data Report,* Washington, DC: American Association of University Women, 1990, pp. 47, 48.

20. Roberta Simmons and Dale Blyth, *Moving into Adolescence: The Impact of Pubertal Change and School Context,* Hawthorne, NY: Aldine de Gruyter Press, 1987, p. 95.

21. For a comprehensive discussion of girls and dating abuse, see Barrie Levy, ed., *Dating Violence: Young Women in Danger.* Seattle, WA: Seal Press, 1991. See also Fern Shen, "Dating Turns Violent for Teens," San Francisco *Chronicle,* reprinted from Washington *Post,* August 17, 1993, p. E1.

4
Confronting Vulnerability
■

1. Nancy Chodorow, *The Reproduction of Mothering: Psychoanalysis and the Sociology of Gender,* Berkeley, CA: University of California Press, 1978. Jean Baker Miller, *Toward a New Psychology of Women,* 2nd ed., Boston: Beacon Press, 1986. Carol Gilligan, *In a Different Voice: Psychological Theory and Women's Development,* Cambridge, MA: Harvard University Press, 1982.

2. Chodorow, *The Reproduction of Mothering.* Chodorow's work is neatly summarized by Carol Tavris in *The Mismeasure of Woman: Why Women Are Not the Better Sex, the Inferior Sex, or the Opposite Sex,* New York: Simon & Schuster, 1992, pp. 80–81.

3. Chodorow, *The Reproduction of Mothering,* p. 4.

4. Carol Tavris, *The Mismeasure of Woman,* pp. 89–90. Moreover, in her clinical work on culturally based gender differences, Sandra Lipsitz Bem has found that traditional femininity does not, in fact, correlate with empathy. Women who, according to her sex-role inventory, were considered "feminine women" were no more likely to be nurturing toward a baby than "androgynous" women and men or "feminine" men, and they were significantly less likely than those other groups to be responsive to a kitten. Sandra Lipsitz Bem, "Probing the Promise of Androgyny," in *Beyond Sex Role Stereotypes,* Alexandra G. Kaplan and Joan B. Bean, eds., Boston: Little, Brown, 1976, pp. 54–56.

5. Carol Tavris, *The Mismeasure of Woman,* p. 65. Tavris cites Sara E. Snodgrass, "Women's Intuition: The Effect of Subordinate Role on Interpersonal Sensitivity," *Journal of Personality and Social Psychology,* 49 (1985): pp. 146–55.

6. Girls, in general, are more vulnerable than boys to intimate involvement in their mother's problems, particularly those regarding family troubles. Susan Gore, Robert Aseltine, and Mary Ellen Colten, "Gen-

der, Social Relational Involvement, and Depression," *Journal of Research on Adolescence,* 3 (1993): pp. 101–25, quoted in Debra L. Schultz, *Risk, Resiliency, and Resistance: Current Research on Adolescent Girls,* New York: Ms. Foundation for Women National Girls Initiative, 1991, p. 3.

7. Wardell Pomeroy, *Girls and Sex,* 3rd ed., New York: Laurel Leaf Books, 1991, pp. 50–51. Although he advocates a positive, healthy attitude toward sexual experimentation and female desire, Dr. Pomeroy dismisses the threat of advances by older males much too blithely. In addition to saying that "half-joking sexual advances from a girlfriend's father may or may not" be degrading or dangerous, he encourages girls to believe they are responsible for inciting adult men (and, presumably, deserve what they get). "Girls are often embarrassed or bewildered about how to handle these situations," he writes, discussing sexual advances made by the father of a child for whom a girl is babysitting, or the unwanted attention of a "loving uncle." "Most likely they'll feel threatened or uncomfortable, at least, particularly since they've neither invited nor expected the advances. *Or so they honestly believe* [emphasis mine]. Yet sometimes a flirtatious girl, full of herself and conscious of her sexual attractiveness, may encourage a man without realizing she's done it. . . . Afterward she'll be much more careful not to let herself be put in such a situation again" (pp. 51–52).

8. By adolescence, masculinity is associated with turning aggression outward while femininity is associated with turning aggression against the self. Girls in distress, then, are most likely to engage in behaviors that are self-destructive rather than destructive toward others. David B. Levit, "Gender Differences in Ego Defenses in Adolescence: Sex Roles as One Way to Understand the Differences," *Journal of Personality and Social Psychology,* 61, 6 (1991): p. 995; Minnesota Women's Fund with the assistance of National Adolescent Health Resource Center, *Reflections of Risk: Growing Up Female in Minnesota,* Minneapolis: Minnesota Women's Fund, 1990, pp. 10, 49.

9. Teenage girls are four to five times more likely than boys to attempt suicide (although, since boys choose more lethal methods, they are

more likely to die). Both adolescent girls and adult women report higher rates of clinical depression than males. The American Association of University Women Educational Foundation, *The AAUW Report: How Schools Shortchange Girls,* Washington, DC: The AAUW Educational Foundation and National Education Association, 1992, p. 79.

5

Bodily Harm

■

1. Joan Jacobs Brumberg, *Fasting Girls: The Emergence of Anorexia Nervosa as a Modern Disease,* Cambridge, MA: Harvard University Press, 1988, pp. 35–37.

2. Boys account for just a small percentage of eating disorders. Eating disorders are also relatively rare in African American and Latina girls, although the stereotype of the affliction as white and upper-middle-class may conspire against detection in girls of color. Lynn Jaffee, "Pivotal Years: Health and Self-Esteem Issues for Adolescent Girls," in *Today's Girls, Tomorrow's Leaders: Symposium Proceedings,* New York: Girl Scouts of the U.S.A. and American Association of University Women, 1991, pp. 72–73; Margaret B. Balentine, Kathleen R. Stitt, Judith Bonner, and Louise J. Clark, "Weight Perceptions and Dietary Practices of Black, Low-Income Adolescents," *School Food Service Research Review,* 14, 2 (1990): pp. 103–7; L. K. George Hsu, "Are Eating Disorders Becoming More Common in Blacks?" *International Journal of Eating Disorders,* 6, 1 (1987): pp. 113–24; Tomas J. Silber, "Anorexia Nervosa in Blacks and Hispanics," *International Journal of Eating Disorders,* 5, 1 (1986): pp. 121–28.

3. Joan Jacobs Brumberg, quoted in Jane E. Brody, "Personal Health," New York *Times,* May 19, 1988, p. B14; Deborah L. Tolman and Elizabeth Debold, "Conflicts of Body and Image: Female Adolescents, Desire, and the No-Body Body," in *Feminist Perspectives on Eating Disorders,* Patricia Fallan, Melanie Katzman, and Susan Wooley, eds., New York: Guilford Press, 1994, p. 302.

4. Richard Cendo, "Eating Disorders Rise in Adolescents," New York *Times*, April 17, 1988, Section 12CN, p. 4. Cendo also notes that, in 1988, girls under fifteen comprised 37 percent of the patients at the Wilkins Center for Eating Disorders in Greenwich, Connecticut, and at the Silver Hill Hospital in New Canaan, the number of eating disorder patients between ages fourteen and eighteen "has exploded."

5. Jean Seligmann, "The Littlest Dieters," *Newsweek,* July 27, 1987, p. 48. Girls as young as seven have adopted prevailing adult perceptions of beauty, including an unnatural standard of thinness. "Girls, at 7, Think Thin, Study Finds," New York *Times,* February 11, 1988, p. B9. The article reports that nearly half of the 271 young girls involved in a Canadian survey believed they were overweight, although nearly 90 percent were not.

6. Tolman and Debold, "Conflicts of Body and Image," p. 302; Minnesota Women's Fund with the assistance of National Adolescent Health Resource Center, *Reflections of Risk: Growing Up Female in Minnesota,* Minneapolis: Minnesota Women's Fund, 1990, pp. 12, 38.

7. Jaffee, "Pivotal Years," p. 74.

8. Minnesota Women's Fund, *Reflections of Risk.* This study of 36,000 students across Minnesota found that girls with negative body images are three times more likely than similar boys to say they feel badly about themselves, and more likely to believe that others see them in a negative light. Further, while negative body image is associated very strongly with suicide risk for girls, it is not for boys (pp. 12, 38). *Shortchanging Girls, Shortchanging America* found that while both boys and girls perceive the changes that boys go through at adolescence as positive, girls see the changes in themselves as negative. Both in the AAUW's focus groups and my own, girls had an easy time identifying the disadvantages of being a girl, but difficulty describing the advantages. They also found it easy to describe the benefits of being a boy. American Association of University Women, *Shortchanging Girls, Shortchanging America: Executive Summary,* Washington, DC: American Association of University Women, 1991, p. 7.

9. Simone de Beauvoir, *The Second Sex,* translated and edited by H. M. Parshley with an introduction by Deirdre Bair, New York: Alfred A. Knopf, 1952; reprint, New York: Vintage Books, 1989, p. 48.

10. Anaïs Nin, *The Diary of Anaïs Nin,* Vol. II, New York: Harcourt Brace Jovanovich, 1967, quoted in Bernice Lott, *Becoming a Woman: The Socialization of Gender,* Springfield, IL: Charles C Thomas, 1981.

11. For more on the conflict between traditional and contemporary notions of femininity, see Kim Chernin, *The Hungry Self: Women, Eating & Identity,* New York: Perennial Library, 1986; and Naomi Wolf, *The Beauty Myth,* New York: William Morrow and Co., 1991, pp. 179–217.

12. Jane E. Brody, "Personal Health," p. B14; Brumberg, *Fasting Girls,* p. 268. For a clinical account of the interrelationship among self-esteem, appearance, perfectionism, and the current epidemic of eating disorders in girls, see Paul E. Garfinkel and David M. Garner, *Anorexia Nervosa: A Multidimensional Perspective,* New York: Brunner/Mazel Publishers, 1982.

13. See Tolmann and Debold, "Conflicts of Body and Image," pp. 301–17.

14. Jaffee cites a study which found that 51.9 percent of non-obese high school girls went to college as opposed to 31.6 percent of girls who were clinically obese. "Pivotal Years," p. 72.

15. John Schwartz, "Obesity Affects Economic, Social Status: Women Fare Worse, 7 Year Study Shows," Washington *Post,* September 30, 1993, p. A1. The article reports on a Harvard School of Public Health study which found that severely overweight women were 20 percent less likely to get married and earned an average of $6,170 a year less than their slimmer counterparts. Overweight men were 11 percent less likely to be married than thinner men, but did not suffer significant economic consequences.

16. Susie Orbach, *Fat Is a Feminist Issue: The Anti-Diet Guide to Permanent Weight Loss,* New York: Paddington Press, 1977, pp. 42–43, 84–85.

17. R. Favazza and K. Conterio, "Female Habitual Self-Mutilators," *Acta Psychiatrica Scandinavica*, 78 (1986): p. 5. Armando R. Favazza, Lori DeRosear, and Karen Conterio, "Self-Mutilation and Eating Disorders," *Suicide and Life Threatening Behavior*, 19, 4 (1989): pp. 352–61. The authors found that self-mutilation typically begins at around age fourteen and about two-thirds of mutilators are female. Just as there is some historical context for female starvation (see Brumberg's *Fasting Girls)*, Favazza and Conterio believe that there is an archetypal backdrop for self-mutilation. Although few of the women in their study had known or read of self-mutilation before practicing it, "the majority of significant, culturally sanctioned mutilative rituals involve children and adolescents, such as initiation rites, scarification, female infibulation. These rituals facilitate acceptance by the adult world, establishment of social identity, and control of sexuality. From this perspective, deviant self-mutilative behavior may represent a culturally embedded phenomenon that addresses the major developmental tasks of adolescence." "Female Habitual Self-Mutilators," p. 6.

18. Favazza and Conterio, "Female Habitual Self-Mutilators," p. 6.

6
Striking Back
■

1. Nan D. Stein, "Sexual Harassment in Schools," *The School Administrator,* January 1993, p. 15. According to Stein, formerly the sex equity/civil rights specialist with the Massachusetts Department of Education, students are also protected from sexual harassment by Title VII of the Civil Rights Act, the Fourteenth Amendment to the Constitution, and numerous state criminal and civil statutes.

2. A 1989 study found that three-quarters of all high schools violate Title IX. Susan Faludi, *Backlash: The Undeclared War Against American Women,* New York: Crown Publishers, 1991, p. xiv.

3. *Franklin* v. *Gwinnett County Public Schools.* Christine Franklin claimed she had been subjected to continual sexual harassment since

tenth grade by her economics teacher, Andrew Hill. She said that, initially, Hill had made a number of sexually oriented comments to her, phoned her at home, and forcibly kissed her in the school parking lot; during her junior year he allegedly forced her to have sex with him in his office. Franklin informed the principal of the sexual assault, but the school dropped its investigation when Hill agreed to resign. Franklin subsequently filed her suit against the district, claiming her school had violated Title IX.

4. Millicent Lawton, "Sexual Harassment of Students Target of District Policies," *Education Week,* February 10, 1993, p. 1.

5. The following is the definition of sexual harassment according to the Equal Employment Opportunity Commission, modified by the Minnesota Human Rights Act to apply to educational institutions:

"Sexual harassment consists of sexual advances, requests for sexual favors, and other inappropriate verbal or physical conduct of a sexual nature (student to student; employee to student or vice versa) when: 1) submission to such conduct is made either explicitly or implicitly a term or condition of an individual's employment or education, or when 2) submission to or rejection of such conduct by an individual is used as the basis for academic or employment decisions affecting that individual, or when 3) such conduct has the purpose or effect of substantially interfering with an individual's academic or professional performance or 4) creating an intimidating, hostile, or offensive employment or educational environment."

6. The American Association of University Women Educational Foundation, *Hostile Hallways: The AAUW Survey on Sexual Harassment in America's Schools,* researched by Harris/Scholastic Research, a division of Louis Harris and Associates, Inc., in partnership with Scholastic, Inc., Washington, DC: American Association of University Women, 1993, p. 12. The report found that classrooms were second only to hallways as a venue for harassment. More than half the students surveyed had been harassed during class. In *Secrets in Public: Sexual Harassment in Our Schools,* Wellesley, MA: NOW Legal Defense and Education Fund and Wellesley College Center for Research

on Women, 1993. Nan Stein, Nancy L. Marshall, and Linda R. Tropp found the classroom to be the most likely single place for harassment to occur (p. 7).

7. Nan Stein, personal interview, June 16, 1993. Minnesota, the first state to enact legislation against sexual harassment in schools in 1989, requires every school to develop a process for discussing the policy with students and employees. The state has also generated a model curriculum, [Susan Strauss] *Sexual Harassment to Teenagers: It's Not Fun/It's Illegal, A Curriculum for Identification and Prevention of Sexual Harassment for Use with Junior and Senior High School Students,* St. Paul, MN: Minnesota Department of Education Equal Educational Opportunities Section, 1988. Individual schools, such as Minuteman Tech and Amherst Regional High School—both in Massachusetts—have also developed sexual harassment policies that are educational rather than merely disciplinary. Both schools place a premium on mediation between students, allowing the harassee to maintain a sense of control over the proceedings.

7
"You People Are Animals"
■

1. Socioeconomic status remains the best predictor of educational outcome. The American Association of University Women Educational Foundation, *The AAUW Report: How Schools Shortchange Girls,* Washington, DC: The AAUW Educational Foundation and National Educational Association, 1992, pp. 34–35.

2. In addition, at Audubon there is a higher proportion of white students in the honors program than in any other eighth-grade class. Teachers often do not see giftedness in minority children or children with limited English-language skills. Claude Steele, "Race and the Schooling of Black Americans," *The Atlantic Monthly,* April 1992, p. 72; Denise De La Rosa and Carlyle E. Maw, *Hispanic Education: A Statistical Portrait, 1990,* Washington, DC: National Council of La Raza, 1990, p. 19.

3. The AAUW Educational Foundation, *The AAUW Report,* pp. 34–35. Although in low-income urban schools black girls perform better than their male classmates, when they attend desegregated schools in more affluent communities, both groups tend to follow the achievement patterns of whites, with boys scoring significantly better than girls in both standardized reading and math tests in middle school as well as high school.

4. In its survey of sexual harassment in public schools, the American Association of University Women found that patterns of abuse differed across racial and ethnic lines. According to the report, African American girls were more likely than Latina or white girls to have been pinched, touched, or grabbed in a sexual way in school. African American girls were also most likely to say that harassment has caused them emotional harm and impaired their ability to achieve. However, the survey also found that African American boys experience higher rates of physical harassment than Latino or white boys, although the experience affects them less profoundly than it does African American girls. The American Association of University Women Educational Foundation, *Hostile Hallways: The AAUW Survey on Sexual Harassment in America's Schools,* researched by Harris/Scholastic Research, a division of Louis Harris and Associates, Inc. in partnership with Scholastic, Inc., Washington, DC: American Association of University Women, 1993, pp. 22–25.

5. As at Weston, the most damning slur used against boys was "fag," which, like "girl," "bitch," or "ho'," has connotations of sexual powerlessness and femininity. According to American Association of University Women, being called "gay" provokes a stronger negative reaction among boys than any other type of harassment, including actual physical abuse. The AAUW Educational Foundation, *Hostile Hallways,* pp. 19–20.

8
Split Loyalties
■

1. Based on the percentage of girls who answered "always true" in response to the statement "I'm happy the way I am." As with whites and Latinos, however, black boys still report stronger self-esteem than black girls, leading them by 18 percent on measures of general happiness and confidence in their ability to do things and 17 percentage points in their satisfaction with their appearance. American Association of University Women, *Shortchanging Girls, Shortchanging America: Full Data Report,* Washington, DC: American Association of University Women, 1990, pp. 19–22. The AAUW results may seem counterintuitive, especially to white readers, but they are not without precedent. In 1971, psychologist Morris Rosenberg was the first to propose that African American children had higher self-esteem than— or at least equivalent self-esteem to—whites. Since then, numerous other studies have confirmed Rosenberg's finding. Morris Rosenberg and Roberta Simmons, *Black and White Self-Esteem: The Urban School Child,* Washington, DC: American Sociological Association, Arnold and Caroline Rose Monograph Series, 1971; Rubén Martínez and Richard L. Dukes, "Ethnic and Gender Differences in Self-Esteem." *Youth & Society,* 22, 3 (1991): pp. 318–38; Rubén Martínez and Richard L. Dukes, "Race, Gender and Self-Esteem among Youth," *Hispanic Journal of Behavioral Sciences,* 9, 4 (1987): pp. 427–43; William E. Cross, "Black Identity: Rediscovering the Distinction Between Personal Identity and Reference Group Orientation," in *Beginnings: The Social and Affective Development of Black Children,* Margaret Beale Spencer, Geraldine Kearse Brookins, and Walter Recharde Allen, eds., Hillsdale, NJ: Lawrence Erlbaum Associates, 1985; Charles L. Richman, M. L. Clark, and Kathryn P. Brown, "General and Specific Self-Esteem in Late Adolescent Students: Race × Gender × SES Effects," *Adolescence,* 20, 79 (1985): pp. 555—66; Jewelle Taylor Gibbs, "City Girls: Psychosocial Adjustment of Urban Black Adolescent Females," *SAGE,* 2, 2 (1985): pp. 28–36; Elsie J. Smith, "The

Black Female Adolescent: A Review of the Educational, Career, and Psychological Literature," *Psychology of Women Quarterly* 6, 3 (1982): pp. 261–88; and Hariette Pipes McAdoo, "The Development of Self Concept and Race Attitudes of Young Black Children over Time," paper presented at Cornell University Conference on Empirical Research in Black Psychology III, October 29, 1976.

2. Mary Williams Burgher, "Images of Self and Race in the Autobiographies of Black Women," in *Sturdy Black Bridges: Visions of Black Women in Literature,* Roseann P. Bell, Bettye J. Parker, and Beverly Guy-Sheftall, eds., New York: Anchor Books, 1979, pp. 107–22. Burgher points out that black women's strong sense of self has been evident since slavery, not only in the narratives of cultural icons such as Harriet Tubman and Sojourner Truth, but in the surviving memoirs of ordinary women. Henry Louis Gates notes that, unlike the European American literary tradition in which memoirs tend to be written late in an author's career, African-American writers' *first* book tends to be an autobiography. The assertion of self is both an act of defiance and a celebration of resilience: as Gates says, the black writer's motto could very well be: "I write my self, therefore I am." Henry Louis Gates, Jr., ed., *Bearing Witness: Selections from African-American Autobiography in the Twentieth Century,* New York: Pantheon Books, 1991, p. 7.

3. Patricia Spacks, "Selves in Hiding," in *Women's Autobiography,* Estelle C. Jelinek, ed., Bloomington: Indiana University Press, 1980, pp. 112–32, quoted in Carolyn G. Heilbrun, *Writing a Woman's Life,* New York: W. W. Norton & Company, 1988, p. 23. In comparing the autobiographies of such twentieth-century heroes as Eleanor Roosevelt, Emmeline Pankhurst, Dorothy Day, Emma Goldman, and Golda Meir, Spacks writes: "Although each author has significant, sometimes dazzling accomplishments to her credit, the theme of accomplishment rarely dominates the narrative. . . . Indeed to a striking degree they fail directly to emphasize their *own* importance, though writing in a genre which implies self-assertion and self-display." Heilbrun goes on to note: "These women accept full blame for any failures in their lives, but shrink from claiming that they either sought the responsibilities they ultimately bore or were in any way ambitious" (p. 23).

4. In *Shortchanging Girls, Shortchanging America,* African American girls' sense of pride in their schoolwork plummets 43 percentage points between elementary and high school. Meanwhile, their belief that their teachers are proud of them fell 38 points—by high school only 12 percent of black girls reacted positively to that statement. It should be noted that this drop is among girls who have, in spite of their low confidence, remained in school. AAUW, *Full Data Report,* pp. 37–38. This jibes with an earlier analysis of the Rosenberg-Simmons data, in which sociologists Janet G. Hunt and Larry L. Hunt found that "embracement of roles linked with school" enhanced white children's self-esteem and efficacy. For African American students, however, distance from roles linked with school was associated with those traits. Hunt and Hunt also note that the higher self-esteem among black children relative to whites is present at all economic levels, and lower efficacy is found at every level except one: underclass black children report slightly higher efficacy than their white counterparts. "Racial Inequality and Self-Image: Identity Maintenance as Identity Diffusion," *Sociology and Social Research,* 61, 4 (1977): pp. 550, 557. See also, Signithia Fordham and John U. Ogbu, "Black Students' School Success: Coping with the Burden of 'Acting White,' " *The Urban Review,* 18, 3 (1986): pp. 176–206.

5. Martínez and Dukes, "Ethnic and Gender Differences in Self-Esteem"; Martínez and Dukes, "Race, Gender and Self-Esteem among Youth." In their study of seventh- through twelfth-grade students in the Pikes Peak region, Martínez and Dukes found that both African Americans and Chicanos have lower levels of self-esteem than whites in the public domain (which they define as "intelligence") but they have higher levels in the private domain (which they define as "satisfaction with self"). The notion of a dual self-esteem among African Americans is not new, but echoes the "double consciousness" W. E. B. Du Bois discussed in his classic work *The Souls of Black Folk,* A. C. McClurg and Company, Chicago: 1903; reprint, New York, Bantam Classics, 1989.

6. In "Race and the Schooling of Black Americans," *The Atlantic Monthly,* April 1992, psychologist Claude M. Steele reports that at

every level of preparation black students' achievement is depressed relative to whites: by sixth grade, black students in many school districts are two grade levels behind their white peers in achievement; in high school they leave school or achieve below grade level at greater rates; in college, 70 percent of black students drop out compared with 45 percent of whites. These deficits occur, Steele says, even when black students are from middle-class families and are not at financial disadvantage. In fact, he notes, class does not act as an insulator against dropping out for blacks in the way that it does for whites. Meanwhile, black students are also more than twice as likely as whites to receive corporal punishment, be suspended, or be labeled mentally disabled. Steele concludes that black students make two discouraging realizations early on in their education which undercut their success: first, that white society (as represented by their teachers) is predisposed to see the worst in them, making recognition of achievement difficult. And second, even if they are acknowledged in one classroom, approval will have to be won anew in the next (p. 68).

7. Fordham and Ogbu, "Black Students' School Success," pp. 176–206; Signithia Fordham, "Racelessness as a Factor in Black Students' School Success: Pragmatic Strategy or Pyrrhic Victory?" *Harvard Educational Review*, 58, 1 (1988): pp. 54–84. The pressure to see mainstream success as a betrayal of one's essential "blackness"—which, Fordham and Ogbu write, is defined by mannerisms, behaviors, and opinions endorsed by a community, rather than by skin color—affects children at all class levels, as well as black adults who have transcended poverty. John Edgar Wideman, for instance, writes about the gulf that has developed between himself and his youngest brother, who remained in the Pittsburgh ghetto where they were raised and was eventually convicted of first-degree murder. ". . . I felt uncomfortable around you. Most of what I felt was guilt. I'd made my choices. I was running away from Pittsburgh, from poverty, from blackness." *Brothers and Keepers,* New York: Penguin Books, 1984, pp. 26–27. See also, Claude M. Steele, "Race and the Schooling of Black Americans," pp. 74–75.

8. Forty-nine percent of all African American teenagers live in single-parent homes, compared with 20 percent of white teens and 30 per-

cent of Latinos. Janet M. Simons, Belva Finlay, and Alice Yang, *The Adolescent & Young Adult Fact Book,* Washington, DC: Children's Defense Fund, 1991, p. 51.

9. In their analysis of the reasons low-income girls leave school, Michelle Fine and Nancie Zane found that 37 percent of female dropouts select "family-related problems" (excluding pregnancy and marriage), versus 5 percent of males. They conclude that "family complexity strains adolescent females and interrupts their educational careers far more dramatically than is true for young men." "Bein' Wrapped Too Tight: When Low-Income Women Drop Out of High School," in *Dropouts from Schools: Issues, Dilemmas and Solutions,* Lois Weis, Eleanor Farrar, and Hugh G. Petrie, eds., Albany, NY: SUNY Press, 1989, p. 27.

10. Similarly, early pregnancy and motherhood can be a strategy for attaining and maintaining feelings of efficacy. Michelle Fine has written that "having a baby at least offers a full-time job and a sense of purpose and competence." "Why Urban Adolescents Drop Into and Out of Public High School," *Teachers College Record,* 87, 3 (1986): p. 339.

11. Other school districts have discovered that the tutoring of younger students can build both academic confidence and engagement among middle school students. Eighth graders who have acted as paid tutors in the decade-old Valued Youth Program (VYP) in San Antonio and McAllen, Texas, have raised their grades and developed better attitudes toward school than similar students not involved in the program. VYP has been especially effective in keeping high-risk students in school. Simons, Finlay, and Yang. *The Adolescent & Young Adult Fact Book,* pp. 18–19.

9
"I Choose Not to Go down That Path"
■

1. Michelle Fine and Nancie Zane, "Bein' Wrapped Too Tight: When Low-Income Women Drop Out of High School," in *Dropouts from Schools: Issues, Dilemmas and Solutions,* Lois Weis, Eleanor Farrar, and Hugh G. Petrie, eds., Albany, NY: SUNY Press, 1989, p. 29, cited in The American Association of University Women Educational Foundation, *The AAUW Report: How Schools Shortchange Girls.* Washington, DC: The AAUW Educational Foundation and National Educational Association, 1992, p. 49. Fine and Zane found that, in one New York City school, 92 percent of the girls—but only 22 percent of the boys—linked their decision to leave school to having been held back.

2. The AAUW Educational Foundation, *The AAUW Report,* p. 70. In her study of first graders, Linda Grant found that black girls initiated a significant amount of contact with teachers early in the school year, but after being continually rejected, they gave up. "Race-Gender Status, Classroom Interaction and Children's Socialization in Elementary School," in *Gender Influences in Classroom Interaction,* Louise Cherry Wilkinson and Cora B. Marrett, eds., Orlando, FL: Academic Press, 1985, p. 69.

3. Linda Grant, "Black Females' Place in Desegregated Classrooms," *Sociology of Education,* April 1984, pp. 98–110.

4. Further, Grant found that black girls were the sole victims of racist remarks in desegregated classrooms. With one exception, the epithets were hurled by low-achieving white boys who were trying to reassert dominance after a teacher complimented a black girl on her schoolwork. "Black Females' Place," p. 109.

5. Many of the black girls in *Shortchanging Girls, Shortchanging America* report stronger feelings of isolation than other children, with two-thirds saying that others "don't know the real me." American Association of University Women, *Shortchanging Girls, Shortchanging*

America: Full Data Report, Washington, DC: American Association of University Women, 1990, pp. 22, 39. See also Diane Scott-Jones and Maxine L. Clark, "The School Experience of Black Girls: The Interaction of Gender, Race, and Socioeconomic Status," *Phi Delta Kappan,* 67, 7 (1986): p. 525; Elsie J. Smith, "The Black Female Adolescent: A Review of the Educational, Career and Psychological Literature," *Psychology of Women Quarterly,* 6, 3 (1982): p. 288; and, for a first-person account of a black girl's experience in a New England preparatory school, Lorene Cary, *Black Ice,* New York, Alfred A. Knopf, 1991.

6. See Beverly Jean Smith, "I Don't Hold My Tongue," paper presented at the annual meeting of the American Psychological Association, Toronto, Ontario, August 1993.

7. AAUW, *Full Data Report,* p. 22. In her study of urban high school students, Michelle Fine found that it is often the most assertive girls who leave school and that "a moderate level of depression, an absence of political awareness, persistent self-blame, low assertiveness and high conformity may tragically have constituted the 'good' urban student at this high school . . . The price of academic 'success' may have been the muting of one's own voice." *Reframing Dropouts,* Albany, NY: SUNY Albany Press, 1991, p. 37.

8. Tracy Robinson and Janie Victoria Ward, " 'A Belief in Self Far Greater than Anyone's Disbelief': Cultivating Resistance among African American Female Adolescents," in *Women, Girls & Psychotherapy: Reframing Resistance,* Carol Gilligan, Annie G. Rogers, and Deborah L. Tolman, eds., New York: The Haworth Press, 1991, pp. 87–103.

9. Among the "quick fix" strategies some girls employ are pregnancy, substance abuse, and overeating. Robinson and Ward note that black girls' pregnancy rates are still double that of white girls, heroin and cocaine use are disproportionately prevalent, and, during the past two decades, obesity has increased 53 percent among African American teenagers. Robinson and Ward, " 'A Belief in Self Far Greater than Anyone's Disbelief,' " p. 95.

10. Robinson and Ward's "resistance for liberation" includes ongoing analysis of the effects of racism on "the economics, culture, family, psyche and spirit of African Americans" as well as extensive study of black women's history and African culture. They suggest that African American girls should be encouraged to adopt the seven principles of the Nguzo Saba, a value system based on traditional African philosophies: unity, self-determination, collective work and responsibility, cooperative economics, purpose, creativity, and faith. " 'A Belief in Self Far Greater than Anyone's Disbelief,' " pp. 97–98.

10
Slipping Away
■

1. American Association of University Women, *Shortchanging Girls, Shortchanging America: Executive Summary,* Washington, DC: American Association of University Women, 1991, pp. 8–9. The sample used by AAUW was primarily Mexican American and may not apply as readily to other Latino subgroups. However, two-thirds of the Latino population in the United States is Mexican American. Further, 90 percent of that group lives in urban areas and, overall, Latino children live in poverty at a rate of nearly 40 percent. Denise De La Rosa and Carlyle E. Maw, *Hispanic Education: A Statistical Portrait, 1990,* Washington, DC: National Council of La Raza, 1990, pp. 6–13.

2. AAUW, *Executive Summary,* pp. 8–9. Minnesota Women's Fund with the assistance of the National Adolescent Health Resource Center, *Reflections of Risk: Growing Up Female in Minnesota,* Minneapolis: Minnesota Women's Fund, 1990, pp. 24, 26, 34, 38, 40, 42. The Minnesota survey found that girls in general were one and a half to two times more likely to feel under emotional stress than boys, with Latina girls feeling the most anxious, followed by white, Asian, and African American girls. Native American girls reported stress rates similar to those of African Americans.

3. Sonia M. Pérez with Luis A. Duany, *Reducing Hispanic Teenage Pregnancy and Family Poverty: A Replication Guide,* Washington,

DC: National Council of La Raza, 1992, p. 9. Pérez notes that, while African American girls' birth rates are slightly higher than Latinas', black teenage mothers are more than twice as likely to eventually complete high school.

4. De La Rosa and Maw, *Hispanic Education,* pp. 18–19, 45, 51, 61. Latina girls are less likely than boys to repeat a grade, but when they do, the retention seems to come as a harsher blow, and they become more likely than boys to repeat two or more grades.

5. U.S. Bureau of the Census, *Educational Attainment in the United States: March 1991 and 1990,* Washington, DC: U.S. Government Printing Office, 1992, pp. 29–35, 68–76. In highly urbanized areas, 56 percent of Latinas leave school before graduation. When smaller cities and rural areas are factored in, boys' dropout rates exceed girls' by less than one-tenth of a percentage point. In spite of this, the myth that "dropping out" is a male-only phenomenon persists and solutions are considered accordingly. In fact, although boys and girls leave school for different reasons, the actual differential in numbers between male and female dropouts of all races and ethnicities is negligible.

6. Although teachers often believe that Latino parents hold low educational aspirations for their daughters, they are, in truth, more likely than Caucasians to want their daughters to attend college, and Latina mothers tend to hold higher educational ambitions for their daughters than they do for their sons. Latina mothers are a decisive motivating factor in their daughters' pursuit of higher education, a correlation stronger for Latinas than for either white or African American girls. Because of this, programs for Latina girls that include their mothers, such as the Mother-Daughter Program developed by the University of Texas at El Paso, have been especially successful in raising the educational attainment rates of Latina girls. Josefina Villamil Tinajero, Maria Luisa Gonzalez, and Florence Dick, *Raising Career Aspirations of Hispanic Girls,* Bloomington, IN: Phi Delta Kappa Educational Foundation, 1991; "Facts and Figures on Hispanic Americans, Women, and Education," in *The Broken Web: The Educational Experience of Hispanic American Women,* Teresa McKenna and Flora Ida Ortiz, eds., Berkeley, CA: Floricanto Press, 1988, pp. 195–209.

7. Although estimates are sketchy at best, newspaper reports have claimed that girls make up 10 percent of gang members nationwide, including some who are in all-girl gangs. Yasmin Anwar, "Female Gangs Fighting for Respect," Oakland *Tribune,* August 15, 1993, p. A1.

8. That same year in San Francisco, the practice expanded beyond a "consensual" initiation, when eight Latino gang members were arrested for allegedly orally, vaginally, and anally raping two fourteen-year-old girls. Twelve other young men are suspected of participating in the attack. Thaai Walker, "Gang Members Charged in Rapes of 2 Girls," San Francisco *Chronicle,* December 15, 1993, p. A23. From the late 1970s to the late 1980s, the FBI reported nearly a 65 percent increase in the arrest rates for attempted rape, assault with the intent to rape, and forcible rape among boys under the age of twelve and more than a 70 percent increase among thirteen- to fourteen-year-old boys. The statistics do not reveal who the boys attacked, but it is likely that their victims were near their own age. Denise A. Alston, "Girls in Society," in *Today's Girls, Tomorrow's Leaders: Symposium Proceedings,* New York: Girl Scouts of the U.S.A. and the American Association of University Women, 1991, p. 62.

11

Rising Above

■

1. Claudia Tate, ed., *Black Women Writers at Work,* New York: Continuum, 1983, quoted in Carolyn G. Heilbrun, *Writing a Woman's Life,* New York: W. W. Norton & Company, 1988, p. 61. Black women have historically higher rates of labor force participation than white women, combining the roles of mother and worker without the luxury of ambivalence. For a thorough chronicling of African American women's economic history, political and church leadership, as well as their participation in the white women's movement, see Paula Giddings, *When and Where I Enter: The Impact of Black Women on Race and Sex in America,* New York: Bantam Books, 1988; and Te-

resa Amott and Julie Matthaei, *Race, Gender, and Work: A Multicultural Economic History of Women in the United States,* Boston: South End Press, 1991.

2. In high school, 58 percent of black girls strongly agree that "I like the way I look," compared with 12 percent of white girls and 11 percent of Latinas. American Association of University Women, *Shortchanging Girls, Shortchanging America: Full Data Report,* Washington, DC: American Association of University Women, 1990, p. 25. For other comparisons of body image by race, see Minnesota Women's Fund with the assistance of the National Adolescent Health Resource Center, *Reflections of Risk: Growing Up Female in Minnesota,* Minneapolis: Minnesota Women's Fund, 1990, p. 32; Maria P. P. Root, "Disordered Eating in Women of Color," *Sex Roles: A Journal of Research,* 22, 7–8 (1990): p. 527; Margaret B. Balentine, Kathleen R. Stitt, Judith Bonner, and Louise J. Clark, "Weight Perceptions and Dietary Practices of Black, Low-Income Adolescents," *School Food Service Research Review,* 14, 2 (1990): pp. 103–7; and L. K. George Hsu, "Are the Eating Disorders Becoming More Common in Blacks?" *International Journal of Eating Disorders,* 6, 1 (1987): p. 120. For an examination of black and white girls' aspirations, see Jewelle Taylor Gibbs, "City Girls: Psychosocial Adjustment of Urban Black Adolescent Females," SAGE, 2, 2 (1985): pp. 28–36; Elsie J. Smith, "The Black Female Adolescent: A Review of the Educational, Career, and Psychological Literature," *Psychology of Women Quarterly,* 6, 3 (1982), pp. 271–72, 282. Smith notes that although African American boys' expectations of success rise when they are enrolled in schools in higher-income communities, the same is not true for black girls, who may be influenced by the undervaluing of female achievement. Further, white and black girls' motivations for employment as adults are different: young white women often work for self-fulfillment, while young black women are motivated by economic responsibility and a recognition of forces that limit black men in the labor force.

3. That fear is well founded: African American and Latina girls are less likely to use birth control and more likely than their white counterparts to give birth if they become pregnant. Meanwhile, teenage moth-

ers are far less likely than other girls—or than teenage fathers—to obtain a high school degree or its equivalent. The combination of early (and usually single) motherhood and low educational attainment virtually guarantees that a teen mother and her children will live in poverty. Sonia M. Pérez with Luis A. Duany, *Reducing Hispanic Teenage Pregnancy and Family Poverty: A Replication Guide*, Washington, DC: National Council of La Raza, 1992, pp. 4–10; The American Association of University Women Educational Foundation, *The AAUW Report: How Schools Shortchange Girls*, Washington, DC: The AAUW Educational Foundation and National Educational Association, 1992, pp. 37–41; Michelle Fine and Nancie Zane, "Bein' Wrapped Too Tight: When Low-Income Women Drop Out of High School," in *Dropouts from Schools: Issues, Dilemmas and Solutions*, Lois Weis, Eleanor Farrar, and Hugh G. Petrie, eds., Albany, NY: SUNY Press, 1989, pp. 25–27.

12
Anita Hill Is a Boy

■

1. Elizabeth G. Cohen, *Designing Groupwork: Strategies for the Heterogeneous Classroom*, 2nd ed., with a foreword by John J. Goodlad, New York: Teachers College Press, 1994.

2. Marcia C. Linn, "Gender Differences in Educational Achievement," in *Sex Equity in Educational Opportunity, Achievement, and Testing*, Princeton, NJ: Proceedings of the 1991 Invitational Conference of the Educational Testing Service, 1992; "MMAP: Middle-School Mathematics Through Applications Project," Palo Alto, CA: Documentation from the Institute for Research on Learning, 1993.

3. Suzanne Alexander, "New Grade-School Sexuality Classes Go Beyond Birds and Bees to Explicit Basics," *The Wall Street Journal*, April 2, 1993, p. B1; [Susan Strauss], *Sexual Harassment to Teenagers: It's Not Fun/It's Illegal—A Curriculum for Identification and Prevention of Sexual Harassment for Use with Junior and Senior High School*

Students, St. Paul, MN: Minnesota Department of Education Equal Educational Opportunities Section, 1988.

4. Michael Winerip. "Public School Offers a Social-Service Model," New York *Times,* December 8, 1993, p. A1; Michael Winerip, "In School: A Public School in Harlem That Takes the Time, and the Trouble, to Be a Family," New York *Times,* January 26, 1994, p. A19. For more on integrating values of home and community into the school setting, see Jane Roland Martin, *The Schoolhome: Rethinking Schools for Changing Families,* Cambridge, MA: Harvard University Press, 1992.

5. Josefina Villamil Tinajero, Maria Luisa Gonzalez, and Florence Dick, *Raising Career Aspirations of Hispanic Girls,* Bloomington, IN: Phi Delta Kappa Educational Foundation, 1991; "Facts and Figures on Hispanic Americans, Women, and Education," in *The Broken Web: The Educational Experience of Hispanic American Women,* Teresa McKenna and Flora Ida Ortiz, eds., Berkeley, CA: Floricanto Press, 1988, pp. 195–209.

6. Judy Logan, *Teaching Stories,* with a foreword by Peggy McIntosh, St. Paul, MN: Minnesota Inclusiveness Program, 1993, p. x. Logan wrote *Teaching Stories* with the aid of an American Association of University Women Eleanor Roosevelt grant.

7. Di Bentley and Mike Watts, "Courting the Positive Virtues: A Case for Feminist Science," *European Journal of Science Education,* 8 (1986), pp. 121–23. See also Sue Rosser, *Biology & Feminism: A Dynamic Interaction,* New York: Twayne Publishers, 1992; Evelyn Fox Keller, *Reflections on Gender and Science,* New Haven: Yale University Press, 1985; Ruth Bleier, *Science and Gender: A Critique of Biology and Its Theories on Women,* New York: Pergamon Press, 1984; Evelyn Fox Keller, *A Feeling for the Organism: The Life and Work of Barbara McClintock,* San Francisco: W. H. Freeman and Co., 1983.

8. Emily Style, "Curriculum as Window and Mirror," in *Listening for All Voices: Gender Balancing the School Curriculum,* proceedings of a conference held at Oak Knoll School, Summit, NJ, June 1988, p. 6.

9. Peggy McIntosh, "Interactive Phases of Curricular Re-Vision: A Feminist Perspective," Working Paper No. 124, Wellesley, MA: Wellesley College Center for Research on Women, 1983; Peggy McIntosh, "Interactive Phases of Curricular and Personal Re-Vision with Regard to Race," Working Paper No. 219, Wellesley, MA: Wellesley College Center for Research on Women, 1990. McIntosh's phases are meant to be applied across the curriculum.

10. Logan, *Teaching Stories*, p. 44.

11. Jamaica Kincaid, "Girl," in *At the Bottom of the River*, New York: Plume Contemporary Fiction, 1992, p. 3.

Bibliography

■

■

■

Adelman, Clifford. "Women at Thirtysomething: Paradoxes of Attainment." Washington, DC: Office of Educational Research and Improvement, 1991.

Alexander, Suzanne. "New Grade-School Sexuality Classes Go Beyond Birds and Bees to Explicit Basics." *The Wall Street Journal*, April 2, 1993, p. B1.

American Association of University Women. *Shortchanging Girls, Shortchanging America: A Call to Action.* Washington, DC: American Association of University Women, 1991.

———. *Shortchanging Girls, Shortchanging America: Executive Summary.* Washington, DC: American Association of University Women, 1991.

———. "Equitable Treatment of Girls and Boys in the Classroom." *AAUW Equity Brief,* June 1991.

———. *Shortchanging Girls, Shortchanging America: Full Data Report.* Washington, DC: American Association of University Women, 1990.

The American Association of University Women Educational Foundation. *Hostile Hallways: The AAUW Survey on Sexual Harassment in*

America's Schools. Researched by Harris/Scholastic Research, a division of Louis Harris and Associates, Inc., in partnership with Scholastic, Inc. Washington, DC: American Association of University Women, 1993.

————. *The AAUW Report: How Schools Shortchange Girls*. Washington, DC: The AAUW Educational Foundation and National Educational Association, 1992.

Amott, Teresa, and Julie Matthaei. *Race, Gender, and Work: A Multicultural Economic History of Women in the United States*. Boston: South End Press, 1991.

Anwar, Yasmin. "Female Gangs Fighting for Respect." Oakland *Tribune,* August 15, 1993, p. A1.

Anzaldúa, Gloria. "Haciendo Caras, una Entrada." In *Making Face, Making Soul = Haciendo Caras: Creative and Critical Perspectives by Women of Color,* Gloria Anzaldúa, ed. San Francisco: Aunt Lute Foundation, 1990, pp. xv–xxviii.

Apter, Terri. *Altered Loves: Mothers and Daughters During Adolescence*. New York: Fawcett Columbine, 1990.

Balentine, Margaret B., Kathleen R. Stitt, Judith Bonner, and Louise J. Clark. "Weight Perceptions and Dietary Practices of Black, Low-Income Adolescents." *School Food Service Research Review,* 14, 2 (1990): pp. 103–7.

Barnes, Edward J. "The Black Community as the Source of Positive Self-Concept for Black Children: A Theoretical Perspective." In *Black Psychology,* Reginald L. Jones, ed. New York: Harper & Row, 1980, pp. 106–29.

Bartky, Sandra Lee. *Femininity and Domination: Studies in the Phenomenology of Oppression*. New York: Routledge, 1990.

Baruch, Grace, Rosalind Barnett, and Caryl Rivers. *Lifeprints: New Patterns of Love and Work for Today's Women*. New York: Signet Books, 1983.

Belenky, Mary Field, Blythe McVicker Clinchy, Nancy Rule Gold-berger, and Jill Mattuck Tarule. *Women's Ways of Knowing: The Development of Self, Voice and Mind.* New York: Basic Books, 1986.

Bell, Lee Anne. "Something's Wrong Here and It's Not Me: Challenging the Dilemmas That Block Girls' Success." *Journal for the Education of the Gifted,* 12, 2 (1989): pp. 118–30.

Bem, Sandra Lipsitz. "Probing the Promise of Androgyny." In *Beyond Sex Role Stereotypes,* Alexandra G. Kaplan and Joan B. Bean, eds. Boston: Little, Brown, 1976, pp. 48–62.

Bentley, Di, and Mike Watts. "Courting the Positive Virtues: A Case for Feminist Science." *European Journal of Science Education,* 8 (1986): pp. 121–23.

Bigler, Mark O. "The Facts: Adolescent Sexual Behavior in the Eighties." *SIECUS Report,* 18, 1 (1989): pp. 6–9.

Bleier, Ruth. *Science and Gender: A Critique of Biology and Its Theories on Women.* New York: Pergamon Press, 1984.

Bower, Bruce. "Gender Paths Wind Toward Self-Esteem." *Science News,* 143, 20 (1993): p. 308.

Bowman, Phillip J., and Cleopatra Howard. "Race-Related Socialization, Motivation, and Academic Achievement: A Study of Black Youth in Three-Generation Families." *Journal of the American Academy of Child and Adolescent Psychology,* 24, 2 (1985): pp. 134–41. "Boys Predominate in a Contest Fueling Complaint of Test Bias." New York *Times,* May 26, 1993, p. B7.

Brandon, P. R., B. J. Newton, and O. Hammond. "Children's Mathematics Achievement in Hawaii: Sex Differences Favoring Girls." *American Educational Research Journal,* 24, 3 (1987): pp. 437–61.

"The Breakdown for Minorities." *USA Today.* February 16, 1994, p. 4D.

Brody, Jane. "Personal Health." New York *Times.* May 19, 1988, p. B14.

Bibliography

Brown, Lyn Mikel, and Carol Gilligan. "The Psychology of Women and the Development of Girls." Paper presented at the Harvard-Laurel Conference on the Psychology of Women, Cleveland, OH, May 1990.

————. *Meeting at the Crossroads: Women's Psychology and Girls' Development.* Cambridge, MA: Harvard University Press, 1990.

Bruch, Hilde. *The Golden Cage: The Enigma of Anorexia Nervosa.* New York: Vintage Books, 1979.

Brumberg, Joan Jacobs. *Fasting Girls: The Emergence of Anorexia Nervosa as a Modern Disease.* Cambridge, MA: Harvard University Press, 1988.

Burgher, Mary. "Images of Self and Race in the Autobiographies of Black Women." In *Sturdy Black Bridges: Visions of Black Women in Literature,* Roseann P. Bell, Bettye J. Parker, and Beverly Guy-Sheftall, eds. New York: Anchor Books, 1979, pp. 107–22.

Callahan, Carolyn M. "The Gifted Girl: An Anomaly?" *Roeper Review,* 2, 3 (1980): pp. 16–20.

Campbell, Patricia B. "Math, Science and Too Few Girls: Enough Is Known for Action." Documentation developed under the auspices of the Women's Educational Equity Act by Campbell-Kibler Associates, Groton, MA, 1991.

Cary, Lorene. *Black Ice.* New York: Alfred A. Knopf, 1991.

Cendo, Richard. "Eating Disorders Rise in Adolescents." New York *Times,* April 17, 1988, p. 12CN4.

Chernin, Kim. *The Hungry Self: Women, Eating & Identity.* New York: Perennial Library, 1986.

Chodorow, Nancy. *The Reproduction of Mothering: Psychoanalysis and the Sociology of Gender.* Berkeley, CA: University of California Press, 1978.

Cohen, Elizabeth G. *Designing Groupwork: Strategies for the Heterogeneous Classroom.* 2nd ed. with a foreword by John C. Goodlad. New York: Teachers College Press, 1994.

Coles, Robert, and Geoffrey Stokes. *Sex and the American Teenager.* New York: Harper Colophon Books, 1985.

Countryman, Joan. *Writing to Learn Mathematics: Strategies That Work, K-12.* Portsmouth, NH: Heinemann Press, 1992.

Cross, William E. "Black Identity: Rediscovering the Distinction Between Personal Identity and Reference Group Orientation." In *Beginnings: The Social and Affective Development of Black Children,* Margaret Beale Spencer, Geraldine Kearse Brookins, and Walter Recharde Allen, eds. Hillsdale, NJ: Lawrence Erlbaum Associates, 1985.

Daley, Suzanne. "Girls' Self-Esteem is Lost on Way to Adolescence, New Study Finds." New York *Times,* National Edition, January 9, 1991, p. B1.

Damico, Sandra, and Elois Scott. "Behavior Differences Between Black and White Females in Desegregated Schools." *Equity and Excellence,* 23 (1987): pp. 520–26.

de Anda, Diane, Rosina M. Becerra, and Eve P. Fielder. "Sexuality, Pregnancy, and Motherhood among Mexican-American Adolescents." *Journal of Adolescent Research* 3, 3–4 (1988): pp. 403–11.

de Beauvoir, Simone. *The Second Sex.* Translated and edited by H. M. Parshley with an introduction by Deirdre Bair. New York: Alfred A. Knopf, 1952; reprint, New York: Vintage Books, 1989.

De La Rosa, Denise, and Carlyle E. Maw. *Hispanic Education: A Statistical Portrait, 1990.* Washington, DC: National Council of La Raza, 1990.

Eaky, Kenneth. "Girls' Low Self-Esteem Slows Their Progress, Study Finds." San Francisco *Examiner,* January 9, 1991, p. A1.

Eisenhart, Dorothy, and Margaret Holland. *Educated in Romance.* Chicago: University of Chicago Press, 1991.

Faludi, Susan. *Backlash: The Undeclared War Against American Women.* New York: Crown Publishers, 1991.

Favazza, Armando R., Lori DeRosear, and Karen Conterio, "Self-Mutilation and Eating Disorders." *Suicide and Life Threatening Behavior,* 19, 4 (1989): pp. 352–61.

Favazza, R., and K. Conterio. "Female Habitual Self-Mutilators." *Acta Psychiatrica Scandinavica* 78 (1986): pp. 1–7.

Featherstone, Heather. "Girls' Math Achievement: What We Do and Don't Know." *The Harvard Education Letter,* January 1986, pp. 1–5.

Feldman, Carole. "U.S. Students Trail Industrial World in Math." Associated Press, December 1, 1993.

Fennema, Elizabeth, and Julia Sherman. "Sex-Related Differences in Mathematics Achievement, Spatial Visualization and Affective Factors." *American Educational Research Journal,* 14, 1 (1977): pp. 51–71.

Fennema, Elizabeth, and Gilah C. Leder, eds. *Mathematics and Gender.* New York: Teachers College Press, 1990.

Fine, Michelle. *Reframing Dropouts.* Albany, NY: SUNY Albany Press, 1991.

———. "Sexuality, Schooling and Adolescent Females: The Missing Discourse of Desire" *Harvard Educational Review,* 58, 1 (1988): pp. 29–53.

———. "Why Urban Adolescents Drop Into and Out of Public High School." *Teachers College Record,* 87, 3 (1986): pp. 393–409.

——— and Pat Macpherson. "Over Dinner: Feminism and Adolescent Female Bodies." In *Disruptive Voices: The Possibilities of Feminist Research.* Ann Arbor, MI: University of Michigan Press, 1992, pp. 175–203.

——— and Nancie Zane. "Bein' Wrapped Too Tight: When Low-Income Women Drop Out of High School." In *Dropouts from Schools: Issues, Dilemmas and Solutions,* Lois Weis, Eleanor Farrar, and Hugh G. Petrie, eds. Albany, NY: SUNY Press, 1989, pp. 23–53.

Fisher, William A., Donna Byrne, and Leonard A. White. "Emotional Barriers to Contraception." In *Adolescents, Sex, and Contraception.* Hillsdale, NJ: Lawrence Erlbaum, 1983, pp. 207–42.

Fordham, Signithia. "Racelessness as a Factor in Black Students' School Success: Pragmatic Strategy or Pyrrhic Victory?" *Harvard Educational Review* 58, 1 (1988): pp. 54–84.

——— and John U. Ogbu. "Black Students' School Success: Coping with the 'Burden of "Acting White."'" *The Urban Review,* 18, 3 (1986): pp. 176–206.

Forrest, Jacqueline Darroch, and Susheela Singh. "The Sexual and Reproductive Behavior of American Women, 1982–1988." *Family Planning Perspectives,* 22, 5 (1990): pp. 206–14.

Garfinkel, Paul, and David Garner. *Anorexia Nervosa: A Multidimensional Perspective* New York: Brunner/Mazel, 1982.

Gates, Henry Louis, ed. *Bearing Witness: Selections from African-American Autobiography in the Twentieth Century.* New York: Pantheon Books, 1991.

Gibbs, Jewelle Taylor. "City Girls: Psychosocial Adjustment of Urban Black Adolescent Females." *SAGE,* 2, 2 (1985): pp. 28–36.

Giddings, Paula. *When and Where I Enter: The Impact of Black Women on Race and Sex in America.* New York: Bantam Books, 1988.

Gilbert, Sandra M., and Susan Gubar. *The Madwoman in the Attic: The Woman Writer and the Nineteenth Century Literary Imagination.* New Haven: Yale University Press, 1979.

Gilligan, Carol. *In a Different Voice: Psychological Theory and Women's Development.* Cambridge, MA: Harvard University Press, 1982.

———. Nona P. Lyons, and Trudy J. Hanmer, eds. *Making Connections: The Relational Worlds of Adolescent Girls at Emma Willard School.* Cambridge, MA: Harvard University Press, 1990.

"Girls, at 7, Think Thin, Study Finds." New York *Times,* February 11, 1988, p. B9.

Gladwell, Malcolm. "Pythagorean Sexism." Washington *Post,* March 14, 1993, p. C3.

Gorman, Christine. "Sizing Up the Sexes." *Time,* January 20, 1992, p. 42.

Gottesman, Jane. "A Harmful 'Blessing' for Women Athletes: Amenorrhea Linked to Osteoporosis," San Francisco *Chronicle,* July 8, 1993, p. C1.

Grant, Linda. "Race-Gender Status, Classroom Interaction and Children's Socialization in Elementary School." In *Gender Influences in Classroom Interaction,* Louise Cherry Wilkinson and Cora B. Marrett, eds. Orlando, FL: Academic Press, 1985, pp. 57–77.

———. "Black Females' 'Place' in Desegregated Classrooms." *Sociology of Education,* 57, 2 (1984): pp. 98–110.

Harter, Susan. "Self and Identity Development." In *At the Threshold: The Developing Adolescent,* Shirley Feldman and Glen Elliot, eds. Cambridge, MA: Harvard University Press, 1990, pp. 352–87.

Heilbrun, Carolyn G. Review of *Meeting at the Crossroads,* by Lyn Mikel Brown and Carol Gilligan. In the New York *Times Book Review,* October 4, 1992, p. 13.

———. *Writing a Woman's Life.* New York: W. W. Norton & Company, 1988.

Hispanic Policy Development Project. *The Research Bulletin,* 2, 1 (1991); 1, 1 (1986); 1, 3 (1989).

Hochschild, Arlie, with Anne Machung. *The Second Shift: Working Parents and the Revolution at Home.* New York: Viking Penguin, 1989.

hooks, bell. *Black Looks: Race and Representation.* Boston: South End Press, 1992.

———. *Talking Back: Thinking Feminist, Thinking Black*. Boston: South End Press, 1989.

Hsu, L. K. George. "Are the Eating Disorders Becoming More Common in Blacks?" *International Journal of Eating Disorders*, 6, 1 (1987): pp. 113–24.

Hunt, Janet G., and Larry L. Hunt. "Racial Inequality and Self-Image: Identity Maintenance as Identity Diffusion." *Sociology and Social Research*, 61, 4 (1977): pp. 539–59.

Jaffee, Lynn, and Rebecca Manzer, "Girls' Perspectives: Physical Activity and Self-Esteem." *Melpomene Journal,* 11, 3 (1992): pp. 14–23.

Jaramillo, Mari Luci. "To Serve Hispanic American Female Students: Challenges and Responsibilities for Educational Institutions." Paper presented at the Symposium on the Educational Experience of Hispanic American Women sponsored by the Tomás Rivera Center, Claremont, CA, October 20–21, 1985.

Keller, Evelyn Fox. *Reflections on Gender and Science*. New Haven: Yale University Press, 1985.

———. *A Feeling for the Organism: The Life and Work of Barbara McClintock*. San Francisco: W. H. Freeman and Co., 1983.

Kelly, Deirdre M. *Last Chance High: How Girls and Boys Drop In and Out of Alternative Schools*. New Haven: Yale University Press, 1993.

Kincaid, Jamaica. "Girl." In *At the Bottom of the River*. New York: Plume Contemporary Fiction, 1992, pp. 3–5.

King, Deborah K. "Multiple Jeopardy, Multiple Consciousness: The Context of a Black Feminist Ideology." *Signs: Journal of Women in Culture and Society,* 14, 1 (1988): pp. 42–71.

Kolata, Gina. "Math Genius May Have Hormonal Basis." *Science* 222, December 23, 1983, p. 1312.

Koromvokis, Lee, producer. "Race Relations." Panel discussion, moderated by Charlayne Hunter-Gault. *The MacNeil-Lehrer NewsHour,* February 6, 1993.

Kozol, Jonathan. *Savage Inequalities: Children in America's Schools.* New York: Crown Publishers, 1991.

Lapointe, Archie E., Nancy A. Mead, and Gary W. Phillips. *A World of Differences: An International Assessment of Mathematics and Science.* Princeton, NJ: Educational Testing Service, 1989.

Lawton, Millicent. "Sexual Harassment of Students Target of District Policies." *Education Week,* February 10, 1993, p. 1.

Lees, Sue. *Losing Out: Sexuality and Adolescent Girls.* New York: Hutchinson, 1986.

Levit, David B. "Gender Differences in Ego Defenses in Adolescence: Sex Roles as One Way to Understand the Differences." *Journal of Personality and Social Psychology,* 61, 6 (1991): pp. 992–99.

Levy, Barrie, ed. *Dating Violence: Young Women in Danger.* Seattle, WA: Seal Press, 1991.

Linn, Marcia C. "Gender and School Learning: Science." In *The International Encyclopedia of Education,* Torsten Husén and Neville T. Postlethwaite, eds. 2nd ed., volume 4. New York: Pergamon Press, 1994, pp. 2436–40.

———. "Gender Differences in Educational Achievement." In *Sex Equity in Educational Opportunity, Achievement, and Testing.* Princeton, NJ: Proceedings of the 1991 Invitational Conference of the Educational Testing Service, 1992.

———. "Gender, Mathematics, and Science: Trends and Recommendations." Paper presented at the Summer Institute for the Council of Chief State School Officers, Mystic, CT, July–August 1990.

——— and Janet S. Hyde. "Gender, Mathematics, and Science." *Educational Researcher,* 18, 8 (1989): pp. 17–27.

Logan, Judy. *Teaching Stories*, with a foreword by Peggy McIntosh. St. Paul, MN: Minnesota Inclusiveness Program, 1993.

Lorde, Audre. *Sister Outsider: Essays and Speeches.* Freedom, CA: The Crossing Press, 1984.

Lott, Bernice. *Becoming a Woman: The Socialization of Gender.* Springfield, IL: Charles C Thomas, 1981.

Luftig, Richard L., and Marci L. Nichols. "Assessing the Social Status of Gifted Students by Their Age Peers." *Gifted Child Quarterly*, 34, 3 (1990): pp. 111–15.

Madhok, Jacqueline. "Group Size and Gender Composition Influences on Discussion." Paper presented at the Berkeley Women and Language Conference: Locating Power, Berkeley, CA, April 1992.

Martin, Jane Roland. *The Schoolhome: Rethinking Schools for Changing Families.* Cambridge, MA: Harvard University Press, 1992.

Martínez, Rubén, and Richard L. Dukes. "Ethnic and Gender Differences in Self-Esteem." *Youth & Society*, 22, 3 (1991): pp. 318–38.

———. "Race, Gender and Self-Esteem among Youth," *Hispanic Journal of Behavioral Sciences*, 9, 4 (1987): pp. 427–43.

McAdoo, Hariette Pipes. *Black Families.* Beverly Hills, CA: Sage Publications, 1981.

———, ed. "The Development of Self-Concept and Race Attitudes of Young Black Children over Time." Paper presented at Cornell University Conference on Empirical Research in Black Psychology III, Ithaca, NY, October 29, 1976.

McIntosh, Peggy. "Interactive Phases of Curricular and Personal Re-Vision with Regard to Race." Working Paper No. 219. Wellesley, MA: Wellesley College Center for Research on Women, 1990.

———. "Interactive Phases of Curricular Re-Vision: A Feminist Perspective." Working Paper No. 124. Wellesley, MA: Wellesley College Center for Research on Women, 1983.

McKenna, Teresa, and Flora Ida Ortiz, eds. *The Broken Web: The Educational Experience of Hispanic American Women*. Berkeley, CA: Floricanto Press, 1988.

Miller, Jean Baker. *Toward a New Psychology of Women,* 2nd ed. Boston: Beacon Press, 1986.

Minnesota Women's Fund with the assistance of the National Adolescent Health Resource Center. *Reflections of Risk: Growing Up Female in Minnesota*. Minneapolis: Minnesota Women's Fund, 1990.

Moore, Elsie G. J., and A. Wade Smith. "Sex and Ethnic Group Differences in Mathematics Achievement: Results from the National Longitudinal Study." *Journal for Research in Mathematics Education,* 18, 1 (1987): pp. 25–36.

National Assessment of Educational Progress. *The Science Report Card: Elements of Risk and Recovery: Trends and Achievement Based on the 1986 National Assessment*. Princeton, NJ: Educational Testing Service, 1988.

National Coalition for Women and Girls in Education. *The Task Force Reports: Teaching Strategies for Girls in Math & Science*. Washington, DC: National Coalition for Women and Girls in Education, 1992.

———. *Title IX: A Practical Guide to Achieving Sex Equity in Education*. Washington, DC: National Coalition for Women and Girls in Education, 1988.

National Science Board. *Science & Engineering Indicators*. Washington DC: National Science Board, 1991.

Ogbu, John U. "Origins of Human Competence: A Cultural-Ecological Perspective." *Child Development,* 52, 2 (1981): pp. 413–29.

Olsen, Tillie. *Silences*. New York: Delacorte Press, 1965; reprint, New York: Delta/Seymour Lawrence, 1989.

Orbach, Susie. *Fat Is a Feminist Issue: The Anti-Diet Guide to Permanent Weight Loss*. New York: Paddington Press, 1977.

Orr, Daniel P., Mary L. Wilbrandt, Catherine J. Brack, Steven P. Rauch, and Gary M. Ingersoll. "Reported Sexual Behaviors and Self-Esteem among Young Adolescents." *American Journal of Diseases of Children,* 143 (1989): pp. 86–90.

Orum, Lori S. *Project EXCEL: A Mid-Course Report.* Los Angeles: National Council of La Raza, 1991.

Pérez, Sonia, with Luis A. Duany. *Reducing Hispanic Teenage Pregnancy and Family Poverty: A Replication Guide.* Washington, DC: National Council of La Raza, 1992.

Pomeroy, Wardell. *Girls and Sex,* 3rd ed. New York: Laurel Leaf Books, 1991.

Reyes, Laurie Hart, and George M. A. Stanic. "Race, Sex and Math," *Journal of Research in Math Education,* 19, 1 (1988): pp. 26–43.

Richman, Charles L., M. L. Clark, and Kathryn P. Brown. "General and Specific Self-Esteem in Late Adolescent Students: Race × Gender × SES Effects." *Adolescence,* 20, 79 (1985): pp. 555–66.

Robinson, Tracy, and Janie Victoria Ward. " 'A Belief in Self Far Greater than Anyone's Disbelief': Cultivating Resistance among African American Female Adolescents." In *Women, Girls & Psychotherapy: Reframing Resistance,* Carol Gilligan, Annie G. Rogers, and Deborah L. Tolman, eds. New York: The Haworth Press, 1991, pp. 87–103.

Root, Maria P. P. "Disordered Eating in Women of Color." *Sex Roles: A Journal of Research,* 22, 7/8 (1990): pp. 525–36.

Rosenberg, Morris. *Society and the Adolescent Self-Image,* rev. ed. Middletown, CT: Wesleyan University Press, 1989.

———, Carmi Schooler, and Carrie Schoenbach. "Self-Esteem and Adolescent Problems: Modeling Reciprocal Effects." *American Sociological Review,* 54, 6 (1989): pp. 1004–18.

———— and Roberta Simmons. *Black and White Self-Esteem: The Urban School Child.* Washington DC: American Sociological Association, Arnold and Caroline Rose Monograph Series, 1971.

Rosser, Sue. *Biology & Feminism: A Dynamic Interaction.* New York: Twayne Publishers, 1992.

Rubin, Lillian B. *Erotic Wars: What Happened to the Sexual Revolution?* New York: Farrar, Straus & Giroux, 1990.

Sadker, David, and Myra Sadker. "Sexism in the Classroom: From Grade School to Graduate School." *Phi Delta Kappan,* 67, 7 (1986): pp. 512–15.

————. "Is the OK Classroom OK?" *Phi Delta Kappan,* 66, 5 (1985): pp. 358–61.

————. "Sexism in the Schoolroom of the '80s." *Psychology Today,* March 1985, p. 54.

Sanford, Linda Tschirhart, and Mary Ellen Donovan. *Women & Self-Esteem: Understanding and Improving the Way We Think and Feel about Ourselves.* New York: Doubleday, 1984.

Sapolsky, Robert. "The Case of the Falling Nightwatchmen." *Discover,* July 1987, p. 42.

Scarf, Maggie. *Unfinished Business: Pressure Points in the Lives of Women.* New York: Ballantine Books, 1980.

Scheier, Michael F., and Charles S. Carver. "Private and Public Aspects of Self." *Review of Personality and Social Psychology,* 2 (1981): pp. 189–216.

Schrof, Joannie M. "The Gender Machine." *U.S. News & World Report,* August 2, 1993, p. 42.

Schultz, Debra L. *Risk, Resiliency, and Resistance: Current Research on Adolescent Girls.* New York: Ms. Foundation for Women National Girls Initiative, 1991.

Schwartz, John. "Obesity Affects Economic, Social Status: Women Fare Worse, 7 Year Study Shows." Washington *Post,* September 30, 1993, p. A1.

Scott-Jones, Diane, and Maxine L. Clark. "The School Experience of Black Girls: The Interaction of Gender, Race, and Socioeconomic Status." *Phi Delta Kappan,* 67, 7 (1986): pp. 520–26.

Seligmann, Jean. "The Littlest Dieters." *Newsweek,* July 27, 1987, p. 48.

Selverstone, Robert. "Adolescent Sexuality: Developing Self-Esteem and Mastering Developmental Tasks." *SIECUS Report,* 18, 1 (1989): pp. 1–3.

"Sexual and Reproductive Behavior Among U.S. Teens." *Fact Sheet.* New York: Planned Parenthood Federation of America, Inc., 1991.

Shapiro, Laura. "Guns and Dolls." *Newsweek,* May 28, 1990, p. 56.

Shen, Fern. "Dating Turns Violent for Teens," Washington *Post,* reprinted in the San Francisco *Chronicle,* August 17, 1993, p. E2.

Silber, Tomas J. "Anorexia Nervosa in Blacks and Hispanics." *International Journal of Eating Disorders,* 5, 1 (1986): pp. 121–28.

Simmons, Roberta, and Dale Blyth. *Moving into Adolescence: The Impact of Pubertal Change and School Context.* Hawthorne, NY: Aldine de Gruyter Press, 1987.

Simons, Janet M., Belva Finlay, and Alice Yang. *The Adolescent & Young Adult Fact Book.* Washington, DC: Children's Defense Fund, 1991.

Smith, Beverly Jean. "I Don't Hold My Tongue." Paper presented at the Annual Meeting of the American Psychological Association, Toronto, Ontario, August 1993.

Smith, Elsie J. "The Black Female Adolescent: A Review of the Educational, Career, and Psychological Literature." *Psychology of Women Quarterly,* 6, 3 (1982): pp. 261–88.

Spelman, Elizabeth V. *Inessential Woman: Problems of Exclusion in Feminist Thought.* Boston: Beacon Press, 1988.

Steele, Claude M. "Race and the Schooling of Black Americans." *The Atlantic Monthly,* April 1992, p. 68.

Stein, Nan. "Sexual Harassment in Schools." *The School Administrator,* January 1993, p. 14.

————, Nancy L. Marshall, and Linda R. Tropp. *Secrets in Public: Sexual Harassment in Our Schools.* Wellesley, MA: NOW Legal Defense and Education Fund and Wellesley College Center for Research on Women, 1993.

Steinem, Gloria. *Revolution from Within: A Book of Self-Esteem.* Boston: Little, Brown, 1992.

Stock, Phyllis. *Better than Rubies: A History of Women's Education.* New York: Capricorn Books, 1978.

[Strauss, Susan]. *Sexual Harassment to Teenagers: It's Not Fun/It's Illegal—A Curriculum for Identification and Prevention of Sexual Harassment for Use with Junior and Senior High School Students.* St. Paul, MN: Minnesota Department of Education Equal Educational Opportunities Section, 1988.

Style, Emily. "Curriculum as Window and Mirror." In *Listening for All Voices: Gender Balancing the School Curriculum.* Proceedings of a conference held at Oak Knoll School, Summit, NJ, June 1988, pp. 6–12.

Tavris, Carol. *The Mismeasure of Woman: Why Women Are Not the Better Sex, the Inferior Sex, or the Opposite Sex.* New York: Simon & Schuster, 1992.

Tinajero, Josefina Villamil, Maria Luisa Gonzalez, and Florence Dick. *Raising Career Aspirations of Hispanic Girls.* Bloomington, IN: Phi Delta Kappa Educational Foundation, 1991.

Today's Girls, Tomorrow's Leaders: Symposium Proceedings. New York: Girl Scouts of the U.S.A. and American Association of University Women, 1991.

Tolman, Deborah Lynne. "Daring to Desire: Culture and the Bodies of Adolescent Girls." In *Sexual Cultures and the Construction of Adolescent Identity,* Janice Irvine, ed. Philadelphia, PA: Temple University Press, forthcoming.

————. Voicing the Body: A Psychological Study of Adolescent Girls' Sexual Desire. PhD Diss, Harvard University, 1992.

————. "Just Say No to What? A Preliminary Analysis of Sexual Subjectivity in a Multicultural Group of Adolescent Females." Paper presented at the American Orthopsychiatric Association, Miami, FL, April 27, 1990.

———— and Elizabeth Debold. "Conflicts of Body and Image: Female Adolescents, Desire, and the No-Body Body." In *Feminist Perspectives on Eating Disorder,* Patricia Fallon, Melanie Katzman, and Susan Wooley, eds. New York: Guilford Press, 1994, pp. 301–17.

U.S. Bureau of the Census. *Educational Attainment in the United States: March 1991 and 1990.* Washington, DC: U.S. Government Printing Office, 1992.

Valdivieso, Rafael. *Must They Wait Another Generation? Hispanics and Secondary School Reform.* New York: Clearinghouse on Urban Education, 1986.

————. "Hispanics and Schools: A New Perspective." *Educational Horizons,* 64, 4 (1986): pp. 190–96.

Valentine Foundation and Women's Way. "A Conversation about Girls." Proceedings of "A Conversation about Girls' Development," Philadelphia, PA, May 3, 1990.

Walker, Thaai. "Gang Members Charged in Rapes of 2 Girls." San Francisco *Chronicle,* December 15, 1993, p. A23.

Wallerstein, Judith S., and Sandra Blakeslee. *Second Chances: Men, Women and Children a Decade after Divorce.* New York: Ticknor & Fields, 1989.

Walters, David C. "Number of Women in MBA Schools Is Dropping." *Christian Science Monitor,* November 16, 1992.

White, Patricia E. *Women and Minorities in Science and Engineering: An Update.* Washington DC: National Science Foundation, 1992.

Wideman, John Edgar. *Brothers and Keepers.* New York: Penguin Books, 1984.

Wilson Sporting Goods Company in cooperation with Women's Sports Foundation. *The Wilson Report: Moms, Dads, Daughters and Sports.* New York: Wilson Sporting Goods Company and Women's Sports Foundation, 1988.

Winerip, Michael. "In School: A Public School in Harlem That Takes the Time, and the Trouble, to Be a Family." New York *Times,* January 26, 1994, p. A19.

————. "Public School Offers a Social-Service Model." New York *Times,* December 8, 1993, p. A1.

————. "Study Finds Boys Receive 75% of New Science Scholarships." New York *Times,* November 17, 1993, p. B7.

Wolf, Naomi. *The Beauty Myth: How Images of Beauty Are Used Against Women.* New York: William Morrow and Company, 1991.

Women's Sports Foundation. *The Women's Sports Foundation Report: Minorities in Sports.* New York: Women's Sports Foundation, 1989.

About the Author

■

■

■

Peggy Orenstein was formerly managing editor of *Mother Jones* magazine, and was a founding editor of the award-winning *7 Days* magazine. She has served on the editorial staffs of *Manhattan,inc.* and *Esquire,* and her work has appeared in such publications as *The New York Times Magazine, Vogue, Glamour, The New Yorker, New York Woman,* and *Mirabella.* She lives in the San Francisco Bay Area.